HISTORICAL VINDICATIONS:

A DISCOURSE

ON THE

PROVINCE AND USES OF BAPTIST HISTORY,

DELIVERED BEFORE THE BACKUS HISTORICAL SOCIETY,
AT NEWTON, MASS., JUNE 23, 1857.
REPEATED BEFORE THE AMERICAN BAPTIST HISTORICAL SOCIETY,
AT NEW YORK, MAY 14, 1859.

WITH

APPENDIXES,

CONTAINING

HISTORICAL NOTES AND CONFESSIONS OF FAITH.

BY

SEWALL S. CUTTING,

PROFESSOR OF RHETORIC AND HISTORY IN THE UNIVERSITY OF ROCHESTER.

BOSTON:
GOULD AND LINCOLN,
59 WASHINGTON STREET.
NEW YORK: SHELDON AND COMPANY.
CINCINNATI: GEORGE S. BLANCHARD.
1859.

ELECTROTYPED BY W. F. DRAPER, ANDOVER, MASS.

Printed By R. M. Edwards.

TO THE

VENERABLE FIRST BAPTIST CHURCH

IN THE CITY OF PROVIDENCE, R. I.,

This Discourse

IS RESPECTFULLY

DEDICATED.

PREFACE.

THIS Discourse is placed in form for preservation at the request of the bodies before whom it was delivered. Prepared for delivery at the Anniversary of the Newton Theological Institution, it is printed as spoken at that time. The historical importance of some of the subjects discussed in the Notes, will justify, it is believed, the extended space which they occupy. The Confessions of 1643 and of 1689 are inserted, because, though absolutely essential to the knowledge of Baptist doctrinal history, they are to most readers now inaccessible. The pages here given to the pûblic are partial fruits of studies pursued through many years by the writer, and he will be abundantly compensated if they shall become the occasion to others of kindred researches, and kindred pleasure and profit. He believes that studies in our denominational history will increase our reverence for those who have gone before us, and contribute, by the blessing of God, to restore somewhat of their superior efficiency in promoting the kingdom of our Lord, and the salvation of men.

S. S. C.

UNIVERSITY OF ROCHESTER,
SEPTEMBER 24, 1859.

CONTENTS.

THE

PROVINCE AND USES OF BAPTIST HISTORY.

I WAS not uninfluenced by personal considerations in accepting the invitation which has brought me to your presence to-day. I came to meet old friends, whose grasp always repays a long journey, needing no pledge of welcome save that which is furnished in recollections of former intimacies, and of labors in a common and blessed service. This hill, whose winding ascent is shaded by venerable elms, — the beautiful panorama which delights the eye from its summit, — are not more familiar than the faces which assemble here on these sacred occasions. They differ in this, that while the former abide with the constancy of nature, knowing no change save that of increasing beauty, the latter reveal the touches of time and care, each year reminding us, by their absence, of some whom we shall not greet again, and whom we in our turn shall successively follow. I may too early attune your thoughts to sadness; but these allusions force to my mind and to yours the name of one whose recent departure, in the very vigor of his days, we all have mourned as the loss of a brother. It is not my province to utter his eulogy; and yet, the part which I have to perform in the exercises of this anniversary, permits and invites a brief reference to his virtues. He was my friend. When he came to the pastorship of the ancient church in Providence, I was the pastor of a rural church in this state, at no great distance from him, and was honored with his confidence. From that time I knew him well. I never knew integrity more perfect than his. Prudent and reserved, when he spoke his words were the exact transcript of his thoughts. Of ripe judgment, he was a sagacious and wise counsellor. With wonderful faith in right and in God, he looked for the triumph of truth and righteousness with a confidence as unquestioning as that of the astronomer looking for the calculated phenomena of the planets. Perhaps it required somewhat of intimacy to know his emotional nature,—the depth, the unchangeableness of his love, which, as a pervading, characterizing sentiment, embraced his friends,—his work as a pastor,—and the cause of Christ, whether as a whole or in its special departments of education or missions, whether as connected with his own denomination, or with that true church catholic which embraces the faithful of every clime and name. He was a rarely developed Christian man, whom, to human seeming, the church on earth could not afford to lose. We feel the pang of his absence here to-day, and before we pass to other themes we pay this brief tribute to the memory of JAMES N. GRANGER.

I had another reason for obeying the summons which called me hither. It was my privilege to bear a part in the formation of this Historical Society; anterior, indeed, to the formation, I bore a part in the public and private discussions which led to that event. There were those among us who felt that materials for our denominational history were dropping away beyond recovery, for the lack of some repository in which they might be gathered, — that we were in danger of losing the historic spirit, for the lack of something to remind us of the names and deeds of our fathers — those true men who, in this and other lands, labored and suffered for our faith. It was our wish to link the living generation with those who in all preceding times have been the representatives of our ideas of the Christian economy, and with those who shall come after us in the same evangelical succession. We believed the purpose a worthy one — one which would minister to faith, and hope, and charity, and which would grow in the interest and regard of the thoughtful and cultivated in our ministry and our churches. I am still impressed by similar convictions, and these gave the weight of authority to your wishes.

In occupying your attention for an hour, I shall restrict myself to topics closely related to the purposes of this society. I propose to offer some remarks on the *Province and Uses of Baptist History;* and if I dwell somewhat disproportionately on a single branch of the former of these topics, it will be from my desire to direct your attention to questions relating to the rise of our denomination which seem to me to have been studied less than they deserve.

By Baptist History, I mean history with the restriction implied by that epithet, taken in its ordinary sense.

In that sense the epithet is modern, belonging wholly to the period of the Reformation and the times succeeding. There are those who regard it as the chief and distinguishing province of Baptist history to trace the stream of our sentiments from their primal fountain in the churches of the apostles, down through successions of organized communities, to the Baptists of modern times. I have little confidence in the results of any attempts of that kind which have met my notice, and I attach little value to inquiries pursued for the predetermined purpose of such a demonstration. The past opens her testimonies not to those who approach her in the spirit of dictation, and to serve the ends of sect or party, but to those who come in a docile temper to accept her lessons, whatever they may be. It is a more legitimate task to search for the good seed of the kingdom, wheresoever or howsoever scattered in the lapse of ages, — whether manifesting itself in individual minds distinguished by faith and genius, in sects struggling to restore the primitive economy, and hunted and destroyed as heretics, or mingled with the mass of evangelical germs which never perished in the great apostasy; and to note how that seed, when the Reformation came to the church like vernal suns and airs to the teeming, waiting earth, started into rank and even unhealthy growth. This is preliminary to Baptist history. It explains how and why there came to be a Baptist denomination, and hence a history with that epithet. In that sense it is within the province of Baptist history, but it is not that history itself. American history falls back upon English, and English in its turn upon Continental, and this again upon Roman, Grecian and Asiatic; but when, in the forces and events of these anterior periods, American history has accounted for its existence and character, its province becomes peculiar and restricted. It is so with Baptist history. It falls back upon the anterior periods with which it is linked, and of which it is the offspring; but, having in this way accounted for its rise, and explained its character, it becomes distinct and substantive, and belongs exclusively to modern times.

It by no means follows, from the distinction which I have named, that this preliminary chapter is in any sense unimportant. I should be misconceived, were it supposed that I am aiming at that inference. It is, on the contrary, with the closing section of that chapter that I am now for some little time, and as a leading topic, to occupy your attention. I shrink from no scrutiny in regard to the principles or the facts which gave rise to the Baptist denomination. I am not unfamiliar with the facile and stereotyped reproaches which are cast upon our pedigree. It is easy for any sectary of the nineteenth century, judging of his own communion as he sees it now, and of other communions as they were, or as they were represented by their enemies to be, two or three centuries ago, to institute offensive comparisons. He may make the Episcopal Church odious, by presenting to the modern sense the revolting scenes of Smithfield, or the more refined atrocities of the period of the Corporation and Test Acts; or the Church of Holland odious, by reminding the world that when the reformed of that country were yet in their deadly struggles with the human fiend of Spain, they were reproaching the great Prince of Orange because he would not let loose the fury of persecution against the Anabaptists; but he has in this process only revealed the unloveliness of his own temper, and engaged in a game at which any number can play. It should rather be our interest to cast the veil over common infirmities, and to look, in that memorable period of the world's commotion, for those better moral forces which, under God, have given us the bloom and beauty of our later Protestant unity. In order to detect these forces, we must learn to go beyond abnormal developments — beyond the abuse of power in church and state, on the one hand, and beyond the excesses of ignorant fanaticism on the other, to that great mass of Christian PEOPLE, as distinguished from priests and rulers, from zealots and madmen, who made little figure in the public affairs which form history, but whose faith and piety constituted in fact the leaven of the world. Those who can trace their spiritual pedigree to such a source, have no occasion to blush for their origin.

I think that the *people* of the period of the Reformation, and of the ages immediately anterior, will rise in our estimation, in proportion as we know them more intimately. Luther sprung from the people, and addressed himself to them. The Reformation embraced doctrines as well as morals, — doctrines relating to the profoundest questions of spiritual life, — and yet the people felt and appreciated the discussions, and were swayed by them as the harvest is swayed by the summer wind. The "guilds of Rhetoric" which flourished in the cities of the Netherlands, and contributed so largely to the religious reformation and the political revolt, furnish a striking illustration of the intelligence and cultivation of Dutch mechanics of that period. "They ridiculed, with their farces and satires," says Motley, "the vices of the clergy. They dramatized tyranny for public execration."[1] Princes could neither seduce them by asking to be admitted as members, nor break them down by power or menace. Earlier than this, in England, the brilliant period of Edward III. was crowned with the rise of Wickliffe. In the minds of most men, Wickliffe stands out solitary, amid general gloom, — one star on the broad face of surrounding night. Such a view of him is a grand historical mistake. Wickliffe rose on a movement which embraced a large portion of the English people, and was himself but the representative of that movement. Old Henry De Knyghton, contemporary and antagonist of the great reformer, declares that the adherents of Wickliffe were so held in honor, and multiplied, that of every two men met in the way, one or the other might be supposed to belong to the sect.[2] Wickliffe translated the Bible for a people whose conscious wants required it. Frag-

1 *Dutch Republic*, Vol. I. p. 89. No unfavorable opinion can be formed as to the culture of a nation, whose weavers, smiths, gardeners, and traders, found the favorite amusement of their holidays in composing and enacting tragedies or farces, reciting their own verses, or in personifying moral and æsthetic sentiments, by ingeniously arranged groups, or gorgeous habiliments. — *Ib.*

2 Secta illa in maxime honore illis diebus habebatur et in tantum multiplicata fuit, quod vix duos videres in via, quin alter eorum discipulus Wyclefi fuerit. Quoted in Gieseler's *Eccl. Hist.*, Vol. III. p. 147.

mentary portions—the work of pious priests, who had sought in this good way to feed the flock of God—had created an appetite for more of that heavenly food. His resistance to the pretensions of monks and friars, was a resistance which he echoed from classes extending downward to the very humblest of the people. This is strikingly illustrated in that curious old poem belonging to this time, the Creed of Piers Ploughman. An humble and earnest inquirer is represented as going, in pursuit of religious instruction, from one order of friars to another, but failing utterly in the search. They are skilled in the art of abusing each other, but not in the divine art of directing the penitent to the way of life. He has parted from the last of the orders, "wepynge for sorowe," when he meets an humble ploughman, who inquires the cause of his grief.

"I can fynden no man,"

the wanderer replies,

"That fulli byleveth,
To techen me the heyghe weie,
And therefore I wepe;
For I have fonded the freres
Of the foure ordres:

* * * * *

And al myn hope was on hem,
And myn herte also;
But thei ben fulli faithles,
And the fend sueth."

Mark, then, how the peasant suddenly interrupts the lamentation:

"A! brother, * *
Beware of tho foles;
For Christ seyde hymself,
'Of swiche I you warne.'"—*L.* 908.

The peasant then proceeds with a terrible picture of their pride, their covetousness, and their inability to teach; and in the end, in answer to the inquirer, explains the simple creed of a Christian man. Such a poem—a poem designed to aid the cause in which Wickliffe was laboring—is altogether inexplicable, except upon the supposition of an amount of religious knowledge among the people of England of that time, far beyond that which is ordinarily attributed to them. If it be asked how they had acquired it, the answer may be found, undoubtedly, in the better character of many of the secular clergy, of some one of whom Chaucer has given the immortal portrait:

"Christes love, and his apostles twelve
He taught; and ferst he folwed it himselve!"

English history is full of intimations of the perpetual restlessness of the English people, under papal domination, and of the presence of a deeper religious life than it was the purpose of the papal hierarchy to originate or to supply. Nor were the life and progress of the English people manifested in religious directions only. Even then, in the popular poem known as the "Vision" of the Ploughman, the poet, as if already recognizing a political axiom destined to triumph in the constitution of his country, writes of a king:

> "Might of the communes
> Made hym to regne."—*L.* 225.

I may refer to another illustration of the growth of religious life among the English people, preparing them for the Reformation, which seems to me to have been singularly overlooked. It is safe to assume that the language of any nation expresses, at any given stage of its history, the aggregate intellectual life of the nation. Its speech is the product, the sign, and the measure of its thought. If, then, we apply this test to the time when Chaucer wrote for the aristocracy, and the authors of Piers Ploughman for the people, and from that period leap forward to the time of Tyndale and Cranmer, we behold at once the indications of great progress. There have been feeble intervening princes; there have been the devastating wars of the Roses; there have been, on the part of the alternately ascendent factions, the most shameless compliances with ecclesiastical demands; the nobles have devoured each other, until not thirty peers are found to sit in parliament; the obsequious legislature has passed the act *de hæretico comburendo*, that the realm may be purified by fire from the heresies of Wickliffe; and literature has drawn on the cowl, and retired to the gloom and the superstitions of the cloister;—but whoso judges the condition of the English people from these chief and most familiar phenomena of history, has done great injustice to a period of popular progress — progress, of which, apart from other proofs, we have an incontestable sign in the growth of the English tongue. The English tongue had become ripe for the expression of religious ideas, because the people, by the growth of their religious life, had religious ideas to express. The language of the Reformation was not now superimposed; it came from within. Artisans, and peasants even, when summoned before priests and magistrates, used the terminology of theological science with the conscious facility of men whose objective knowledge was grounded in a profound subjective experience. When the Reformation of England is attributed to the lust of a brutal king, or even when better men, like Tyndale and Cranmer, and the gentle Josiah of the British throne, are regarded as essential ministers of its induction and progress, the grand forces of the period are overlooked. These forces were in the people, who were now, by the discipline of Providence, prepared for that great event; and kings, prelates, and scholars, were but the unconscious ministers of their will. Henry and Edward, Tyndale and Cranmer, were incidents; the Reformation, with or without them, was a necessity. The lust of Henry might be the occasion and instrument of its precipitation; the event itself lay in the destinies of the world, and the fulness of the time had come.

Contemplate, then, the Reformation as a great popular movement — a movement for which the people, whether on the continent or in England, had become ripe. Let it not be accounted a strange thing that its progress was marked by many events to be regretted. It was a divine work, but wrought through human agency, and bore, as was inevitable, the marks of human infirmity. It had been the aim of the spiritual tyranny which ruled over Europe, to suppress all freedom of thought and discussion; and the design seemed well-nigh accomplished. Babylon, as in her pride she surveyed the subject peoples of Christendom, sung exultingly, "I sit a queen, and shall see no sorrow." Suddenly her plagues came. The nations, awaking to the consciousness of their strength, broke the withes by which they had been bound, and cast them beneath their feet. Freedom of thought was the distinction and the triumph of Protestantism. It is no marvel that, in the delirium of new-found liberty, excesses of opinion and conduct were exhibited, which contemporary conservatism and reäction, and the cooler judgment of modern times, have alike condemned. If the excesses, under the circumstances of the case, had been less violent or less blamable, the Reformation would have been anomalous in human history.

Some of the chief excesses of the period of the Reformation were manifested, under various forms, by individuals and communities who were distinguished by the name of *Anabaptists.* It is undeniable that fanatics, under this name, became the reproach of Protestantism, and the terror of civil society. But, on the other hand, it is not less certain that better people, against whom no crimes against Protestantism or the state could be alleged, were compelled by their enemies to share the title and the reproach; and historians have not always been sufficiently careful to discriminate between these distinct classes. The student of human nature, who observes its workings under the powerful influence of religious controversy, will not be surprised that hard names were made a substitute for arguments; but the student of history may well wonder that historical justice has been so tardy and so reluctant. There were but few crimes charged against the Anabaptists of the Reformation, which were not charged against dissenters in England, under the reigns of the last Stuarts. In their case, however, history has been more ready to vindicate the wronged from unjust aspersions, and already the slanders of that day are refuted forever. There is a similar work to be done for the Anabaptists,—the work of distinguishing between those Christian people whose simple and earnest practical piety adorned the Reformation, and those fanatics and madmen whose delusions and misdeeds dishonored it, and of giving the former their true place among the world's worthies.

There have not been wanting, in our times, writers who have thought it their mission, in utter disregard of historical facts, to connect the Baptists of this day with the madmen of Münster; and, with an equal misconception of the truth of history, some among ourselves have sought to escape from that disgraceful genealogy, by denying any historical connection whatever with any body of that name in the period of the Reformation. To them, our English Baptist ancestors, like Melchizedec, were without father, without mother, without pedigree, — genuine autochthones, sprung from English soil, with no relations on the face of the earth. The fabled origin of the Athenians was not more certainly a mistake. The rise of the Baptist denomination in England — in part, undoubtedly, indigenous, the result of principles recognized as belonging logically to the Reformation — was occasioned, likewise, by intercourse with the Anabaptists of the Continent, of the better class to which I have referred. Sometimes these people came to England, driven thither by persecution, and became, by their testimony and their blood, the apostles of their faith. Sometimes English Christians, driven from their own country by priestly intolerance, became, on the Continent, the docile pupils of Anabaptists there, and then, returning to England, embodied their doctrinal progress in corresponding ecclesiastical organizations. Suffer me to detain you for a few moments with indications of the historical proofs of these statements.

It is impossible to determine at how early a period, in the progress of the Reformation, Anabaptists, under that name, made their appearance in England. Nor is the solution of this problem necessary to our present purpose. Henry had been warned against them, by advices from the Continent, and had taken such decisive measures as he knew too well how to take, to prevent the spread, in his kingdom, of the dangerous heresy. He had been so far unsuccessful, however, that, according to the testimony of Burnet, there were many, in the reign of Edward VI., in several parts of England. Having stated that they were generally Germans, who had been compelled, by revolutions in their own country, to seek homes abroad, he says: "Upon Luther's first preaching in Germany, there arose many, who, building on some of his principles, carried things much further than he did. The chief foundation he laid down was, that the Scripture was to be the only rule of Christians." On this foundation, he proceeds to state, many rejected certain received religious opinions, as without warrant; of those so rejected, infant baptism being one. "They held that to be no baptism," says Burnet, "and so were rebaptized; but from this, which was the most taken notice of, as being a visible thing, *they carried all the general name of Anabaptists.*" "Of these," he adds, "there were *two sorts* most remarkable." One sort, according to his description, "only thought that baptism ought not to be given but to those of an age capable of instruction, and who did earnestly desire it. This opinion"—I am still quoting his words —"they grounded on the silence of the New Testament about the baptism of children; they observed that our Saviour, commanding the apostles to baptize, did join teaching with it: and they said the great decay of Christianity flowed from this way of making children Christians before they understood what they did. These," he says, "were called the gentle, or moderate Anabaptists." This representation makes these Christians different from Protestants generally, by their views of baptism, and the composition of the Christian Church, and in so far, I need not say, they answer to the faith and practice of the Baptists of later times. "But others," he proceeds, "who carried that name [of Anabaptists], denied almost all the principles of the Christian doctrine, and were men of fierce and barbarous tempers. * * These," he adds, "being joined under the common name of Anabaptists, with the other, brought them also under an ill character."[1]

Having given to his readers this distinction, — a distinction required by that truth of history which Bishop Burnet reverenced, — he proceeds to state that, at the period in question, these people were disseminating their errors in England, and making proselytes, and that fresh measures were taken for removing this danger. He says, however, that he knows of no severities used against the moderate or gentle kind, — that these were met by the more legitimate argument of books, to which they wrote replies.[2] We should be glad to give entire credit to his information on this point. Unfortunately, however, under the description of the "fierce and barbarous," he sets down the name of the sufferer, Joan of Kent, with whose death stern history sadly connects the name of Cranmer. Authorities are not agreed as to the character of that unhappy woman, — some making her an example of consistent and zealous piety, and giving her a rank among the martyrs. Un-

1 The testimony from Burnet here cited may be found in his *History of the Reformation*, Vol. II. p. 176. His recognition of the distinction between different sorts of Anabaptists, coincides strikingly with that of Lord Brooke, in his *Treatise on Episcopacy*. This nobleman was a commander in the Parliamentary Army, and fell at Litchfield, in 1643. The tolerant sentiments of his treatise were praised by Milton, in his *Speech for the Liberty of Unlicensed Printing*. See Supplement to Neal's *History of the Puritans*, Vol. II. p. 365.

2 *Hist. Ref.*, Vol. II. p. 179.

doubtedly she hesitated to accept the common faith in regard to the mystery of Christ's human nature. The papist imagines that he honors the Lord by attributing sinlessness to the nature of the virgin mother of whom he took his flesh, and Joan, as I suppose, imagined that she honored him by denying that he took flesh of that mother at all, and requiring a higher miracle as the true solution of the incarnation. Her error was the natural rebound from the Romish Mariolatry. But this error by no means justifies the historian in ranking her with the fanatical Anabaptists. It is not to be denied that her doubts on these questions were shared by a large portion — we know not how large — of those who were called "the gentle." On the Continent, as well as in England, this was charged against them as a distinctive Anabaptist heresy, and in their examinations before priests and magistrates was generally made a chief point. Whether it justifies the inference of their denial of the Divinity of Christ, is another question, not to be answered without discrimination. In the examination of Claes de Praet, at Ghent, in 1556, the priest alleged, "Your people do not believe that Christ is God and man." — "I believe," answered the martyr, "that Christ is truly God and man."[1] Another of the martyrs, in his confession of faith, written subsequently to his examination, and giving an account of that transaction, affirms his belief in the Divinity of Christ, in terms unquestionable for their orthodoxy.[2] Pieters and

[1] *Baptist Martyrology*, Hanserd Knollys Society's ed., Vol. II. p. 88.
[2] Ib., p. 256.

Terwoort — Flemish Anabaptists who had sought a refuge in England, the sufferers in that sad tragedy of the year 1575, which stains the reign of Elizabeth — declared, "We believe that Jesus Christ is true God and man."[1] All these persons, however, decline to concede that Christ took his flesh of the virgin. That, say they, is not revealed. "We ought rather," urge the last named of these martyrs, "to mark and appropriate the fruits of the incarnation and sufferings of Christ, than pertly to dispute of the derivation of his flesh; which," they add, "we nevertheless confess, so far as Scripture hath testified thereon, being satisfied with what you desire, that he is come in the flesh." Then they exclaim, with touching pathos, "Would that the people were also content with that, and not urge us to confess that Christ derived his flesh from the 'substance of the Virgin Mary,' which we can neither comprehend nor believe; since the word 'substance' is not to be found in the holy Scripture."[2] We certainly could not defend, indiscriminately, the soundness of Anabaptist views on the question of the Divinity of Christ; but the testimonies are ample and incontestable, that their questionings about the mystery of his birth did not necessarily involve the denial of his Divinity.

This incidental point, however, is perhaps a digression. We have found Anabaptists in England, distinguished from the "fierce and barbarous," as "moderate and gentle." We have found them propagating their

1 *Broadmead Records,* Hanserd Knollys Society's ed., *Hist Int.,* p. lxvii.
2 Letter of the martyrs to John Fox, *ib.,* Appendix, p. 505.

doctrines and making proselytes. Whatever questions may arise as to the previous existence of persons of similar faith in England, from the time of Wickliffe down, it is certain that the seeds of Baptist faith now scattered germinated in English soil, and became ineradicable. There are numerous incidental proofs of their activity and increase during the reign of Elizabeth. Bishop Jewel ranks them among the "pests" that sprang up, like mushrooms, "in the Marian night," and we may add, that not only sermons and books, but prisons and flames also, were witnesses of the prevailing zeal to pluck them up during the Elizabethan day. Whitgift declared that Puritanism would draw in Anabaptism, and he was right. "In the summer time," says Underhill, "they met in the fields. Seated on a bank, they read, and listened to exhortations, from the word of God, by some of their number. In the winter they assembled in a house, at the early hour of five; the day was passed in prayer and Scripture exposition. They dined together, then collected money to pay for their food, carrying the surplus to any of their brethren who were in bonds for the testimony of a good conscience."[1]

We have thus the proofs of a connection in England between the moderate Anabaptists of the Continent and our English progenitors. We are now to see that Puritan exiles from England, dwelling amid such Anabaptists on the Continent, imbibed their views, and returned to establish Baptist churches in their own land.

[1] *Broadmead Records, Hist. Int.*, pp. l., lxxi.

The limits within which I am necessarily confined do not permit me to enter at length on the perplexing question of the Continental Anabaptists. The analysis already cited indicates the classes under which, with all their multiform varieties, they naturally fall. This general allusion, however, is hardly sufficient for our present purposes, and I may be pardoned, therefore, for recalling that question to your consideration, in order to determine more specifically the character of the people with whom the English exiles came in contact. The world has heard so much of frantic proceedings on the Continent, which dishonored the name of Anabaptists, that the name has come to be very generally regarded as applicable to madmen only, and the error can be corrected in no other way than by perpetual iteration.

The rejection of infant baptism, at the period of the Reformation, did not manifest itself as a mere vulgar error. It was so natural a development of the principles of the Reformation, that it could not but suggest itself to the learned, and, at the same time, was so startling a development as to cause the conservative and the timid to hesitate before committing themselves to such a result. Melancthon acknowledged this as "a weak point." "The questions concerning baptism affected me, and, in my opinion," said he, "not without good reason."[1] It is melancholy to reflect that the same gentle name is associated in the proceedings of

1 Hague's *Hist. Discourse*, pp. 65, 67, 173. The authorities referred to by Dr. Hague, are, Neander, in a conversation and in a letter, and Planck's *History of Protestant Theology*, Vol. II. p. 47.

the Diet of Homburg, with the sentiment, "that the Anabaptists may and ought to be restrained by the sword."[1] Zwingle, too, bitterly as he afterwards persecuted the Anabaptists, was at first agitated by their questions, and inclined to their views.[2] The same was true of Oecolampadius.[3] It was no easy thing to reconcile the involuntary rite with the obligations of a personal and voluntary profession, resulting logically from the doctrine of justification by faith. Men of learning and ability, friends and coadjutors of these reformers, gave up the attempt in despair, and committed themselves to their principles, whithersoever they might lead.

It was such men with whom the Anabaptists had their origin at Zurich. Mantz and Grebel, Hetzer and Hubmeyer, were all able and learned men.[4] Mantz, in opposition to Zwingle's "indiscriminate church con-

1 *Baptist Martyrology,* Vol. I. p. 164.

2 *Ib.*, pp. 66, 71.

3 *Ib.*

4 "The question of pædobaptism began to be agitated in Switzerland in 1523 or 1524. Among its earliest opponents were Balthasar Hubmeyer, Conrad Grebel, Felix Mantz, and Louis Hetzer, — all men of learning and ability."—*Baptist Martyrology,* Vol. I. p. 6. In the ample and elaborate editorial additions and notes contained in the Hanserd Knollys Society's editions of these volumes, will be found biographical sketches, which remove the heavy weight of reproach under which party spirit has for long buried some of these reformers. Hubmeyer was a brilliant scholar and preacher, and though there is reason to believe he partially recanted under torture, he reäffirmed his faith, and died a martyr. The monstrous and incredible charges against Hetzer seem to have been a later invention, to remove the ignominy of his condemnation. "No one," wrote an eye-witness, "has with so much charity, so courageously, or so gloriously laid down his life for Anabaptism, as Hetzer. He was like one who spake with God and died." See Vol. I. pp. 4—11, 12—16, 61—75, 97—101.

stitution," allied to the state, and upheld and promoted by its power, demanded a church composed of spiritual persons only, introduced into it by a voluntary baptism. He was reproached, in reply, as "wishing a church free from sin," and his followers as exalting themselves in point of holiness above their neighbors. He denied the right of the magistrate to interfere in matters of religion, and this was stigmatized as contempt by the civil authority. His career was short. The magistrates issued their edicts against the Anabaptists, and persecution was commenced. Nevertheless, "in fields and in woods, as occasion offered, with the Hebrew and Greek Scriptures in his hand, he expounded the word of God to the people who flocked to hear him." Seized and imprisoned, tried and condemned, he died serenely, as became a Christian martyr. His death was by drowning. Zwingle, his old friend, the companion of his earlier studies, who, in the sacred relations of friend and fellow-student, had known his doubts on baptism, and had himself felt their force, is reported by Brandt to have pronounced his sentence in the four words, scarcely less impious than unfeeling, "*Qui iterum mergit, mergatur.*"[1] Erasmus, startled by these transactions in Zurich, in a letter to his friends in East Friesland, exhorting them to abide in the Ark, paid incidentally his tribute to the character of the sufferers: "a people," said he, "against whom there is very little to be said, and concerning whom we are assured there are many who have been reformed from

[1] Brandt's *Hist. Ref.*, fol. ed., Vol. I. p. 57.

the worst to the best lives; and though perhaps they may foolishly err in certain opinions, yet have they never stormed towns nor churches, nor entered into any combinations against the authority of the magistrate, nor driven anybody from his government or estate."[1]

Contemporary with this movement in Switzerland, a similar people appear in the Netherlands. I cannot here pursue the history of their sufferings. It is among the most melancholy recitals of a period of horrors. Conceding the abuse of their principles by multiform sects who sprung from even the better class of them, and the extravagance and madness of others, between whom and these Christians there was never either connection or sympathy, it is sufficient for the present purpose to say that exemplary and suffering people, known by this name, transmitted their faith and their virtues to descendants in the Low Countries, with whom, three-fourths of a century later, our English progenitors came in contact. And yet I ought not to pass in utter silence over that great intervening period. The history of English liberty links itself indissolubly with the rise of the Dutch Republic. The impulses of that movement were felt across the channel, quickening the preparations for the Commonwealth and the English and American Revolutions. The history of that period indicates an honorable connection of the Anabaptists with the cause of the great Prince of Orange. When gloom rested heavily on his affairs; when his plans

1 Quoted in Brandt, Vol. I. p. 58.

demanded pecuniary supplies, for which he appealed to the rich and the great with little success; when nobles and gentlemen, once foremost in his support, were now wavering and inactive,—we behold in his presence humble Anabaptist pastors, who, at the risk of their lives, had brought to his camp the contributions of their brethren. "They prayed him to take in good part that small present [of over a thousand guilders], declaring that they esteemed his favor greater than the gift, and that they never desired to be repaid." When the prince asked them what return he could make, they replied, "Nothing but his protection, in case God bestowed upon him the government of these provinces."—"That," said the prince, "would he show to all men, especially to them that were exiles and refugees as well as he."[1] Nobly did he fulfil that pledge. Once and again he was importuned to prosecute the Anabaptists, and once and again he repelled the proposition. His testimony is conclusive as to their loyalty, their industry, and their virtue,—reminding us, by the terms in which it was given, of that of the Dutch ambassador Van Beuning, as furnished, at a later period, in his conversation on Toleration in the Netherlands, with the French warrior Turenne. "Why," said he, "should they not be tolerated? They are very good and quiet people. They do not aspire to dignities; an ambitious man never meets them in his way; they never oppose us by any competition and canvassing. * * We do not fear the rebellion of a sect that

[1] Brandt's *Hist. Ref.*, Vol. I. p. 295. Motley's *Dutch Republic*, Vol. II. p. 250.

teaches, among other things, that one ought never to bear arms. * * We raise troops with their money, which do us more service than they would by listing themselves. They edify us by their simplicity; they apply themselves to arts and trades, without lavishing away their estates by luxury and debauchery. * * These people think themselves as much bound by their promise to speak the truth, as if they took an oath."[1] We may well repeat his question, "Why should they not be tolerated?" It is a mournful reflection, that those who were urging William to persecute these quiet people, were themselves, at the very time, hunted by the sanguinary bigot who sat upon the Spanish throne, and were pleading, in their own behalf, the rights of conscience.

Among those whom William was asked to persecute, and of whose industry and thrift he is the witness, were the Anabaptists of Middelburg. In this very city occurred the first intercourse of the English exiles with the Dutch Anabaptists, of which we have knowledge. Here Robert Browne, with his followers, towards the close of the sixteenth century, found a refuge from persecutions at home. Their views of the spiritual character of the church rendered them peculiarly susceptible to the influence of the Anabaptists, who formed at Middelburg "a flourishing community," and whose views "the greater part" of the exiles adopted.[2] We cannot suppose, however, that this occurrence at Middelburg was singular, even thus early in the history of

[1] Bayle, Art. *Anabaptists*, note.

[2] *Broadmead Records, Hist. Int.*, p. xxxv.

the exiles. For only a few years later (1597), John Payne, addressing, from Harlaem, his brethren who frequent the Royal Exchange [of London], warns them to avoid "the new English Anabaptists." "I wish you beware," he says, "of the dangerous opinions of such English Anabaptists, *bred here*, as whose parsons, in part, with more store of their letters, doth creep and spread among you, in city and country."[1] Perhaps it was this "creeping and spreading" of opinions in England which gave rise to the mission of Mr. Richard Blount, who is said to have been sent to Holland to receive baptism, and who, on his return, baptized Mr. Samuel Blacklock,—the two then baptizing the rest of the company, fifty-two in number.[2] Certain it is, that ten years later than the warning missive of Mr. John Payne, a schism among the Brownists of Amsterdam, kindred to that of Middelburg, resulted in the formation of an English Baptist Church in that city. This church, gathered by Mr. John Smyth, and after his death under the ministry of Mr. Thomas Helwisse, was composed of that noble company of exiles, who, doubting their right to enjoy their asylum in Holland while their brethren were hunted and oppressed at home, resolved to return to their own country, "to challenge"—the words are their own—"to challenge king and state to their faces, and not give way to them—no, not a foot." They did return, proclaiming, in their Confession of Faith, "that the magistrate is not to meddle with religion, or matters of conscience, nor compel men to this or that form

[1] *Broadmead Records, Hist. Int.*, p. lxxiii.

[2] Neal's *History of the Puritans. Supplement.* Vol. II. p. 361.

of religion, because Christ is the King and Lawgiver of the church and conscience." It was this return to the dangers of persecution, and this proclamation of the rights of conscience, to which the pilgrim pastor, John Robinson, replied, in a publication which places him, in regard to the question of religious liberty, in unfavorable contrast with his Baptist brethren.[1] Of the active correspondence of those who composed this church of the exiles with the Dutch Anabaptists of Amsterdam, interesting evidences have been discovered within a few years, tending, among other things, to lift from John Smyth, that man "of able gifts," the reproach of *self-baptism*, under which he had lain for more than two centuries,—"*se ipsos baptizare*," meaning only, it is contended, that it was lawful for the company of Christians to which he belonged, converted to Scriptural views of baptism in their exiled condition, to institute baptism *among themselves*, instead of receiving it from their Dutch brethren. The Dutch denied this, and John Smyth, on whom the reproach of *self-baptism* abides, was convinced by their arguments, and acknowledged that he was mistaken.[2]

The return of this church from Holland, in 1611, may be accepted as the date of the permanent establishment of distinct Baptist churches in England.

Arrived at this period, we cannot but pause to notice the character of the elements now combined for the complete development of our denominational faith.

1 See Mr. Robinson's "Religious Communion," etc. *Works*, Doctrinal Tract and Book Society's ed. Vol. III. p. 277.

2 See Appendix I., A.

We have seen the unquestionable proofs of the intercourse of our English progenitors with the Dutch Anabaptists, and of the powerful influence of that intercourse in moulding their views of the Christian Church. The Baptist denomination of to-day is, however, by no means the simple development of Dutch Anabaptism. Our ecclesiastical relations to that people are analogous to our political relations to the Dutch Republic. It is impossible to read the history of that republic without observing the identity of the principles there at work, with those which, at a later day, triumphed permanently under Cromwell, William and Mary, and Washington. And yet those principles did not so triumph on the Continent. The Dutch seemed to be wanting in the power of bringing those principles within the grasp of their consciousness, and in that sturdy practicalness of the English mind, which is never content until a principle becomes an embodied fact, adjusted to its relations to other principles and to other facts. The growth of our constitutional liberties could not have been what it was without the prior existence and influence of the Dutch Republic; nor could these liberties have become what they are without the more potent conditions of English thought and life. The dependence and the *in*-dependence of the English Baptists were not different. When the exiled Brownists of Middelburg and Amsterdam, holding the doctrine of a church composed of spiritual persons, came in contact with the Dutch Anabaptists, they found a people in advance of themselves in the development of that principle, by the logical and Scriptural exclusion of infants from baptism, and they at once followed the new light. But in the further development of that principle, they parted from the Dutch where the Dutch parted from Christ and his apostles. They repelled the curious speculations of the Continental Anabaptists, in regard to the mode of the incarnation, and affirmed the lawfulness to Christian men of holding civil offices, and exercising the functions of civil magistrates. The mode of baptism, unsettled and various on the Continent, became with them the fixed mode of immersion, — with the greater facility, perhaps, because dipping had been preserved to about that time in the Church of England,[1] but especially for the reason that a voluntary profession of personal faith must be in exact accordance with the statutes of the great Lawgiver himself. The English mind thus dropped off at once the leading eccentricities of the Continent; and as we trace the history of the English Baptists, we find, within a very brief time, that they have brought their new position into harmony, theologically and socially, with the great mass of reformed Christendom, while at the same time they have preserved the integrity and consistency of their principles. At the first, sympathizing with the Remonstrants, and therefore followers of Arminius, they became not long afterwards, in common with all Protestants, divided on the theological questions involved in that great controversy, constituting permanently two bodies, known as the General and the Particular Baptists. The church of the latter, consti-

[1] See Appendix I., B.

tuted in London in the year 1633, by a secession from the Independent Church gathered by the Rev. Mr. Jacob, may be regarded as fixing the epoch of our own distinct denominational life, and as closing, therefore, the preliminary chapter of our denominational history.

We have seen, in the inquiries thus far pursued, that the Reformation was the work, not wholly or chiefly of princes, divines, or scholars, but of peoples of various nations, whose intellectual and religious life had attained a development which demanded freedom from the restraints of the apostate hierarchy, and required ecclesiastical institutions in nearer accordance with the word of God. I think we have seen, likewise, that an ecclesiastical ancestry, found among those who had reached such a development, may be wanting in princely or priestly patronage, as were the primitive founders of the Christian Church, and yet not be wanting in true worth and honor.

I have consumed, according, indeed, to my intimation at the outset, so large a portion of my time on the views now presented, that I am obliged to hasten over my remaining topics with very summary statements.

Having thus accounted for its own rise, it belongs further to Baptist history to define, by a thorough analysis and exposition, the matured faith of the founders of the denomination, and to exhibit their true relations to other branches of the one Christian family. What was the position which our progenitors, by these manifold developments, and through these long struggles, had attained, at the period which we have named as the epoch of our distinct and recognized denominational origin? What ideas did they represent? What mission did they undertake? How far were those ideas and that mission the common distinctions of Protestantism, and how far peculiar to themselves? Happily, the materials for solving questions like these are abundantly supplied in our formularies and our literature.

The rapid increase of Baptists from 1633 to 1643, had brought upon the rising sect the bitter reproaches of an age bitter with religious controversy. Charged with being Pelagians, Socinians, Arminians, Soul-sleepers, and the like, and ridiculed as ignorant and fanatical, seven churches of London, in the latter year, issued their Confession of Faith, the first published by the Particular Baptists, and the type of all which have since followed.[1] Preceding the Westminster Confession, it is not less sound in the fundamentals of Christianity, as may be seen by comparing it with the work of the Westminster Assembly. It is remarkable for clearness, breadth, and acuteness, the production of cultivated minds, and an effectual answer to the reproaches which occasioned its issue. Among the names appended to it we observe those of Benj. Cox and Hanserd Knollys, distinguished as scholars and preachers; Samuel Richardson, a voluminous and able writer; and William Kiffin, who stood honored in the presence of kings. From this Confession, and from contemporary controversial works, the productions of men of learning and

[1] See Appendix I., C.

ability, it is clear that the founders of the denomination demanded only a consistent and completed Reformation, — the restoration of evangelical faith and of apostolic order. They accepted the principles of the Reformation, with the design of carrying them out, and parted company with their brethren only when their brethren declined to follow those principles to their results. It is sometimes said that Baptists are not Protestants. I think it more just to say that they are Protestants by eminence, — protesting against, not Rome only, but against everything *of* Rome which Anglicans, Lutherans, or Calvinists, retained in their ecclesiastical structure, their scientific theology, or their religious life. They accepted the apostolic as the model church; and, with a total irreverence of popes, councils, and fathers, leaped the chasm of sixteen centuries, and planted themselves on the immovable rock of the Divine Word. In that Word they found simple and intelligible statements, — that apostles and evangelists went everywhere preaching the gospel, addressing to the consciences and hearts of intelligent and responsible men and women, the claims of the divine law, and the necessity of faith in Christ; that those who accepted Christ by a personal faith, professed him before the world by a voluntary baptism; and that Christian churches were communities of men and women so converted and so baptized. These statements gave to them the law of their ecclesiastical polity. They protested, therefore, against the attempt, by a mechanical process, to make Christians of unconscious infants, as impossible in itself, and as filling the church, which ought to be holy and separate from the world, with unconverted persons; and against all ecclesiastical authority, existing or traditional, which enjoined or tolerated such a process. Since justification was by personal faith, since baptism was a voluntary act, since religious service could be accepted only as it was free, — they protested against all coercion in religion, whether themselves or others were the objects at which it was aimed. The baptism of infants, state churches, and persecution for religious opinions, they regarded as utterly irreconcilable with New Testament Christianity, and as retained from the apostate church, — the Babylonish garments and wedges of gold, destined to be the weakness and discomfiture of the Christian Israel. Alas! it was this radical demand, this demand for a reformed Reformation, which arrayed against them the timid and the conservative, and that larger class who had not stated fully to their own minds the principles for which they were contending, and who remind us of Milton's lion, in process of creation, half formed, uprearing his noble head, shaking his brinded mane, pawing to get free, but fast bound to earth by parts yet unfinished.

Having thus explained the origin, and the distinctive character and mission of the denomination, it is, finally, the province of Baptist history to trace the progress of our principles, both in our own denominational growth, and in the influence of these principles on other communions, and on the civilization of modern times. Planting himself at the period of the Confession of the Seven Churches, the Baptist historian, as he looks down the line of coming years, beholds struggles which might appall the stoutest heart, and, at the same time, triumphs, which, had they been uttered in prophecy, would have been scarcely less wonderful than those ancient ones in which the seers of the captivity proclaimed the return to Zion. Their scanty numbers, increased, sometimes rapidly, sometimes slowly, for a hundred years, he sees then, under the impulse of a second Reformation, embodying more fully their ideas of a spiritual church, augmented by ratios which, at the end of a second century, give us adherents embracing millions, and an honorable rank among the forces of Protestant Christendom. The rapid spread of Baptist sentiments during the period of the English Commonwealth; the maturing, strengthening, consolidating process of the succeeding period of persecution; the ministry and the dreams of Bunyan; the General Assembly of 1689, representing more than one hundred congregations, met to celebrate their release from oppression, by organizing missionary labors, and providing for the education of their ministry; the embodying of the distinctive sentiments of the Baptists on liberty of conscience in a civil state on this side of the Atlantic; the great names which adorn our history, in the departments of literature, in civil station, in commerce, and in works of evangelical charity, — these are events and themes which arrest the attention of the historian, and invite and repay his labors. If their influence on other communions, and on society at large, is sought, it is seen in what they have done to raise the views of evangelical Christians generally, in regard to the spiritual character of the Christian Church; in the desuetude of infant baptism; in the growth of that tree of liberty which they planted on the shores of the Naragansett, until a whole nation reposes under its shadow; and in the great questions of the church, and of church and state, which, in our own time, they have excited on the Continent of Europe, which even now are agitating synods, consistories and cabinets, in France, Germany, Denmark and Sweden, and which are manifestly destined to become the occasions of new triumphs. With enough of human infirmity and sin in our history to make us humble, there has been, by the blessing of the Divine Master whom we serve, enough of honorable success to inspire our hearts with higher hopes, and to encourage steadfastness and zeal in our future labors.

With these brief references to the last topics adduced, we must pass from the consideration of the Province of Baptist History, to a few remarks on its Uses. I regret that my limits will not permit the ampler consideration of this theme which I had designed.

I think that at the end of two hundred years we may fairly be summoned to show, by its practical workings, the superiority of the church-system which it is our mission to embody and illustrate. The friends of hereditary and of national churches — Lutheran, Calvinistic, and Anglican — have from the beginning objected to the theory of churches composed of spiritual members only, that in this world of universal frailty it was visionary and impracticable. Even at the dawn of the Anabaptist movement in Switzerland, Zwingle made this a distinct point with the Anabaptist Reformers; and within the last year, the shrill voice of the Swiss Presbyterian has been echoed from the banks of the Ohio, by the learned and evangelical bishop who presides over the diocese of Kentucky. The latter, contending as earnestly as we for justification by faith, and regeneration by the Holy Spirit, would nevertheless make churches *national*, — bringing children within the church in order to their conversion under its means of grace, and leaving the separation of the tares from the wheat to the harvest-day of the world. If your theory is the correct one, he argues, your churches, composed of those only who have been spiritually enlightened and renewed, and have made profession of personal faith in voluntary baptism, ought to be more distinguished than others by the practical fruits of Christian piety, by the graces of love and union and Christian zeal. He demands, with propriety and force, have the facts answered to the theory? Has "the life of God in the soul of man" been better developed and illustrated with you than with those whose theory admits a more comprehensive and indiscriminate membership? I cannot deny the justice of the appeal; nor can I answer it without a familiar acquaintance with our history. I do not shrink from the historical scrutiny to which it invites. Marred our history is by backslidings, which remind us of our full share in human frailty; but when I contemplate our beginnings, the reproaches and persecutions through which we passed, the disadvantages of many kinds under which we have since labored, and then review our growth, with its beneficent results to the church catholic and to mankind, I cannot but admire the testimonials which it furnishes in praise of the glory of His grace who has made us a separate and peculiar people. Our church-system has its adequate vindication in our history.

I think, in the second place, that the study of our history will aid us in the settlement of practical questions, relating to polity, and to agencies and methods of evangelization. We have been from the first a practical people, and as exigencies have arisen, they have been met by courses of policy determined by men who bowed with reverence to the authority of the Divine Word, who prayed much, and were earnest in their work. The recorded experience of such men opens a mine of practical wisdom which we cannot afford to neglect. Take, for illustration, the single question of an educated ministry. I do not say that nothing on that subject is to be learned beyond what our fathers have taught us, but I think it safe to say that we shall go into error when we stray from the path which they opened. Their views and plans were conformed equally to the spirit and procedure of primitive Christianity, and to their own condition and necessities. They neither repelled from the ministry, for the lack of intellectual culture, good men who, in their "aptness to teach," furnished evidence of a divine call to the sacred office, nor did they fail either to recognize the advantages to the ministry of liberal learning, or to provide the best means in their power for securing those advantages. A considerable number of the early ministers of the Baptist churches, such as Cox, Knollys, Tombes, and Jessey, were graduates of the English universities, and some of them ranked high among the learned men of a learned age. Many of their controversial works were written with masterly ability. Vavason Powell's examination of the Prayer Book was not less keen and effective than it was sententious and logical, and De Laune's Plea for the Non-conformists honors the verdict of Defoe, who ranked him among the first of thinkers and scholars. Recall our progress. The first Particular Baptist church was organized, as we have seen, in 1633. In ten years seven churches in London united in a Confession. In the period of the Commonwealth they had increased so rapidly that it becomes impossible to trace their growth or to estimate their numbers. Hunted and oppressed during the succeeding reigns of Charles and James, their men of learning and influence fined and imprisoned, they had nevertheless increased in numbers, and so consolidated their organizations, that more than one hundred congregations[1] were represented in the General Assembly of 1689. It was impossible for a people, mainly of the middle and humbler classes, so persecuted and impoverished, and shut out from the endowed schools and universities, to provide a learned ministry for the demands of such a growth. And yet the desirableness of learning to the ministry seems never even then to have been forgotten. Mr. Tombes, so early as 1650, had three young men under his personal instruction, two of whom subsequently rendered eminent service in our

[1] All the Particular Baptist churches of the kingdom were not represented in this Assembly.

churches. It is stated further, that in those days of common peril and suffering, this only practicable method was followed by Baptist and Pedobaptist pastors, without distinction of sentiment, on the part of the pupils, as to the points at issue between them. In 1675, letters were sent by the Baptist ministers of London to the churches throughout England and Wales, inviting their brethren to a meeting, in the month of May following, to take measures "for the providing an orderly standing ministry in the church, who might give themselves to reading and study, and so become able ministers of the New Testament." Dyke and Kiffin were among the signers of this call. Whether the meeting was held, or what was the result, we do not know. In 1686, the venerable Terrill, of the Broadmead church, whose pastor, a man "of great learning,"[1] died in prison, for the testimony of Jesus, and who, himself a man of very considerable acquirements, appreciated the value of learning to a minister of Christ, had left by his will the provision which subsequently became the foundation of the Baptist College at Bristol. As soon as the heavy weight of persecution was removed by the glorious Revolution of 1688, the General Assembly, already alluded to, met in London, and took vigorous measures for the education of the ministry of our churches. The benefactions of Hollis to Harvard College and to the Philadelphia Association; the early efforts of that Association, prompted by these benefactions, to secure an educated ministry; the Education Society at Charles-

[1] *Broadmead Records*, p. 493.

ton, which a hundred years ago supported Samuel Stillman in his studies;[1] the call for an educated ministry which succeeded the astonishing growth of our denomination about the middle of the last century, and led to the establishment of Brown University, — these are links in an unbroken chain, connecting this honored theological institution, whose anniversary we now celebrate, devoted to the highest professional learning of our times, with the humbler labors in the same cause of Terrill and Knollys, Dyke and Tombes. We perfect their work; we do not depart from their principles. They demanded grace before learning, and then learning to the utmost practicable extent. This principle pervades our history with the uniformity of a law. We have never had a ministry universally learned. Besides that this has been forbidden by our rapid growth, we may doubt whether, in any conceivable stage of human progress, such a ministry will be found in accordance with the divine plan. No church-system can be a divine one which is not adapted to universality, and none can be adapted to universality which is not exclusive of castes, high or low — which does not welcome alike to its fellowship the cultivated and the rustic, and furnish to all their suitable aids to edification, and their fitting spheres of service for Christ. As matter of fact, he calls to his ministry men of all ranks, all conditions, all grades of culture not below "aptness to teach." He did it in the first age, and has done it since in all the active ages of his church. We may

[1] Benedict's *History of the Baptists*, ed. 1813, Vol. II. p. 136.

infer that he always will do it. Our system requires us to welcome to the service all whom he calls, and then to raise all to the highest possible intellectual efficiency, by the highest culture practicable for each. With the advance of popular intelligence, "aptness to teach," which is but relative, must require higher preparations for the duties of the sacred office, and the aggregate culture of the ministry must rise in proportion. Always for them to whom the completest education is possible, the completest education is a duty; for, in learning, sanctified, in earnest, and practical, lies the greatest human power. I understand this to have been the theory of our fathers, the earliest and the best of them, and the theory of our whole history. I believe there can be no better. It seems to me to reconcile views at present conflicting among us, by opening wide the door for all true laborers, while at the same time, wherever practicable, it demands the most thorough preparatory and life-long discipline.

And as on the subject of ministerial education, so on various others, our history is replete with discussions and experiences, in which we may find lamps for our own paths, which will neither grow dim nor mislead us.

Finally, the study of our history will evoke and sustain a true denominational spirit, and so minister effectively to the progress and triumph of our distinctive principles. The great truths of Christianity — those which pertain to our salvation, and so lie at the basis of Christian character and Christian brotherhood — we hold in common with other branches of the one household of faith. In urging an awakened denominational spirit, I shall not, I trust, be suspected of a wish to violate the charity of this comprehensive and sacred relationship. What I ask is that we may understand ourselves, and perform in the spirit of Christianity our distinctive mission. As it was the maintenance and spread of certain principles which justified the original formation of Baptist churches, so, if their continuance is to be justified, it must be on similar grounds. Our fathers formed churches not to supplement the gospel of the Reformation, but to give it free scope and power, — to rescue it from perversions and additions, and to embody it in institutions of Divine appointment, and therefore of greater efficiency in the world's regeneration. The principles for which they contended were the unshared authority of the Word of God, the personal character of faith and a religious profession, and the inviolability of the rights of conscience. They demanded that Christ alone be King in Zion, reigning over voluntary subjects, by laws of his own ordination. The Christian world more nearly accords with us now on all these questions than it did two hundred years ago; especially is this true in this country and in Great Britain, the more immediate sphere of our influence. The practices of our brethren around us have burst the restraints of their written formularies, and some of them have but to state their positions to their own consciousness, and they are Baptists at once. It is a striking fact, that at the very time when the desuetude of infant baptism in evangelical churches is arresting attention and challenging inquiry, the work of

Litton,[1] one of the most elaborate and scientific works on the church which have appeared in our language for two centuries, takes fundamental grounds which, by a logical and by a well-nigh admitted necessity, make the church Baptist. We have gained much, but not all. In Germany, Denmark, and Sweden, our controversies of one and two centuries ago are renewed to-day. The field of religious liberty with us is won; but even here tradition has not given place to the complete supremacy of Scripture, nor is the spiritual character of the primitive churches fully restored. We have a great work still before us. We may increase our numbers, while we fulfil but imperfectly this distinctive mission. We may stand on an equal footing with our brethren in the matters of wealth, culture, and social position — in the learning of our ministry, and in the luxury and elegance of our appointments for worship, and yet may fail to bear our proper part in that great purpose which justified and demanded our denominational origin, and which has illustrated and adorned our denominational history. It was the aim of our progenitors to restore the order of apostolic churches, and so to bring back the power of primitive Christianity. "I believe and

[1] The Church of Christ, in its Idea, Attributes, and Ministry: with a Particular Reference to the Controversy on the Subject between Romanists and Protestants. By Edward Arthur Litton, M. A., Perpetual Curate of Stockton Heath, Cheshire, and late Fellow of Oriel College, Oxford. Philadelphia, 1856.

Mr. Litton's work coincides in important particulars with the work of the Rev. John S. Stone, D. D., on the True Comprehension of the Church, printed several years ago, for his own congregation, — that of Christ Church, Brooklyn. It is to be regretted that portions of Mr. Litton's work are omitted in the American edition.

know," said Hubmeyer, "that Christendom will not receive its rising aright, till baptism and the Lord's Supper are restored to their original purity."[1] In that faith, seeking a perfected reformation, our fathers labored. Whether preaching to little congregations in England, gathered privately to avoid the interruptions of officials and the penalties of the law, or itinerating among the new settlements of this country, and planting the seeds of the gospel with the first opening of the soil to cultivation, everywhere they understood, with remarkable distinctness, the character of their work, and felt its high inspiration. We shall catch their spirit by studying their deeds. We shall then imitate their zeal, and renew their successes. We shall gain, not a mere party triumph, which is unworthy of Christian men, but the increase of that moral power in the church, which, under the blessing of God, will the sooner achieve the world's regeneration. Let our name[2] and our memory perish, if only Christ reigns in an obedient and sanctified church. And he must so reign; for, in the glorious words of the same martyr, "DIVINE TRUTH IS IMMORTAL; IT MAY, PERHAPS, FOR LONG, BE BOUND, SCOURGED, CROWNED, CRUCIFIED, AND FOR A SEASON BE ENTOMBED IN THE GRAVE; — BUT ON THE THIRD DAY IT SHALL RISE AGAIN VICTORIOUS, AND RULE AND TRIUMPH FOREVER."[3]

[1] *Baptist Martyrology,* Vol. I. p. 72.

[2] See Appendix I. D.

[3] Quoted by E. B. Underhill, Esq., *Christian Review,* 1852, p. 48.

APPENDIX I.

NOTES.

A. THE ALLEGED SELF-BAPTISM OF JOHN SMYTH.

B. THE HISTORICAL BAPTISM OF THE ENGLISH PEOPLE.

C. CREED-STATEMENTS IN THE BAPTIST DENOMINATION.

D. "BAPTISTS."

A.

THE ALLEGED SELF-BAPTISM OF JOHN SMYTH.

THE charge of self-baptism is sustained by the testimony of the Pilgrim pastor, John Robinson, in his work on "Religious Communion," etc. The following is his language:

"Lastly, If the church be gathered by baptism, then will Mr. Helwisse's church appear to all men to be built upon the sand, considering the baptism it had and hath; which was, as I have heard from themselves, on this manner: Mr. Smyth, Mr. Helwisse, and the rest, having utterly dissolved and disclaimed their former church state, and ministry, came together to erect a new church by baptism; unto which they also ascribed so great virtue, as that they would not so much as pray together before they had it. And, after some straining of courtesy who should begin, and that of John Baptist (Matt. iii. 14) misalleged, Mr. Smyth baptized first himself, and next Mr. Helwisse, and so the rest, making their particular confessions."—*Works*, vol. iii. p. 168.

This language is, certainly, not ambiguous: "Mr. Smyth baptized *first himself*, and next Mr. Helwisse, and so the rest." In reference to the source of his information, he says, "as I have heard from themselves."

The biographers of Mr. Smyth, and the Baptist Historians, Crosby and Ivimey, have been entirely skeptical in regard to this alleged self-baptism. It has been argued that the charge has proceeded from enemies only, and that, if there had been any truth in it, some intimation of the propriety of such an act would have been found somewhere in the writings of Mr. Smyth, or in those of his friends. Speculations of this sort, however, are hardly a reply to the express testimony of Mr. Robinson. Was Mr. Robinson mistaken? He was not an eye-witness, — he was a resident of Amsterdam for a brief time only, and then went to Leyden, — he "heard" the manner of establishing the new church narrated. Did he understand correctly what he heard? Or, did he misinterpret *instituting baptism among themselves*, by supposing it to mean *self-baptism?* The controversy seems to be narrowed down to this single question. No inference can be drawn from the silence of Mr. Smyth after Mr. Robinson's book was written; — Mr. Smyth was already dead, and Mr. Helwisse, if still alive, was in England. It is not certain, however, that Mr. H. was still living. On the supposition that Mr. Robinson misinterpreted what he had heard, the circumstances of the case render it easy enough to suppose the statement might pass to history uncontradicted.

Recent testimony, referred to in the foregoing discourse, reaches the point in question. Edward Bean Underhill, Esq., an English Baptist, whose historic researches render him authority, in a letter to the Rev. David Benedict, D. D., dated London, Oct. 13, 1849, and published in the *New York Recorder* of Nov. 21, writes as follows:

"In a visit I lately paid to Amsterdam, I found some more interesting manuscripts relative to the church of which John Smyth was pastor, with the original Confessions of Faith, published by him and his 'Company.' I was also able to discover and elucidate the name of Se-Baptist, given to John Smyth, and so often used as a name of reproach. As these documents are now being copied for me, I am not able to send you the particulars, but the general facts are as follows:

"On Smyth and his people becoming Baptists, the question arose how they were to commence the practice of the rite, and by whom it should be administered. The Dutch Baptists, or Mennonites, held at the time the opinion, that baptism should be administered only by a minister or elder in office. As Smyth did not agree, in several matters, with the Dutch, they were unwilling to resort to them for baptism, and became of the opinion that it might be originated *among themselves;* they were therefore called *Se*-Baptists — persons baptizing themselves; — not that each one dipped or baptized himself, but among them they commenced the practice. After this, Smyth and several more came to be of the same opinion, on this and other points, with the Dutch, and applied to be admitted to communion with them. The Dutch received them, but at the same time required a recantation of their error. A fac-simile of this document I possess. The heading is in Latin, purporting that the persons whose names are subscribed renounce the sentiment that they may *se ipsos baptizare,* — baptize themselves, — as contrary to the order of Christ. It thus appears that the equivocal phrase, "se ipsos baptizare," became the foundation of the charge that Smyth baptized himself. But, from the controversy which arose, it is evident that the meaning of the words is as I have stated it. Among the names which follow is the autograph of John Smyth and his wife Mary. A few remained of the first opinion, among whom was Thomas Helwisse. I have seen a MS. letter of his, in which this subject is taken up and argued with the Dutch pastors to whom this letter is addressed, and he also treats of the succession of the ministry in reference to the same subject, in a printed work still extant. A copy of this letter I hope soon to possess. I may, therefore, confidently affirm, that the charge of baptizing himself, is, with respect to Smyth, a calumny; but arose from the circumstance referred to. In no other way can we account for the silence with respect to it, observed by himself in his writings, and in those of his friends."

B.

THE HISTORICAL BAPTISM OF THE ENGLISH PEOPLE.

THE Latin origin of Christianity in England would lead very naturally to the use of Saxonized forms of the Greek-Latin *baptizo*, at least occasionally, during the Anglo-Saxon period. That they were so used, is certain. Bosworth, in his Anglo-Saxon Dictionary, has "Baedzere, baezere, es; m. baezera, an; m. *A baptizer*, *baptist*, R." — the "R." referring to the Rushworth, or Northumbrian Gloss or version of the Four Gospels, written in the tenth century. The use of these transferred forms seems, however, to have been very limited. The common words were, *fullian*, *fulwian*, *fulluht*, *fulwiht*, *fulwere*, etc., all translations into the vernacular of the original words denoting the Christian rite. They occur, in numberless instances, in Anglo-Saxon literature, and do not disappear from the language until the incoming of the Norman French element, with which came in our present terms denoting baptism, has fully constituted the English language. For a time, the Saxon terms for baptism were used interchangeably with those of the Norman French; but, in the full development of the language, the latter gained the permanent place, and the former faded utterly away. A few notes of this process may be of interest to the reader:

The Anglo-Saxon language and literature were at their zenith at the period of Alfred the Great, who died 901. The language, however, remained Anglo-Saxon, until the Norman Conquest, which occurred in 1066, had begun to impress its permanent marks on the life of the people. Then commenced the changes which ultimately ripened into the language which we now speak. Sir Frederic Madden, in his Preface to *Layamon's Brut*, denotes these changes thus:

Semi-Saxon, from	A. D. 1100,	to	A. D. 1230.
Early English,	"	1230,	"	1330.
Middle English,	"	1330,	"	1500
Later English,	"	1500,	"	1600.

We shall trace the words, used by our forefathers to express the rite of baptism, from Anglo-Saxon times, down through these successive periods.

ANGLO-SAXON.

The word used in the Anglo-Saxon Version of the New Testament — a version belonging to the eighth century — was usually *fullian.* In one instance baptism was denoted by a word denoting *washing*, and in one instance *Baptistam* occurs in translating the name and title of John the Baptist.[1] As this version was translated from the Latin, it is by no means singular that such a Latin form should have been brought into it. That no more were brought in, shows how much such forms were strangers to the people for whom the version was designed.

[1] Gotch's *Critical Examination* in Appendix to *Bible Question*, pp. 200, 201.

Mr. Gotch refers, likewise, to Anglo-Saxon Gospels, found in the Bodleian Library, and in the Public Library at Cambridge, in which the words *dyppan* and *depan*, to *dip*, are used in two or three instances, to translate *baptizare*. These translations were not usual, but they indicate, beyond question, the *act* by which the Christian rite was in those days performed. The word which was commonly used by the Anglo-Saxons, *fullian*, denoted not only *drenching*, but the process of *cleansing* accomplished by it, and we may suppose, therefore, was chosen as expressing their notion not only of the visible act of baptism, but also of the spiritual effects accomplished by it. This view is confirmed by one of the extracts from the Vision of Piers Ploughman, to be presently given.

A specimen of Anglo-Saxon of the tenth century, in which the word denoting baptism occurs, is accessible to readers generally, in Chambers' *Cyclopædia of English Literature*.[1] The author was Alfric, Archbishop of Canterbury, who died in the beginning of the eleventh century.

"Haethen cild bith *ge-fullod*, ac hit ne braet na his hiw with-utan, dheah dhe hit beo with-innan awend. Hit bith ge-broht synfull dhurh Adames forgaegednysse to tham fant fate. Ac hit bith athwogen fram eallum synnum withinnan, dheah dhe hit with-utan his haw ne awende. Eac swylce tha halige fant waeter, dhe is gehaten lifes wyl-spring, is ge-lic on hiwe odhrum waeterum, and is under dheod brosnunge; ac dhaes halgan gastes niht ge-nealaecth tham brosnigendiclum waetere dhurh sacerda bletsunge, and hit maeg sythan lichaman and sawle athwean fram eallum synnum, dhurh gastlice mihte."

1 Vol. I. p. 3.

The degeneracy of Anglo-Saxon in this passage is not less noticeable than the degeneracy of its theology. The passage serves, however, the present purpose, by illustrating the use of the term denoting baptism. Reduced to English, the passage is as follows:

"A heathen child is christened (baptized, *ge-fullod*), yet he altereth not his shape without, though he be within changed. He is brought sinful through Adam's disobedience to the font-vessel. But he is washed from all sins inwardly, though he outwardly change not his shape. Even so the holy font-water, which is called life's fountain, is like in shape to other waters, and is subject to corruption; but the Holy Ghost's might comes to the corruptible water through the priest's blessing, and it may afterwards wash body and soul from all sin, through ghostly might."

SEMI-SAXON.

The Norman Conquest had now occurred, and changes induced by that event had begun to take place. *Layamon's Brut*, a metrical Chronicle of Britain, belonging to the close of the twelfth or the beginning of the thirteenth century, will furnish the necessary illustrations. Sir Frederic Madden, from whose edition I quote, says: "The language of Layamon belongs to that transition period in which the ground-work of Anglo-Saxon phraseology and grammar still existed, although gradually yielding to the influence of the popular forms of speech."[1] The popular forms of speech, there is reason to believe, were somewhat in advance of Layamon's style; that is, more of the Norman and accompanying elements had been introduced

[1] Preface, p. xxviii.

into the spoken language of the mingled Saxon and Norman people, than the style of Layamon would seem to indicate. Layamon seems almost to avoid Norman words, when certainly it is impossible to suppose that they had not become common. I do not find that he ever used the words *baptize*, *baptism*, etc., though it cannot be doubted that they had already begun to find a place in ordinary language. The rite of baptism is frequently mentioned, but, so far as I have discovered, always with the Saxon terms. The following extracts, accompanied with translations, will show the state of the language, as indicated by his writings:

and the feire Austin,
the *fulluht* broute hider in.

And the fair Austin, who brought *baptism* in hither.[1]

and thus heo wuneden here
an hundred and fif yere
that neuere com here cristindon
i cud i thissen londe.
no belle i-rungen,
no masse isunge
na chirche ther nes ihaleyed
no child ther nes *ifuleyed*.

And thus they dwelt here an hundred and five years, so that never Christendom came here to be known in the land, nor bell rung, nor church was there hallowed, nor mass sung, nor child was there *baptized*.[2]

Austin wede wide
yeond Englene-londe

1 Vol. I. p. 2.   2 Vol. III. p. 180.

he *fullehtede* kingges
and heore here-dringes;
he *fullehtede* eorles;
he *fullehtede* beornes;
he *fullehtede* Englisce men;
he *fullehtede* Sexisce men,
and sette an godes honde
al that was on londe.
Tha wes he ful blithe-mod
that folc he hafde iblessid.

Austin proceeded wide over England; he *baptized* kings and their chieftans; he *baptized* earls; he *baptized* barons; he *baptized* Englishmen; he *baptized* Saxish men, and set in God's hand all that was in the land. Then was he of full blithe mood, that he had rendered the folk joyful.[1]

EARLY ENGLISH.

We come now to the word *baptize*, used in an early English poem, the production of Robert of Gloucester, whose period is fixed at about 1280. His work is a Metrical History of England, and has been commonly held as the oldest extant work which may properly be regarded as in the English language. This writer uses the word *baptize* as one entirely familiar, though he uses *fulled* likewise.

Costantyñ ne com nower in batail non
That he nadde thorg the crois the maistri of fon,
So that he hym vnderstood of the beste won
And of Seynt Siluestre the pope hym let *baptize* anon,
And he was (as yt is ywrite) pur mesel tho,
An he bi com in hys *baptizing* hol of ys wo,
Seynt Siluestre was pope tho, and the first that ther com
Of alle popes that deide with oute martirdom,

[1] Vol. III. p. 190, 191.

For ther was non by fore him that he martired nas,
Of the luther emperoures, for eche hethene was
A chirche of Seynt Ion the *baptist* Constantyn let rere
And clepude yt Costantiniane, for he was *ybaptized* there.[1]

The following is from Robert Manning (Robert de Brunne), another of the Rhyming Chroniclers, who flourished at the close of the reign of Edward I., and throughout the reign of Edward II. Edward I. died in 1307, and Edward II in 1327.

Certes Saladyn, said the kyng Richere,
To make partie ageyn myn yit ha thou gode powere,
And for the pes to seke has thou no mystere,
Ther tille to mak me meke, my herte to yit in wehere.
Tho has power inouh, whereto askes thou pes?
And my wille wille not bouh, to grant that thou ches.
If thou the lond wille yeld, thereof is to speke,
And sithen if thou wild thy lay forsak and breke,
And take our *bapteme* of funte, as childre ying,
I sall gyue the a reame, and do the coroun kyng.[2]

MIDDLE ENGLISH.

The Vision of Piers Ploughman leads us along another step in the growth of our language. This poem belongs to the latter part of the fourteenth century — probably to the year 1362. It is "peculiarly a national work. It is the most remarkable monument of the public spirit of our forefathers in the middle, or, as they are often termed, dark ages. It is a pure specimen of the English language at a period when it had sustained few of the corruptions which have disfigured it since we have had writers of 'Grammars.' * * * * It is, moreover, the finest example

[1] Hearne's Ed., 1724, p. 86. See likewise Glossary, *fulled*.

[2] *R. of Brunne*, Hearne's Ed. p. 193.

left of the kind of versification which was purely English, inasmuch as it had been the only one in use among our Anglo-Saxon progenitors, in common with the other people of the North."[1] The great popularity which it attained continued for near a century, and was afterwards renewed at the period of the Reformation. It was still a popular poem in the days of Spenser, Shakspeare, and Ben Jonson. In this poem *baptism* and the old Saxon *fulling* are used interchangeably, as the one or the other occurs to the writer's mind, or sounds the more agreeably in his verse.

> Trojanus was a trewe knyght,
> And took nevere Cristendom,
> And he is saaf, so seith the book
> And his soule in hevene.
> For ther is *fullyinge* of font,
> And *fullynge* in blood shedyng,
> And thorugh fir is *fullyng*,
> And that is ferme bileve. — [L. 7998.

In the following passage, baptism is compared to the literal process of fulling:

> Al was hethynesse some time
> Engelond and Walis,
> Til Gregory garte clerkes
> To go here and preche;
> Austyn at Caunterbury
> Cristnede the kyng,
> And thorugh miracles, as men now rede,
> Al that marche he tornede
> To Crist and to cristendom,
> And cros to honoure;
> And *follede* folk faste,
> And the feith taughte,

[1] Wright's Ed., 1856, Introd. pp. xxvii., xxviii.

Moore thorugh miracles
Than thorugh much prechyng
As wel thorugh hise werkes
As with hise holy wordes,
And seid hem what *fullynge*
And feith was to mene.
  Clooth that cometh fro the wevying
Is noght comly to were
Til it be *fulled* under foot
Or in *fullying* stokkes,
Wasshen wel with water,
And with taseles cracched,
Y-touked and y-teynted,
And under taillours hande;
Right so it fareth by a barn,
That born is of a wombe,
Til it be cristned in Cristes name,
And confermed of the bisshope,
It is hethene as to hevene-ward
And help-lees to the soule. — [L. 10541.

In the next quotation, the word *baptism* is used:

Fendes and fyndekynes
Bifore me shal stande
And be at my biddyng
Wher so evere me liketh;
And to be merciable to man
Thanne my kynde asketh.
For we be the bretheren of blood,
But noght in *baptisme* alle.
Ac alle that beth myne hole bretheren,
In blood and in *baptisme*,
Shul noght be dampned to the deeth,
That is withouten ende. — [L. 12839.

In the following, *fullynge* and *baptisme* are used interchangeably:

The Jewes that were gentil men,
Jhesus thei despised,
Booth his loore and his lawe;

Now are thei lowe cherles.
As wide as the world is,
Noon of hem ther wonyeth
But under tribut and taillage,
As tikes and cherles;
And tho that bicome cristene
Bi counseil of the *baptisme*
Aren frankeleyns, free men,
Thorugh *fullynge* that thei toke,
And gentil men with Jhesu;
For Jhesu was *y-fulled*,
And upon Calvary on cros
Y-crowned kyng of Jewes. — [L. 13041.

Chaucer wrote a little later, and in language with much larger admixtures of foreign elements. In his Persones Tale, he says:

"And now, sith I hau delared you what thing is penance, now ye shal understand, that there ben three actions of penance. The first is, that a man be *baptised* after that he hath sinned. Seynt Augustine sayth: 'But he be penitent for his old sinful lif, he may not beginne the newe clene lif; for certes, if he be *baptised* without penitence of his old gilt, he receiveth the marke of *baptisme*, but not the grace, ne the remission of his sinnes, til he hau veray repentance.' Another defaute is, that men don dedly sinne after that they hau received *baptisme*. The thridde defaute is, that men fall in venial sinnes after hir *baptisme*, fro day to day. 'Thereof,' sayth Seynt Augustine, 'that penance of good and humble folk is the penance of every day.'"[1]

Gower belonged to the same period, and thus writes:

For all his hole hirte he laide
Upon Constance; and saide he shulde,

[1] Tyrwhitt's Ed., 1822, Vol. IV. p. 6.

For love of hire, if that she wolde
Baptisme take, and Christes faith
Beleve.[1]

We have now reached the period when already that series of translations of the Holy Scriptures, which ultimately ripened into our present received version, had commenced. *Fullynge*, as we have seen, is still used, but the tendency of the language is to its rapid and final displacement. Fragmentary translations, belonging to the first half of the fourteenth century, types and precursors of Wickliffe's, are preserved in the British Museum. Examples of these are given in the Historical Account of English Versions, which accompanies Bagster's English Hexapla.[2]

John i. 19–28.—And this is the testimoninge of Ion whan the Iues of ierulm sent prestes and dekenes vnto Ion *baptist* for to ask him what ertow. * * * Thes thinges ben done in bethaine beyond iordan ther Ion *baptised*.

Wickliffe, the date of whose version is 1380, used *baptize*, sometimes, however, substituting as its synonym, *wash*. Thus:

Matt. iii. 5.—Thanne ierusalem wente out to hym, and all iudee, and all the cuntre aboute iordan; thei weren *waischen* of him in iordan, knowlechiden hir synnes. 11. I *waisch* you in water unto penaunce, but he that schal com after me, is stronger than I, whos schoon I am not worthi to bere, he schal *baptize* you in the holi goost and fier.

The period of what is termed "Middle English," is the period of transition from *fullynge* to *baptism*. When we reach the later period of the Reformation, and the Tyndale, Cranmer, and Genevan versions, the present usage has become unalterably fixed.

[1] Gower, Con. A. b. iii. [2] P. 8.

What, then, was the *act* which was denoted to the English people by these terms *fullynge* and *baptism?* In other words, what was the mode of baptism practised by the English people from Anglo-Saxon times down to the period of the Reformation? An article in the London *Baptist Magazine* for February 1850, prepared with manifest care, by a scholar of recognized reputation, answers very fully this question.

EARLY MODE OF BAPTISM IN ENGLAND.

BY THE REV. F. BOSWORTH, M. A.

The venerable Bede describes Paulinus as baptizing in the Glen, Swale, and Trent. That this must have been performed by immersion, is evident from the practice of the Romish Church at the time, and from the subsequent practice of the Anglo-Saxons. Gregory, the very Pope who sent Paulinus, thus speaks of the ordinance: "But we, since we immerse (mergimus) three times, point out the sacrament of the three days' burial."

Bede, although in his works he seldom refers to the mode of baptism, gives sufficient evidence of the practice of his church at the time he lived. In his Commentary on John, he finds a striking resemblance between the account of the pool of Bethesda and the rite of baptism (Works, v. 581). So, also, when treating on John xiii. 1—11, he speaks of a man as being altogether washed in baptism (Works, v. 710). Furthermore, he runs a parallel between baptism and Naaman's washing in Jordan (Works, viii. 388). Forty-six years after Bede's death, the following canon was passed by Pope Clement: "If any bishop or presbyter shall baptize by any other than trine immersion (immersionem), let him be deposed." Some few years afterwards, Pope Zacharias, speaking of baptism, refers to an English Synod, in which it was strongly commanded that whoever should be immersed (mersus) without the invocation of the Trinity, should not be regarded as having enjoyed the sacrament of regeneration (Zach. Papa, in Syn. de Conc., dis. 4).

The writings of Alcuin, born at York, A. D. 735, and educated there by Bishop Egbert, abound in references to the mode of baptism. In his sixty-ninth epistle, he says: "Trine immersion (demersio) resembles the three days' burial." His Expositio de Baptisterio, Ep. 70, contains the following language: "And so, in the name of the Holy Trinity he is baptized by trine immersion" (submersione). In his work, De Divinis Officiis, he is still more explicit: "Then the priest baptizes him by trine immersion (mersione) only." Indeed, in his epistle to Odwin he relates the whole process of immersion, and its attendant rites.

At the commencement of the ninth century (A. D. 816), a canon was passed at the Synod of Celichyth, to the following effect: "Let also priests know that when they administer holy baptism they pour not holy water on the heads of infants, *but always immerse them in the font.*" With these notices, the Saxon writings themselves agree; for though, in the laws of Alured and Ina, the Council between Alured and Godrum, and very many other Saxon documents, the word used for baptism refers rather to its supposed effects, than to the mode, yet, in two Anglo-Saxon manuscripts of the Gospels, the word *dyppan* (our English *dip*) is, according to Lye, used four times for baptism. Well does Lingard, in his work on the Anglo-Saxon Church, say: "The regular manner of administering it (baptism) was by immersion."

During the Norman rule, the same method of observing the ordinance in question obtained. A Council, held in London A. D. 1200, passed the following regulation: "If a boy is baptized by a layman, the rites preceding and following immersion (immersionem) must be performed by a priest." A similar article was adopted in 1217, by the diocese of Sarum. In 1222, a Council at Oxford ordered that the rites following immersion (immersionem), not preceding, should be performed by a priest. The Provincial Constitutions of the Archbishop of Canterbury, passed 1236, contain the same reference to immersion as the mode of baptism. In the Constitutions of the Bishop of Wigom, 1240, we find written: "We order that in every church there be a baptismal font, of proper size and depth (profunditatis), and that trine immersion (immersio) be always practised." So also, in the Constitutions of Archbishop Peckham, 1279, the same language is used. The Synodus Exoniensis, 1257, calls baptism submersio. Furthermore, in the Constitutions of Woodlake, Bishop of Winton, 1308, and in a provincial Scotch Council, held in the reign of Alexander II., precisely the same term (immersio) is employed.

Lyndwood, who lived in the sixteenth century, in his Provincial Constitutions, ed. 1679, p. 242, composed by order of the Archbishop of Canterbury, explains a canon of Archbishop Edmund, in the reign of Henry III., as requiring baptisteries that would admit the dipping of the candidate (sic quod baptizandus possit in eō mergi). A drawing still exists in the Cotton MSS. of the British Museum, describing the baptism of the Earl of Warwick, in the reign of Richard II. (1381), in which the mode is evidently by immersion.[1] Prince Arthur, eldest son of Henry VII., was thus baptized. An old manuscript descriptive of the ceremony says: "Incontinent after the prince was put into the font." So, also, was Mayant, afterwards Queen of Scotland — "as soon as she was put into the font," says the account of an eye-witness. The Princess Elizabeth and Edward VI. were also immersed.

Robinson's great work, the History of Baptism, abounds in testimony establishing the conclusion of Professor Bosworth. He refers to fonts, and to constitutions, canons, and other historical records, all going to show that from the earliest times to the period of the Reformation, that which our ancestors called "fullynge" and "baptism," was *dipping*, — this being the hereditary practice, with exceptions in the case of weak or sick children. He says:

"In this country (England), ordinary baptism was always understood to mean immersion, till after the Ref-

[1] This work is a pictorial history of the Earl of Warwick, from the cradle to the grave. It is executed in a very spirited manner, and is well worth seeing. It will be found marked Julius, E. 4.

ormation, and though the private pouring on infants in danger of death was called baptism, yet it was accounted so only by courtesy. Pope Stephen had said, 'If it were a case of necessity, and if it were performed in the name of the Trinity, pouring should be held valid.'"[1]

"In brief, it may with great truth be affirmed, that during the whole establishment of the Catholic religion in England, that is, from the close of the sixth to the middle of the sixteenth century, a period of nearly a thousand years, baptism was administered by immersion, except in cases of necessity; the first converts were catechised in person, and baptized in rivers; the last were infants, catechized by proxy, and dipped in fonts."[2]

"The introduction of sprinkling instead of dipping, in ordinary cases, into this island, seems to have been effected by such English, or, more strictly speaking, Scotch exiles, as were disciples of Calvin at Geneva, during the Marian persecution. In the fourth year of the reign of Queen Mary, the year fifteen hundred and fifty-six, they published at Geneva a book entitled: '*The Form of Prayers and Ministration of the Sacraments, etc., used in the English Congregation at Geneva: approved, by the famous and godly learned man, John Calvyn. Imprinted at Geneva by John Crispin.*' In the order of baptism are the following words: 'N. I baptize thee in the name of the Father, and of the Sonne, and of the Holy Ghoste. And as he speaketh these woords, he taketh water in his hand, and layeth it upon the childes forehead, which done he giveth thanckes as followeth.'"[3]

William Wall, author of the History of Infant Baptism, was a Church of England Clergyman of the period of Queen Anne. He was a man of admitted learning and

[1] Quarto ed. Lond. 1790, p. 441. [2] P. 445. [3] P. 436.

of remarkable candor. He would even go out of his way to correct an error, though the error made for his side. Thus, some had argued from a remark in Wickliffe's writings, that that reformer held dipping and sprinkling indifferent. Wall denies that that was Wickliffe's meaning. He only testified that the "church had ordained" that in case of necessity any *faithful* person might baptize, and that *in such case* dipping or affusion *availed equally to salvation.* "Such words do not suppose any other way than dipping used *ordinarily*," says Wall. Even so late a writer as Sharon Turner,[1] perverts this testimony of Wickliffe — probably following without examination some writer less careful or less candid than Wall.

What, then, on the point under review, is the testimony of Wall?

"England, which is one of the coldest (countries), was one of the latest that admitted this alteration of the ordinary way" (that is, from dipping to affusion).[2]

He cites Erasmus, who, speaking of England in the time of Henry VIII., says of the baptism of infants, "in England they are dipped" (merguntur apud Anglos).[3]

He further cites Erasmus, who, in his Colloquy, *writing in England*, in the time of Henry VIII., says, "We dip children all over into cold water, in a stone font."[4]

"In that king's reign (Henry VIII.) the general custom was to dip infants. And it so continued for two reigns more" (Edward VI., and Mary).

The Zurich Letters contain a paper, written by the English Bishop Horn, and addressed to Henry Bullinger, of Switzerland, which is conclusive as to the mode of baptism at the period to which it refers. The paper is enti-

[1] *Middle Ages*, Vol. V. p. 183.
[2] Oxford Ed. 1844, Vol. II. p. 392.
[3] *Ib.*
[4] P. 392.

tled: "*The order of Administration of Common Prayer and the Sacraments in the Church of England in the time of Edward VI.*"

"The Ministration of Baptism" is set forth in the following terms:

"If there are any infants to be baptized, they are brought on each Sunday, when the most people are come together to the morning or evening prayers. The minister reads an exhortation to the people, in which he teaches them what is the condition of those who are not born again in Christ, and what the sacrament of regeneration signifies. He adds with the church a prayer for the infants, rehearses the gospel from the tenth chapter of Mark, upon which he makes a brief exhortation, followed by a general giving of thanks. The godfathers and godmothers then approach, and demand the sacrament in the name of the infants. The minister examines them concerning their faith, and *afterwards dips the infant in the water*, saying, 'I baptize thee in the name of the Father, and of the Son, and of the Holy Ghost.' He then makes the sign of the cross upon the child's forehead; after which the Lord's Prayer and a general thanksgiving is repeated by all. These infants are brought to the bishop to be confirmed, as soon as they are old enough to repeat and make answer to the catechism in their mother-tongue.

"Then follows the ministration of baptism in private houses, by women, in time of necessity, which is only ministered by the woman baptizing the infant who is like to die, with calling upon the name of God, and baptizing in the name of the Father, Son, and Holy Ghost."[1]

[1] *The Zurich Letters (Second Series), Comprising the Correspondence of Several English Bishops and others with some of the Helvetian Reformers, during the reign of Queen Elizabeth.* Parker Society, 1845, p. 356.

No known Service Book of the English Church gave authority to substitute something else for dipping, down to the period of the Reformation. The *Manuale ad Usum Sarum*, printed in 1530 (21 of Henry VIII.), directs dipping. Simpson, in his elegant work on *Baptismal Fonts*,[1] says: "Not one of the rituals which we have examined (he is alluding to those preceding the Prayer Book of Edward VI.) contains any permission to use pouring or sprinkling when the child is brought to the church."[2] Dipping was the law and the custom, affusion being exceptional.

[1] *A Series of Ancient Baptismal Fonts*, Chronologically Arranged, Drawn by F. Simpson, Jr., and Engraved by R. Roberts, London: Septimus Prowett, 1828, fol.

This superb volume, dedicated by permission to the Marchioness of Exeter, contains engravings of a large number of Fonts, commencing with the Norman era, and extending down to the period of the Reformation. Connected with each engraving is a full explanation, giving the period to which each Font belonged, with its materials, dimensions, etc. The dimensions are the important consideration in this connection, showing their capacity for immersion. For example, the Font in the Lincoln Cathedral, a Font belonging to the Norman era, is two feet eight inches in diameter, in the inside, and one foot one inch in depth. To the Norman succeeded the Early English Style, the style of the thirteenth century, and here we have the Font of All Saints, Leicester, two feet one inch in diameter, and one foot one inch in depth. The fourteenth century was the period of the Decorated Style, and belonging to this style is the Font of Nosely, Leicestershire, two feet in diameter, and one foot three inches deep. The last Font given in the work is that of St. Mary's, Beverly, Yorkshire, a very splendid one, bearing the date of 1530, in the Perpendicular Style of that period, three feet two inches in diameter, and one foot two inches in depth. The sizes of the whole series range from one foot seven inches in diameter and ten inches in depth, to that of St. Mary's, above named, which is the largest — the more usual size being a little over two feet in diameter, and a little over one foot in depth; all being, however, of sufficient capacity for the immersion of infants, and intended for that purpose.

[2] Preface, p. xv.

In the Prayer Books of Edward VI., the exceptional affusion was first put in the rubric. In the first of these Prayer Books *three* dippings were commanded; in the second, *one* dipping. And in both it was then added: "And if the childe be weake, it shall suffice to pour water upon it." "This," says Simpson, "was the first instance of pouring being allowed in public baptism." Treating then of private baptism, the Prayer Book prescribes the ceremony of baptizing infants in danger of death, still again preferring dipping, but allowing pouring if necessity requires. And then, as the final process, if the child lives, this private baptism is to be subjected to a public scrutiny. The priest is to inquire into the circumstances of the baptism, and if he is satisfied that the requisite forms were observed, then he is to ratify the baptism; but if he is not satisfied, then he is commanded himself to baptize the child, and the command is TO DIP, with no option of pouring.

Thus stood King Edward's Prayer Books. The exceptional substitute, pouring, was now in the rubric. Two circumstances contributed to exalt this exceptional substitute into an unintended general practice. "It being allowed," says Wall, "to weak children (though strong enough to be brought to church) to be baptized by affusion, many fond ladies and gentlewomen first, and then by degrees the common people, would obtain the *favor* of the priest, to have their children pass for weak children, too tender to endure dipping in the water."[1] Another more marked occasion of the change was the influence of Calvin. In this opinion Wall agrees with other writers. Calvin's influence with the exiles who resided in Geneva during the Marian persecutions, was immense. His Ser-

[1] Vol. II. p. 400.

vice Book was the first in the world to appoint sprinkling to the exclusion of other modes. The exiles, more or less of them, returned to England, converts to sprinkling. The views thus imported, falling in with the wishes of parental fondness, began to spread, and, as Wall testifies, the custom, hitherto dipping, began to alter in Elizabeth's reign. "In all probability," says Simpson, "dipping was from this time (the time of the rubrical change) by degrees abandoned; but many years elapsed ere it was so entirely." "Dipping," says Wall, "must have been pretty ordinary during the former half of King James's reign." Mr. Blake, writing on this subject in 1645, says: "I have been an eye-witness of many infants dipped, and know it to have been the constant practice of many ministers in their places for many years together."[1]

This reduction of the mode of baptism from dipping to affusion, did not take place without remonstrance. During all the process of reduction, there was a party in the church which steadily opposed the innovation. It was a part of the innovation to substitute the novel "basin" for the "font" of "immemorial usage," and to place the former near the chancel, whereas the font had always stood at the door of the church, to symbolize, by that circumstance, the baptized child's admission into the Church of Christ. The basin was for affusion — the font for immersion. On this point there is an instructive passage in Simpson's *Fonts.* He says:

"From the time of the Reformation to the days of puritanic fury in the reign of Charles I., there was a strong propensity to remove or neglect the Font, and use a basin instead. This was checked so long as it was possible; thus in 1565 it was directed, 'That the fonte be not

[1] P. 403.

removed, nor the curate do baptize in the parishe churches in any basons, nor in any other forme than is alreadie prescribed.' In 1570 it was directed: 'Curabunt (Œditui) ut in singulis ecclesiis sit sacer fons, non pelvis, in quo baptismus ministretur, isque ut decenter et munde conservetur.' Again, the eighty-first canon of 1603 says: 'According to a former constitution, too much neglected in many places, we appoint that there shall be a Font of stone in every church and chapel, where baptism is to be ministered, the same to be set in the ancient usuall places. In which onely Font the minister shall baptize publicly.' Among the inquiries directed to be made by the church-wardens, one is, whether the Font has been removed from its accustomed place, and whether they use a basin or other vessel."[1]

Having occasion, in an editorial article in the *New York Recorder* of May 8, 1850, to refer to the former usage of the Church of England, in respect to the mode of baptism, I maintained the same positions with those here stated, and generally upon the same authorities. I received very soon afterwards, from a learned Episcopalian, of eminent standing in his church, a letter referring to the article, in which he says:

"It is able and true. Some little modifications and additions would, to my mind, have made it more perfect. The writer, unfortunately, had not the use of the words 'office' and 'rubric,' but only 'canon' and 'liturgy.' The history of the 'Rubrics' of the Baptismal 'Offices' of all Christendom, eastern and western, would greatly strengthen his argument. He cannot too severely censure the influence of the returned Geneva Puritans in undermining the *doctrine* and *practice* of the Church of England.

1 Preface, pp. xvi., xvii.

He might have added (and I think from Wall), that not only was the 'Rubric' in the Genevan 'Office' for baptism the first in the world which *directed* (instead of *permitting*) *sprinkling*, but that the church of Calvin was the first in the world which ever witnessed the use of the basin. He might also have gone further, and proved, that just dipping the tips of the fingers in water (in the excepted cases) instead of pouring it freely, had the same origin.

"England (and Wales especially), where the hold of the ancient British and Asiatic rite had never been much relaxed, clung with much greater tenacity to the immersion of infants, than any other part of Christendom subject to Rome, except Bohemia, Moravia, etc., and Milan, where the great name of Ambrose in many things has successfully resisted the encroachments of Rome, but in nothing more than this, that all infants are there still immersed in fonts, some of which are larger than the interesting specimens to which your writer refers, and are rather in the shape of baths than fonts. The Rev. Dr. —— once gave me a most interesting account of an immersion of some eight or ten infants, in this manner, and in such a baptismal font, in one of the principal churches of Milan, but not in the cathedral.

"I suppose you know that there is not a well-read Episcopal minister in America that does not cheerfully admit all these facts. * * * The true issue between profoundly learned men is only between adult and infant immersion.

"The simple fact is, that the Church of England, with

extreme reluctance, has consented to regard *pouring* as VALID, though very *irregular* baptism."[1]

The testimony embraced in this extended note may be fittingly closed with a passage from the *Mercersburgh Review* for May 1850. It is from the pen of that accomplished scholar, the Rev. John W. Nevin, D. D., of the German Reformed Church:

"Several of the earlier Protestant church services call for *dipping*. In the first English Reformed Liturgy, a. 1547, a *trine immersion* of the child is prescribed, cases of infirmity only excepted; and it was not till the beginning of the seventeenth century that sprinkling gained the upper hand for reasons of convenience and health. Gradually the usage of the Protestant Church settled down upon the same practice which had already begun to prevail in the Church of Rome, with the exception only of the Anabaptists."[2] * * * * *

Admitting always the tolerated exceptional affusion in the cases of weak or sick children, no historical proposition is better sustained than that dipping was the baptism of the English people from the very introduction of Christianity down to the period of the Reformation. The occasions, the progress, and the consummation of the reduction from dipping to affusion, which then took place, are not less indubitable. In the earlier years of the seventeenth century, when all but they had veered away from the hereditary mode of the English nation, little companies of persecuted Christians, then taking organized form as churches, alone stood fast. With their retention of the hereditary mode they cast away all traditional accompa-

[1] This letter may be found at greater length in the *New York Recorder* of June 5, 1850.

[2] P. 238.

niments and perversions, and planting themselves on the strong foundation of Apostolic Christianity, they practised *believers' baptism.* Strong in their conviction that with them baptism was restored to its original form and significance, they denied the name to that which, in their belief, was not the thing, and called themselves by distinction, "*baptized* Christians" — "BAPTISTS."

C.

CREED-STATEMENTS IN THE BAPTIST DENOMINATION.

An interesting and a very profitable inquiry might be instituted in regard to the question of Confessions, or Articles of Faith, in the Baptist denomination. The unshared supremacy of the Word of God, held universally and with so much tenacity by us from the beginning, has undoubtedly, by a mistaken logic, led some individual churches, and the churches of some particular localities, to dispense with creed-statements altogether. Facts like these, however, have sometimes led to general inferences in regard to Articles of Faith in the Baptist denomination which are unauthorized by our history. I think we were the earliest of the dissenting bodies of England in the issuing of Confessions; and from the first, our Confessions have been not only significant of our doctrinal unity, but a condition of acceptance in our fellowship. The separation from us, in this country, of the Old School Baptists on the one hand, and of the Free Will Baptists on the other, and the falling away of the Campbellites, or Reformers, are conspicuous signs of established and authoritative doctrines in our communion; and signs as real may be found, likewise, in the doctrinal examinations at every ordination, at every church-recognition, and even at the reception in our churches of candidates for baptism. We shall see that this doctrinal unity has been a declared unity, and that the declarations have had a reflex authoritative influence.

Passing by the Confession of 1611, which belongs to the Arminian branch of the Baptist family, the Confession of the Seven Churches, issued in 1643, presents itself as the first authorized creed-statement of the Particular Baptists of England. Older than the Westminster Confession, and therefore independent of it, it is interesting, as showing how thoroughly the earliest Baptist fathers preserved the orthodox historical theology of all ages, and how readily they brought it into relations with the restored primitive polity of their churches. The Seven Churches of London, however, are not to be supposed as comprising the whole of the Particular Baptist denomination of that time. There were certainly several churches besides these, and their increase at a period immediately succeeding was very rapid. Among these churches the Confession of 1643 seems to have been generally recognized, until it was superseded by the more elaborate Confession which generally, though erroneously, bears the date of 1689. This Confession, entitled "A Confession of their Faith, set forth by the Elders and Brethren of many Congregations of Christians, baptized upon Profession of their Faith, in London and the Country," was in fact issued in the year 1677. The "General Assembly" of 1689, composed of ministers and messengers of more than one hundred churches, gave it by their sanction such an increase of weight and authority, that it has been, not unnaturally perhaps, regarded as their work, and called by their name. It is altogether more elaborate, and more logical in form and structure, than its predecessor of 1643. It became at once the acknowledged formulary of the denomination.

Before remarking upon its character, we may advert for a moment to the dates of other Confessions to which this is nearly related. The Westminster Assembly had closed its labors in 1647, giving to the world the Presbyterian Confession. The doctrinal views of John Robinson, who was "terrible to the Arminians," had crossed the Atlantic with his disciples, the Congregational founders of New England, and in 1648 delegates of the New England churches, assembled at Cambridge, framed a Confession, which, in its doctrinal articles, followed the Westminster. In the year 1658 the elders and messengers of the Congregational churches in England issued the Savoy Confession. Goodwin and Owen, their great leaders, were members of this assembly, and of the committee appointed to draw up the formulary. Agreeing with the Presbyterians on the great questions of theology, the assembly instructed their committee to keep close to Westminster on doctrinal points, engrafting the Congregational polity upon the historical Calvinism which they shared with their brethren of that Confession. In 1680, a Confession to a greater extent original, though modelled after that of Westminster and Savoy, was set forth by a Massachusetts Synod, assembled at Boston; and twenty-eight years later, this platform of doctrines was adopted by the Synod met at Saybrook, to draw up a Confession for the Congregational churches of Connecticut.

The real date, therefore, of the Baptist Confession — 1677 — places it next in order after the Savoy. With that Confession it is most nearly allied. By reference to the preliminary address to the reader, it will be seen that this Confession is the declared successor of that of 1643, — "divers" of those who framed the first taking part in the setting forth of the second. Issued in a time of persecution, it breathes the spirit of Christian manliness and of Christian meekness; the production of a period of religous controversy, it is a beautiful illustration of comprehensive Christian charity. Its framers declare that in "substance and matter" it is the same with the Confession of 1643, — in "method and manner" it varies, and for reasons which they proceed to assign. Not only for the purpose of a clearer exposition to others, but also for the better instructing of the members of their own communion, they deem it necessary to express themselves "more fully and distinctly." Approving the method and comprehension of the Westminster Confession, reproduced in the Savoy — observing that the latter follows the former not in sense only, but for the most part in terms, they in like manner follow the example of their Congregational brethren, "in making use of the very same words with them both, in those articles (which are very many) wherein our faith and doctrine is the same with theirs." "And this we did," they proceed to say, "the more abundantly to manifest our consent with both, in all the fundamental articles of the Christian Religion, as also with many others, whose orthodox Confessions have been published to the world, on behalf of the Protestants in divers nations and cities." In regard to those points respecting which they differ, they express themselves "with candor and plainness," suppressing nothing whatever, and yet, as they trust, with becoming "modesty and humility." The names subscribed to the recommendation, "in the name and behalf of the whole assembly," embrace the great lights of our churches in those days.

We are now to consider the extent to which this Confession became the authorized exposition of the faith of our churches on this side of the Atlantic.

In the first place, however, it must be premised that the Baptist denomination in America had its early growth from two principal centres,—one in Massachusetts and Rhode Island, the other in Pennsylvania and the Jerseys, —and that between the Baptists of New England and those of the other colonies named, very little intercourse was then maintained. The numbers of their churches were probably, at the commencement of the Great Awakening, 1741, about alike in these two sections,—not far from twenty in each.[1]

To what extent Confessions of Faith were declared or received by the early churches of New England, I have not the means of knowing. Backus states[2] that Mr. Clarke, the first Baptist pastor of Newport, and the chief founder of the colony on Rhode Island, "left a Confession of his faith in writing, from whence an extract was inserted in the records of his church," and a similar document, written by Obadiah Holmes, his fellow-sufferer for Jesus' sake, and successor in the pastoral office, is likewise preserved. It is certain that controversies sprung up among them, involving the questions of Arminianism and Calvinism, as well as those of the "Six Principles" and the "Seventh Day," and that these controversies were continually tending to the permanent divisions by which the different branches of the Baptist family came ultimately to be distinguished. "Most of the old Baptists," says Backus, speaking particularly of those of Massachusetts prior to 1741, "were not clear in the doctrines of grace."[3]

1 The number that were Calvinistic in doctrine in New England was considerably smaller. In 1729 there were but three such.—See Benedict, ed. 1813, Vol. I. p. 508.

2 Backus *Hist.*, Vol. I. pp. 255—260.

3 Abridged *History*, chap. xi.

The same was undoubtedly true in Rhode Island.[1] The very dawn of that great movement in New England, from which Baptist churches sprung so rapidly, connects itself incidentally with the Confession of 1689. The young and saintly Comer, pastor at Newport, had both held a correspondence for several years with ministers in New Jersey, and had visited them in 1731, travelling as far as Philadelphia, and returning delighted with "the faith and order of those churches."[2] Retiring from Newport, in part because "some could not bear his preaching the doctrines of grace," he became the founder of the Rehoboth Church, and died before he had completed his thirtieth year. There can be no question, I think, either of his influence in the doctrinal revival in New England, or of the previous influence upon his own faith and zeal, of his correspondence with the churches of the Philadelphia Association. "The pastor of the Baptist Church in Boston," says Backus, "was dark in doctrine, and opposed the revival of religion there in 1740."[3] This doctrinal darkness became the occasion of a secession from the First Church, and of the formation of the Second Baptist Church in Boston, in the year 1742. The documents which relate to this event are deeply interesting. Among the founders of this church was John Proctor, schoolmaster, a man of some estate, who, in conveying the site on which the house of worship of this church was built, *made the title of the church conditional on its continued adherence to the Confession of* 1689.[4] This church grew rapidly. Its doctrinal

[1] Backus *History*, Vol. II. p. 121. [2] *Ib.*

[3] Abridged *History*, chap. xi.

[4] See title-deed of the land on which the Baldwin Place Baptist Church now stands. It bears date July 1745, and may be found in the Suffolk Records. I am indebted for the following extract to a communication in the *Watchman and Reflector* of November 4, 1858:

position was in harmony with that of the Separates in the Congregational churches, and these in great numbers becoming Baptists, the denomination in New England soon assumed a distinctive Calvinistic character. Its first Association of Churches, formed at Warren, R. I. twenty-five years later, with the advice and coöperation of the Philadelphia Association, declared as its doctrinal basis the Confession of 1689.[1] Thus, incontestably, this Confession links

"For the uses, interest and purposes herein mentioned, expressed and Declared, and to no other use, benefit or purpose whatever.

"That is to say, to the Public use, benefit and behoof of that Church or Society whereof the said Ephraim Bound, Ephraim Bosworth and myself do now stand related as members, and of which said Church or Society the said Ephraim Bound is the present Ordained Pastor or Elder, for so long time as the said Church shall hold to, and walk in the faith which they now profess, and are agreeable in principle and practice to their Confession of faith heretofore put forth by the Baptized Churches in England, entitled 'A Confession of faith put forth by the Elders and Brethren of many Congregations of Christians Baptized upon Confession of their faith in London and the country.' But in case they apostatize and decline from the said principles of faith and practice, or in case of annihilation, then the said Land and House and premises herein granted, revert and remain to the only proper use, benefit and behoof of the next and right heirs of me the said John Proctor, their heirs and assigns forever.

"Saving, however, that upon or in case of the Churches declining from her faith, principles and practice, as contained and held forth in the Confession of faith aforesaid, if it shall please God our Saviour that there should remain three or four brethren faithful to the principles, practice and Confession of faith before mentioned, that they shall have, hold and enjoy the said land, meeting-house and premises, and their successors, forever, for the like uses, and under the same limitations, as above particularly mentioned."

[1] The following is from the "Original Platform" of the Warren Association. See Minutes, 1857:

"7. The faith and order of this Association are expressed in a confession put forth by upwards of a hundred congregations (in Great Britain) in the year 1689, and adopted by the Association of Philadelphia in 1742. Some of the principles in said confession are — The imputation of Adam's sin to his posterity — The inability of man to recover himself — Effectual

itself with the first real progress of the Baptists in New England. Prior to 1741, few in numbers, divided on doctrinal questions, and weak in influence, they enter then upon their course of remarkable development, raising aloft this venerable formulary as the acknowledged exposition and embodiment of their views of Divine truth. That acknowledgment abides to this day in the platform of the Warren Association, and its influence remains in the faith of all the Baptist Associations of New England.

The other principal centre from which the Baptist denomination in America proceeded, was, as has been stated, in Pennsylvania and the Jerseys. The Philadelphia Association, embracing the churches of this region, was formed in 1707. The eldest of these churches was gathered in 1687, by Elias Keach, son of the celebrated Benjamin Keach, who was one of the signers of the Confession of 1689. Mr. Keach returned to England in 1692, and became an influential minister there. He was the author of an abridgment of the Confession,[1] which abridgment was early in use in this country, and was referred to as authority.[2] The date at which the Confession of 1689 was

calling by sovereign grace — Justification by imputed righteousness — Immersion for baptism, and that on profession of faith and repentance — Congregational churches, and their independency — Reception into them upon evidence of sound conversion, etc."

[1] "A short Confession of Faith, containing the Substance of all the Fundamental Articles in the larger Confession, put forth by the Baptized Churches owning personal Election and final Perseverance. Subscribed by about thirty Persons, in behalf of the whole Church assembled at *Tallow Chandlers Hall*, upon *Dowgate Hill*, under the pastoral Care of *Elias Keach*."

This is the title, as given in an advertisement which I find at the end of the Fifth Edition of the Confession of 1689, printed at London, 1720.

[2] *Minutes of the Philadelphia Association*, from A. D. 1707 to A. D. 1807. Published by the American Baptist Publication Society, 1851. See the account given of the settlement of a difficulty at Middletown in 1712. I

formally adopted by the Philadelphia Association, I am unable to determine. The common impression that this adoption occurred in 1742, is manifestly a mistake. The following extracts from the minutes will indicate its earlier adoption, and the extent and character of its authority:

1724. "In the year 1724, a query, concerning the fourth commandment, whether changed, altered, or diminished.

"We refer to the Confession of Faith, set forth by the elders and brethren, met in London, 1689, and *owned by us*, chap. 22, sects. 7 and 8."

1727. "In answer to a query from the Great Valley, viz.: How far the liberty of marriage may be between a member and one that is not a member? Answered, by referring to our Confession of Faith, chapter 26th, in our last edition."[1]

1729. "Query from the church at Philadelphia: Suppose a gifted brother, who is esteemed an orderly minister by or among those that are against the laying on of hands in any respect, should happen to come among our churches; whether we may allow such a one to administer the ordinances of baptism and the Lord's Supper, or no?

"Answered in the negative; because it is contrary to the rule of God's word. See Acts xiii. 2, 3, xiv. 23, compared with Titus i. 5, 1 Tim. iv. 14,—from which prescribed rules we dare not swerve. We also refer to the Confession of Faith, chap. 27, sect. 9."

would suggest the inquiry, whether Keach's abridgment cannot be found in extensive use at the present time, in the older churches in New England, and more generally in the Southern States.

[1] Of the original edition, the twenty-fifth chapter is the one which treats "Of Marriage," and the numbering was not changed till 1742. The Minutes were revised in 1749, and "in our last edition" was doubtless added to explain the change in the reference from the twenty-fifth to the twenty-sixth chapter.

1742. "A motion was made in the Association for reprinting the Confession of Faith, set forth by the elders of baptized Congregations, met in London, A. D. 1689, with a short treatise of Church Discipline to be annexed to the Confession of Faith. Agreed that the thing was needful, and likely to be very useful; and in order to carry it on, it is ordered to send it to the several churches belonging to this Association, to make a trial of what sums of money can be raised, and to send an account to Mr. Jenkin Jones, to the intent, that when the several collections are completed, if it be found sufficient to defray the charges of the work, that then it shall go on; if not, then to drop it for this year; and if it be carried on, that then an addition of two articles be therein inserted; that is to say, Concerning Singing of Psalms in the Worship of God, and Laying on of Hands upon Baptized Believers. Ordered, also, that the said Mr. Jones and Benj. Griffith do prepare a short Treatise of Discipline, to be annexed to the said Confession of Faith."

1743. "Tuesday, the house met according to appointment, at eight o'clock A. M., to consider further the affair begun yesterday, touching the differences at Montgomery. After some time spent in debate thereon, brother Joseph Eaton stood up, and freely, to our apprehension, recanted, renounced and condemned all expressions which he heretofore had used, whereby his brethren at Montgomery, or any persons elsewhere, were made to believe that he departed from the literal sense and meaning of that fundamental article in our Confession of Faith, concerning the eternal generation and Sonship of Jesus Christ our Lord; he acknowledged with grief his misconduct therein, whether by word or deed. We desire that all our churches would take notice thereof, and have a tender regard for him in his weak and aged years, and in particular, of that great truth upon which the Christian religion depends; without which it must not only totter, but fall to the ground; which he confesses he was sometimes doubtful of. Our brother Butler gave his acknowledgment, written in his own hand, in the following words: 'I freely confess that I have given too much cause for others to judge that I contradicted our Confession of Faith, concerning the eternal generation of the Son of God, in some expressions contained in my paper, which I now with freedom condemn, and am sorry for my so doing, and for every other misconduct that I have been guilty of, from first to last, touching the said article or any other matter.'

"We had a copy of Discipline designed to be annexed to our Confession of Faith, by an order of a former Association, read and considered at this meeting, and approved by the whole house."

1752. In answer to a query from the church in Kingwood, the Association having referred to our ruin in Adam and our recovery in Christ, by the Sovereign election and grace of God, adds: "Upon which fundamental doctrines of Christianity, next to the belief of an eternal God, our faith must rest; and we adopt, and would that all the churches belonging to the Baptist Association, be well grounded in accordance to our Confession of Faith, and Catechism, and cannot allow that any are true members of our churches who deny the said principles, be their conversation outward what it will."

1761. The Association, writing to the Board of Particular Baptist Ministers, London, say: "Our numbers in these parts multiply; for when we had the pleasure of writing to you in 1734, there were but nine churches in our Association, yet now there are twenty-eight, all owning the Confession of Faith put forth in London in 1689."

It is not necessary to multiply these citations. The cordial reception, and the authoritative character of the creed-statements embraced in the Confession, are beyond question. From a period a little later than this to the end of the century, nearly every year a chapter of the Confession was made the subject of a Pastoral Address to the churches. This venerable formulary never indeed usurped the place of the Word of God; but distinctly, cordially, and always, it was a declaration to the world of the doctrines which the Association regarded as taught in the Bible.

By reference to the extract from the Minutes of 1742, above given, it will be seen that the action of the Association was not an *adoption* of the Confession, but only a "*reprinting*," and that that which made it from that period specially a *Philadelphia* Confession, was the insertion of two new articles, and provision for the elaborate treatise on Discipline, the work of the Rev. Benjamin Griffith,[1] which was formally adopted in 1743. The new articles inserted were written, many years before, by the Rev. Abel Morgan, a native of Wales, born in 1637, who had been a minister of the gospel in his own country, and who had translated the whole Confession into the Welsh language.

I have not the materials at hand for tracing, so particularly as I could desire, the course of doctrinal history in the churches of other sections which sprung more or less directly from the Philadelphia Association. The New York Association, formed in 1791, was distinctly an off-

[1] Mr. Griffith acknowledges the aid derived from the writings of the Rev. Elias Keach, the Rev. Abel Morgan, and Drs. Goodwin, and Owen.

shoot from the Philadelphia, and the inheritor of its doctrines; and the Hudson River Association, next in descent, was accustomed to publish annually, on its title-page, a summary of its faith, in harmony with the venerablé formulary of 1689.

In Virginia the Baptists had a double origin, — partly from zealous Separates from New England, who bore with them to the South the spirit of the Great Awakening, and partly from sources in connection with the Philadelphia Association. They were accordingly known as Separate Baptists, and Regular Baptists, each having a distinct organization. The Regular Baptists seem to have been the more intelligent and better organized, — the Separates the more zealous, perhaps, and more efficient. Attempts at union between these bodies were for some time unsuccessful, the chief obstacle being the rigid adherence of the Regulars to the Philadelphia Confession. Some particulars of the history of their attempts at union are found in Semple's History of the Virginia Baptists (1810), and in the original edition (1813) of Benedict's History of the Baptists, — the latter following chiefly the accounts given in the former.

The General Association of the Séparate Baptists had become so large in 1783, that it was deemed advisable to dissolve it, and form distinct Associations, with a General Committee to be composed of delegates from the several district Associations, this committee to meet annually "to consider matters that may be for the good of the whole society." This action having been taken, the doctrinal unity of these brethren was guarded as follows:

"A motion was made by John Williams: That as they were now about to divide into sections, they ought to adopt some Confession of Faith, by way of affording a standard of principles to subsequent times.

"They then agreed to adopt the Philadelphia Confession of Faith, upon the following explanations:

"'To prevent its usurping a tyrannical power over the consciences of any: we do not mean that every person is to be bound to the strict observance of everything therein contained, nor do we mean to make it in any respect superior or equal to the Scriptures, in matters of faith and practice; although we think it the best human composition of the kind now extant, yet it shall be liable to alterations, whenever the General Committee, in behalf of the Associations, shall think fit.'"[1]

What may have been the effect upon the Regulars, of this action of the Separate brethren, which seems to have been spontaneous among themselves and in view of their own purposes, I have not the means of knowing. It is certain, however, that the union of the two bodies soon followed. In 1786 the Ketocton, or Regular Baptist Association, which had adopted the Philadelphia Confession at its origin,[2] sent delegates to the General Committee, who were received on equal terms by that body. This event gave rise to the following recommendation:

"It is recommended to the different Associations to appoint delegates to attend the next General Committee, for the purpose of forming a union with the Regular Baptists."[3]

In August 1787 the General Committee met again, delegates being present from the Regular, and from all the Separate Associations. The following is Dr. Semple's account of the proceedings:

[1] Semple, p. 68. [2] Benedict, ed. 1813, Vol. II. p. 35.
[3] Semple, p. 73.

"Agreeably to appointment, the subject of the union of Regular and Separate Baptists was taken up, and a happy and effectual reconciliation was accomplished.

"The objections on the part of the Separates related chiefly to matters of trivial importance, and had been for some time removed, as to being a bar to communion. On the other hand, the Regulars complained that the Separates were not sufficiently explicit in their principles, having never published or sanctioned any Confession of Faith, and that they kept within their communion many who were professed Arminians, etc. To these things it was answered by the Separates, that a large majority of them believed as much in their Confession of Faith as they did themselves, although they did not entirely approve of the practice of religious societies binding themselves too strictly by Confessions of Faith, seeing there was danger of their finally usurping too high a place; that if there were some among them who leaned too much towards the Arminian system, they were generally men of exemplary piety and great usefulness in the Redeemer's kingdom, and they conceived it better to bear with some diversity of opinion in doctrines, than to break with men whose Christian deportment rendered them amiable in the estimation of all true lovers of genuine godliness. Indeed, that some of them had now become fathers in the gospel, who, previous to the bias which their minds had received, had borne the brunt and heat of persecution, whose labors and sufferings God had blessed, and still blessed, to the great advancement of his cause. To exclude such as these from the communion, would be like tearing the limbs from the body.

"These and such like arguments were agitated both in

public and private, so that all minds were much mollified before the final and successful attempt for union.

"The terms of the union were entered on the Minutes in the following words, viz:

"'The committee appointed to consider the terms of union with our Regular brethren, reported, That they conceive the manner in which the Regular Baptist Confession has been received by a former Association, is the ground-work for such union.'"[1]

The manner in which the Separates had adopted the Philadelphia Confession, at their last General Association, in 1783, has already been stated on a previous page of this note,[2] and should be referred to in this connection, in order to a full understanding of the present action.

Dr. Semple's narrative proceeds:

"After considerable debate as to the propriety of having any Confession of Faith at all, the report of the committee was received, with the following explanation:

"'To prevent the Confession of Faith from usurping a tyrannical power over the conscience of any, we do not mean that every person is bound to the strict observance of everything therein contained; yet that it holds forth the essential truths of the gospel, and that the doctrine of salvation by Christ, and free, unmerited grace alone, ought to be believed by every Christian, and maintained by every minister of the gospel. Upon these terms we are united, and desire hereafter that the names Regular and Separate be buried in oblivion; and that from henceforth we shall be known by the name of the United Baptist Churches of Christ in Virginia.'"[3]

This union was satisfactory to the Philadelphia Asso-

[1] Semple, pp. 74, 75. [2] See ante, p. 98 [3] Semple, p. 75.

ciation, which expressed its pleasure by vote, and entered the "plan of union" upon its records.[1] The doctrinal agreement of the Regulars and Separates was always nearer than the use of the word "Arminian" in the discussions would seem to imply. Those of the Separates who were regarded as "tending to Arminianism," would probably have accepted cordially the doctrinal theology of Andrew Fuller, as distinguished from that of Dr. Gill.[2]

The Charleston Association—the oldest of Baptist Associations in the United States, excepting the Philadelphia—was formed in 1751. Its oldest church, the venerable first church in Charleston, was organized about 1683. The Rev. William Screven, the first pastor, in "An Ornament for Church Members," printed after his death, said: "And now for a close of all (my dear brethren and sisters, whom God hath made me, poor unworthy me, an instrument of gathering and settling in the faith and order of the gospel), my request is, that you, as speedily as possible, supply yourselves with an able and faithful minister. Be sure you take care that the person be orthodox in faith, and of blameless life, and does own the Confession of Faith put forth by our brethren in London in 1689."[3] Mr. Screven died in 1713.

"In 1767 the Association, having previously called the serious attention of the churches to the subject, formally adopted the Confession of Faith published by the London Assembly of 1689. This had been previously held by the churches in their individual capacities, particularly

[1] *Minutes*, 1787, pp. 227, 233.

[2] See accounts of a discussion of the question, "Is salvation by Christ made possible for every individual of the human race?" given in Semple, p. 60, and in Benedict, Vol. II. pp. 56, 57.

[3] Benedict's *Hist.*, Vol. II. p. 123.

that of Charleston, from the beginning of the eighteenth century. The church at Ashley River adopted it March 18, 1737. Messrs. Hart and Pelot were appointed to draw up a system of Discipline agreeable to Scripture, to be used by the churches. This they brought forward in 1772, and Rev. Morgan Edwards and Mr. David Williams were requested to assist the compilers in revising it. In 1773 it was examined by the Association, and adopted. That and the Confession of Faith were printed under the inspection of Mr. Hart."[1]

The doctrinal differences of the Regulars and Separates of the Atlantic States reproduced themselves in the migrations to the Mississippi Valley. The Regulars carried with them and renewed the Confession, while the Separates hesitated, as their brethren had done in Virginia, or refused altogether. The Holston Association, first in Tennessee, organized in 1786, adopted the Philadelphia Confession. The Tennessee, formed from the Holston in 1802, did not adopt the Confession, but professed to hold its substance and spirit, with some modifications of some of the articles which it contains. In West Tennessee, the Associations adopted an "Abstract of Principles," in the form of creed-statements, very brief indeed, but, by the use of general expressions, furnishing a basis of harmony for those who construe orthodoxy with Gill, and for those who construe orthodoxy with Fuller. The Elkham Association, in Kentucky, formed in 1785, adopted the Philadelphia Confession, while the South Kentucky, or Separate Association, formed in the same year, had no Confession. Attempts to unite the Regulars and the Separates of these

[1] Benedict's *Hist.*, p. 136. See also pp. 143 and 149, where are accounts of measures for reprinting the Confession, etc., in 1793 and 1810. I have no later authorities.

Associations, as their brethren of the Atlantic States had become united, were made without success. "The Separates were afraid of being bound and hampered by Articles and Confessions, and the Regulars were unwilling to unite with them, without something of the kind." In 1801 the union was effected by mutual concessions, the fruit, it is said, of brotherly kindness and charity induced by the Great Revival of that period, and of the discovery that their doctrinal differences were less than they had supposed. The basis of union was a brief series of creed-statements, imperfect, certainly, in form, but undoubtedly intended to set forth the substance of orthodoxy. This union effected, the appellation "Separate Baptists," which had distinguished a portion of the Baptist family for half a century, passed finally away.[1]

It is manifest, from the testimony adduced in this note, that the Baptist denomination, with very rare exceptional instances, has been from the first accustomed to the utterance of its doctrinal convictions in the form of Confessions or Articles of Faith, and that these have exerted a powerful reflex influence. Even the Separates of Virginia, by their own spontaneous act, adopted conditionally the Philadelphia Confession, and their successors in the Mississippi Valley, when uniting with the Regulars, did not hesitate to set forth creed-statements of briefer form. I am not particularly informed in regard to later usages of the Baptists of the South and South West. My limited information coincides with what might be supposed the natural results of the causes here narrated. I think

[1] See Benedict's *History of the Baptists*, ed. 1813, Vol. II. pp. 216, 217, 225, 237, 238, 239, 243. See also an interesting and valuable article on the Baptists of the Mississippi Valley, written by the late Rev. John M. Peck, D. D., and published in the *Christian Review* of October 1852.

the Philadelphia Confession entire, Mr. Keach's, and perhaps other abridgments of it, preserving its language and spirit, and briefer creed-statements, like those already referred to, will be found variously intermixed. Of these last I have a recent illustration, in the "Abstract of Principles"[1] set forth by the Carey Baptist Association, Alabama, at its formation in 1855, which preserves almost the exact words of the "Abstract of Principles" set forth by the Associations of West Tennessee at an early period in their history.[2] Few things are more tenacious of life than creed-statements in religion.

In Ohio, Indiana, Illinois, and the states lying northwest of them, we may, in like manner, look for institutions and habits kindred to those of the eastern sections from which the first Baptist settlers proceeded, — sometimes modified by later and influential intermixtures from other sections. Where the eastern Baptist element was from Virginia, ordination will be by a Presbytery; where it was from New England, it will be by a Council. In reference to Confessions, the same rule will undoubtedly prevail. The East reproduces itself in the West. Whoever will accumulate facts bearing upon this point, will make a most important contribution to our doctrinal history.

This sketch would be imperfect without a reference to the Declaration of Faith, known at the present time as the New Hampshire Confession, which was issued a quarter of a century since by the Baptist Convention of that state. The work of the Rev. John Newton Brown, D. D.,

[1] For which I am indebted to the politeness of the Hon. Jabez L. M. Curry, Member of Congress from Alabama.

[2] The same is true of the "Articles of Faith" of the Coosa River Association, for the Minutes of which I am indebted likewise to the Hon. Mr. Curry.

it was written by him when a pastor in New Hampshire, with a view to pending controversies with the Free Will Baptists, who there are numerous. It has been sometimes criticized as aiming at the difficult task of preserving the stern orthodoxy of the fathers of the denomination, while at the same time it softens the terms in which that orthodoxy is expressed, in order to remove the objections of neighboring opponents.[1] Published in the Encyclopedia of Religious Knowledge, of which its author was editor, it has been circulated in many editions of that work, — published too by booksellers, in small pamphlet form, convenient for distribution in churches, it has been still more widely diffused, — and in churches of late origin it has been extensively adopted in the Northern and Western States.

In Appendix II. will be found at length the Confessions to which reference has been made in this work. The Confession of 1643 is reprinted from the Appendix to the Second Volume of Choules' edition of Neal's History of the Puritans, corrected, however, by collation with the Hanserd Knollys Society's copy in their volume of Confessions. The Confession of 1689, corrected in the same manner, is reprinted from the Pittsburg edition of 1831, in the form known in this country as the Philadelphia Confession, except that the two articles added by that body, on Laying on of Hands and on Singing, are inserted separately at the end. The Confession has been compared with the London (fifth) edition of 1720, for a copy of which I am indebted to the Rev. Wm. R. Williams, D. D., LL. D., of New York. The New Hampshire Declaration of Faith is reprinted from the edition of the American

[1] See *Christian Review* for April 1859.

Baptist Publication Society, revised by the author himself, and including two new articles, one on Repentance and Faith, and the other on Sanctification.

The Confessions here given are not to be understood as all which have been issued by churches, or other bodies, connected with the Baptist denomination. There were other Confessions issued in England[1] in the period between 1643 and 1689; and in this country Confessions have been published by Associations, churches and individuals in the denomination, variously modified, indeed, but preserving a substantial unity. Those which are here given, have had a historical character as acknowledged formularies. The laxity in respect to the ministerial office, indicated in the Confession of 1643, it will be observed, disappears in the Confession of 1689. On the question of laying on of hands, there has never been unanimous consent in the denomination, and the article on that subject in the Philadelphia Confession would be accepted now by a very limited number of our people.

[1] Some of these Confessions may be found in a volume issued by the Hanserd Knollys Society, under the title, "Confessions of Faith, and other Public Documents, illustrative of the History of the Baptist Churches of England in the seventeenth century. Edited by Edward Bean Underhill." London, 1854.

D.

"BAPTISTS."

THE name "Baptists" is both a protest against the misnomer "Anabaptists," aud a euphemism for "Baptized." It was very natural that those who believed in the validity of infant baptism, should regard as "anabaptists" those who renounced that baptism, and were baptized again on personal profession of their faith. It was equally natural, too, that these last should repel the epithet as in nowise significant of their belief and practice. As matter of fact, we find the epithet so applied and so repelled. This was true on the Continent, and true in Great Britain. "On account of your baptism of infants," said the martyr Jan Gerrits, "you cause us to be called Anabaptists, though we baptize once, not twice, nor allow baptism more than once, and that according to the truth, and agreeably to the command and practice of the apostles."[1] "It is commanded, and will be found throughout the New Testament," said another martyr, Hans Schlaffer, answering under torture, "that men should first teach the Word of God, and they alone that hear, understand, believe and receive it, should be baptized. This is the true Christian baptism, and no rebaptism."[2] "Commonly, but most falsely, called Ana-

[1] *Baptist Martyrology,* Vol. II. p. 386. [2] *Ib.,* Vol. I. p. 50.

baptists,"[1] say our English progenitors, in their Persecution for Religion Judged and Condemned, published in 1615. "Unjustly called Ana-baptists,"[2] say they in their address to the king, 1620. Whatever their baptism might be to others, to them it was no *ana*-baptism. They did not *rebaptize*, they simply *baptized;* they were not *Anabaptists*, but only *Baptists.* Distinguished by the restoration of the rite to its primitive form and significance, they very naturally took the name of the rite as their true and lawful designation. They called themselves first "*the Baptized*," and then "*the Baptists*." In 1654 "the *Baptized* churches in this nation" (England) issued their Humble Representation and Vindication.[3] "By John Sturgion, one of the *Baptized People*,"[4] was the form of authorship on the title-page of Sturgion's Plea for Toleration, 1661. "Of the persuasion *commonly called the baptized*,"[5] says the royal license to the Rev. Mr. Hardcastle, the Broadmead pastor, 1671–2. "Brother Gifford, pastor of the other *baptized congregation*," say the Broadmead Records, of the sister church in Bristol, and its minister. In this country, the title "*Baptized congregations*," or "*Baptized churches*," was preserved in the Minutes of the Philadelphia Association,[6] long after the name "*Baptists*" had come into common use. Indeed, that title is preserved occasionally, though very rarely, in the present generation, by persons who desire to be specially precise. The title

1 *Tracts on Liberty of Conscience*, Hans. Knollys Society's ed., p. 101.

2 *Ib.*, 231.

3 *Confessions of Faith*, etc., p. 327.

4 *Tracts on Lib. of Conscience*, p. 311.

5 *Records*, p. 217.

6 The Philadelphia Association has been called, though I cannot say how frequently, or how generally, the Association of "Baptized Congregational Churches." I remember the fact distinctly, but am unable to recall the reference.

"*Baptists*," so far as I can judge, is of uncertain date. I find it first in the Broadmead Records. "At that juncture of time (1640) the providence of God brought to this city one Mr. Canne,. *a baptized* man; it was that Mr. Canne that made notes and references upon the Bible." * * * * "a *baptized* man by them called an Anabaptist, which was to some a sufficient cause of prejudice; because the truth of believers' baptism had been for a long time buried; yea, for a long time by popish inventions, and their sprinkling brought in the room thereof." "This godly, honorable woman, perceiving that Mr. Canne was a *baptist*."[1] * * * Here we have the protest against *Anabaptist*, the descriptive title *Baptized*, and the euphemism *Baptist*, all within narrow space. Mr. Terrill, who made these records, became a member of the Broadmead Church in 1658. The exact date of the use of these words by him cannot, perhaps, be determined. "Once a member amongst the *Baptists*," appears on the title of a book or pamphlet published in 1655,[2] which is my earliest trace of the name. It is here, however, without any appearance of novelty. From a pamphlet entitled "Behold a Cry," etc., published in 1662, Crosby[3] quotes these words: "On the third day of the month called August, 1662, when the prisoners in Newgate, called *Baptists*, were in their chamber, seeking the Lord." * * * The name occurs likewise in the titles of works published by Rev. Daniel Dyke, in 1674 and 1675.[4] The Rev. Andrew Gifford's license from Charles R., in 1672, says: "of the persuasion commonly called *Baptists*."[5] Mr. Henry Morris, writing in 1675, used the title *Baptist* frequently, in speaking of the churches in

1 *Records*, pp. 18, 19, 21.
2 *Ib.*, p. 55.
3 *History of the Baptists*, Vol. II. p. 178.
4 *Ib.*, Vol. I. p. 359.
5 *Ib.*, Vol. III. p. 154.

Wales.[1] In 1696 and 1701, "ministers of the *Baptist* denomination" sent congratulatory addresses to William III.[2] William Wall, writing a little later, says: "As they disown the name of *Anabaptists*, or *Rebaptizers*, so I have nowhere given it to them; as, on the contrary, I do not give them the name of *Baptists*, nor of the *Baptized* people: for that is to cast a reproach upon their adversaries, as concluding that they are not so."[3] He calls them *anti-pædo-baptists.* The common use of the word in this country must have followed close upon the common use of it in England. "Our Anabaptists," says Cotton Mather, "when somewhat of exasperation was begun, formed a church at Boston on May 28, 1665, besides one which they had before at Swanzey. Now they declared our infant baptism to be a mere nullity, and they arrogate unto themselves the title of *Baptists*, as if none were *baptized* but themselves."[4] The earliest use of this title in the Philadelphia Minutes appears under the date 1712. "*Baptized congregations*," "*Baptized churches*," are then the usual forms; but in 1749, when the Rev. Benjamin Griffith, by direction of the Association, prepared his Association Book, he describes it as "containing a brief account of the beginning and progress of the churches holding and practising adult baptism, and COMMONLY CALLED BAPTISTS."

1 *Broadmead Records*, p. 511.

2 Quoted in Crosby.

3 I quote from Crosby without having Wall at hand.

4 *Eccles. Hist.*, Book VII.

APPENDIX II.

CONFESSIONS.

I. THE CONFESSION OF THE SEVEN CHURCHES, 1643.

II. THE CONFESSION OF THE ASSEMBLY OF 1689, CALLED IN AMERICA THE PHILADELPHIA CONFESSION.

III. THE NEW HAMPSHIRE DECLARATION OF FAITH.

IV. DISCIPLINE ADOPTED BY THE PHILADELPHIA ASSOCIATION.

I.

A CONFESSION OF FAITH

Of Seven Congregations or Churches of Christ in London, which are commonly, but unjustly, called Anabaptists; published for the Vindication of the Truth and Information of the Ignorant: likewise for the taking off of those Aspersions which are frequently, both in Pulpit and Print, unjustly cast upon them. Printed at London, Anno 1646. *(Second edition.)*

I. The Lord our God is but one God, whose subsistence is in himself; whose essence cannot be comprehended by any but himself; who only hath immortality, dwelling in the light which no man can approach unto; who is in himself most holy, every way infinite, in greatness, wisdom, power, love; merciful and gracious, long-suffering, and abundant in goodness and truth: who giveth being, moving, and preservation to all creatures.[1]

II. In this divine and infinite Being there is the Father, the Word, and the Holy Spirit; each having the whole Divine essence, yet the essence undivided; all infinite without any beginning, therefore but one God, who is not to be divided in nature and being, but distinguished by several peculiar relative properties.[2]

III. God hath decreed in himself, before the world was, concerning all things, whether necessary, accidental, or voluntary, with all the circumstances of them, to work, dispose, and bring about all things according to the counsel of his own will, to his glory (yet without being the author of sin, or having fellowship with any there-

1 1 Cor. viii. 6; Isa. xliv. 6, and xlvi. 9; Exodus iii. 14; 1 Tim. vi. 16; Isaiah xliii. 15; Psalm cxlvii. 5; Deut. xxxii. 3; Job xxxvi. 5; Jeremiah x. 12; Exodus xxxiv. 6, 7; Acts xvii. 28; Rom. xi. 36.

2 1 Cor. i. 3; John i. 1, and xv. 26; Exod. iii. 14; 1 Cor. viii. 6.

in): in which appears his wisdom in disposing all things, unchangeableness, power, and faithfulness in accomplishing his decree; and God hath, before the foundation of the world, foreordained some men to eternal life, through Jesus Christ, to the praise and glory of his grace: leaving the rest in their sin, to their just condemnation, to the praise of his justice.[1]

IV. In the beginning God made all things very good: created man after his own image, filled with all meet perfection of nature, and free from all sin; but long he abode not in this honor, Satan using the subtlety of the serpent to seduce first Eve, then by her seducing Adam, who, without any compulsion, in eating the forbidden fruit, transgressed the command of God, and fell, whereby death came upon all his posterity: who now are conceived in sin, and by nature the children of wrath, the servants of sin, the subjects of death, and other miseries in this world and forever, unless the Lord Jesus Christ set them free.[2]

V. God, in his infinite power and wisdom, doth dispose all things to the end for which they were created; that neither good nor evil befalls any by chance, or without his providence; and that whatsoever befalls the elect is by his appointment, for his glory, and their good.[3]

VI. All the elect, being loved of God with an everlasting love, are redeemed, quickened, and saved, not by themselves, nor their own works, lest any man should boast, but only and wholly by God, of his free grace and mercy, through Jesus Christ, who is made unto us by God, wisdom, righteousness, sanctification, and redemption and all in all, that he that rejoiceth might rejoice in the Lord.[4]

VII. And this is life eternal, that we might know him the only true God, and Jesus Christ whom he hath sent. And on the con-

1 Isa. xlvi. 10; Eph. i. 11; Rom. xi. 33; Psalm xxviii. 15, cxv. 3, cxxxv. 6, and cxliv.; 1 Sam. x. 9, 26; Prov. xvi 4, 33, and xxi. 6; Exod. xxi. 13; Isa. xlv. 7; Matt xvi. 28, 30; Col. i. 16, 17; Numb. xxiii. 19, 20; Rom. iii. 4; Jer. x. 10, xiv. 22; Eph. i. 4, 5; Jude 4, 6.

2 Gen. i. 1, and iii. 1, 4, 5; Col. i. 16; Isa. xlv. 12; 1 Cor. xv. 45, 46; Eccl. vii. 29; 2 Cor. xi. 3; 1 Tim. ii. 14; Gal. iii. 22; Rom. v. 12, vi. 22, and xviii. 19; Eph. ii. 3.

3 Job xxxviii. 11; Isa. xlvi. 10, 11; Eccl. iii. 14; Matt. x. 29, 30; Exod. xxi. 13; Prov. xvi. 33; Rom. viii. 28.

4 Jer. xxiii. 6, and xxxi. 3; Eph. i 3, 7, and ii 4, 9; 1 Thess. v. 9; Acts xiii 38; 2 Cor. v. 21; Jer. ix. 23, 24; 1 Cor. i. 30, 31.

trary, the Lord will render vengeance, in flaming fire, to them that know not God, and obey not the Gospel of Jesus Christ.[1]

VIII. The rule of this knowledge, faith, and obedience concerning the worship of God, in which is contained the whole duty of man, is (not men's laws or unwritten traditions, but) only the Word of God contained in the Holy Scriptures: in which is plainly recorded whatsoever is needful for us to know, believe, and practise; which are the only rule of holiness and obedience for all saints, at all times, in all places, to be observed.[2]

IX. The Lord Jesus Christ, of whom Moses and the prophets wrote, the apostles preached, he is the Son of God, the brightness of his glory, etc., by whom he made the world; who upholdeth and governeth all things that he hath made; who also, when the fulness of time was come, was made of a woman, of the tribe of Judah, of the seed of Abraham and David; to wit, of the Virgin Mary, the Holy Spirit coming down upon her, the power of the Most High overshadowing her; and he was also tempted as we are, yet without sin.[3]

X. Jesus Christ is made the mediator of the new and everlasting covenant of grace between God and man, ever to be perfectly and fully the prophet, priest, and king of the Church of God for evermore.[4]

XI. Unto this office he was appointed by God from everlasting; and in respect of his manhood, from the womb called, separated, and anointed most fully and abundantly with all gifts necessary, God having without measure poured out his Spirit upon him.[5]

XII. Concerning his mediatorship, the Scripture holds forth Christ's call to his office; for none takes this honor upon him but he that is called of God, as was Aaron, it being an action of God, whereby a special promise being made, he ordains his son to this

1 John vi. 36; and xvii. 3; Heb. v. 9; 1 Thess. i. 8.

2 Col. ii. 23; Mat. xv. 9, 6; John v. 39; 2 Tim. iii 15—17; Isa. viii. 20; Gal. i. 8, 9; Acts iii. 22, 23.

3 Gen. iii. 15; xxii. 18, and xlix. 9, 10; Dan. vii. 13, and ix 24—26; Prov. viii. 23; John i. 1—3; Heb. i. 8, ii. 16, iv. 15, and vii. 14; Gal. iv. 4; Rev. v. 5; Rom. i. 3, and ix. 10; Matt. i. 16; Luke iii. 23, 26; Isa liii. 3—5.

4 1 Tim. ii. 5; Heb. ix. 15; John xiv. 6; Isa. ix. 6, 7.

5 Prov. viii. 23; Isa. xi. 2—5, xli. 6, xlix. 15, and lxi. 1, 2; Luke iv. 17, 22; John i. 14, 16, and iii. 34.

office; which promise is, that Christ should be made a sacrifice for sin; that he should see his seed, and prolong his days, and the pleasure of the Lord shall prosper in his hand; all of mere free and absolute grace towards God's elect, and without any condition foreseen in them to procure it.[1]

XIII. This office to be mediator, that is, to be prophet, priest, and king of the Church of God, is so proper to Christ, that neither in whole, nor any part thereof, can it be transferred from him to any other.[2]

XIV. This office to which Christ is called is threefold — as a prophet, priest, and king: this number and order of offices is necessary, for in respect of our ignorance, we stand in need of his prophetical office; and in respect of our great alienation from God, we need his priestly office to reconcile us; and in respect of our averseness and utter inability to return to God, we need his kingly office, to convince, subdue, draw, uphold, and preserve us to his heavenly kingdom.[3]

XV. Concerning the prophecy of Christ, it is that whereby he hath revealed the will of God, whatsoever is needful for his servants to know and obey; and therefore he is called not only a prophet and doctor, and the apostle of our profession, and the angel of the covenant, but also the very wisdom of God, in whom are hid all the treasures of wisdom and knowledge, who forever continueth revealing the same truth of the gospel to his people.[4]

XVI. That he might be a prophet every way complete, it was necessary he should be God, and also that he should be man: for unless he had been God, he could never have perfectly understood the will of God; and unless he had been man, he could not suitably have unfolded it in his own person to men.[5]

That Jesus Christ is God, is wonderful clearly expressed in the

1 Heb. v. 4—6; Isa. liii. 10, 11; John iii. 16; Rom viii. 32.

2 1 Tim. ii. 5; Heb. vii. 14; Daniel vii. 14; Acts iv. 12; Luke i. 33; John xiv. 6.

3 Deut. viii. 15; Acts iii. 22, 23, xxvi. 18; Heb. iii. 3, and iv. 14, 15; Psalm ii. 6; 2 Cor. v. 20; Col. i. 21; John xvi. 8; Psalm cx. 3; Cant. i. 3; John vi. 44; Phil. iv. 13; 2 Tim. iv. 18.

4 John i 18, xii. 49, 50, and xv., and xvii. 8; Matt. xxiii. 10; Deut. xviii. 15; Heb. iii. 1; 1 Cor. i. 24; Col. ii. 3; Mal. iii. 1.

5 John i. 18; Acts iii. 22; Deut. xviii. 15; Heb. i. 1.

Scriptures. He is called the mighty God.[1] The Word was God.[2] Christ, who is God over all.[3] God manifested in the flesh.[4] The same is very God.[5] He is the first.[6] He gives being to all things, and without him was nothing made.[7] He forgiveth sins.[8] He is before Abraham.[9] He was, and is, and ever will be the same.[10] He is always with his to the end of the world.[11] Which could not be said of Jesus Christ, if he were not God. And to the Son he saith, Thy throne, O God, is forever and ever.[12]

Also, Christ is not only perfectly God, but perfect man, made of a woman.[13] Made of the seed of David.[14] Coming out of the loins of David.[15] Of Jesse and Judah.[16] In that the children were partakers of flesh and blood, he himself likewise took part with them.[17] He took not on him the nature of angels, but the seed of Abraham.[18] So that we are bone of his bone, and flesh of his flesh.[19] So that he that sanctifieth, and they that are sanctified, are all of one.[20]

XVII. Concerning his priesthood, Christ, having sanctified himself, hath appeared once to put away sin by that one offering of himself a sacrifice for sin, by which he hath fully finished and suffered all things God required for the salvation of his elect, and removed all rites and shadows, etc., and is now entered within the veil into the holy of holies, which is the presence of God. Also, he makes his people a spiritual house, an holy priesthood, to offer up spiritual sacrifice acceptable to God through him. Neither doth the Father accept, or Christ offer to the Father, any other worship or worshippers.[21]

XVIII. This priesthood was not legal or temporary, but according to the order of Melchisedeck, and is stable and perfect, not for a time, but forever, which is suitable to Jesus Christ, as to him that ever liveth. Christ was the priest, sacrifice, and altar; he was a priest according to both natures; he was a sacrifice according to his

1 Isa. ix. 6.
2 John i. 1.
3 Rom. ix. 5.
4 1 Tim. iii. 16.
5 1 John v. 20.
6 Rev. i. 8.
7 John i. 2.
8 Matt. ix. 6.
9 John viii. 58.
10 Heb. xiii. 8.
11 Matt. xxviii. 20.
12 Heb. i. 8; John i. 18.
13 Gal. iv. 4.
14 Rom. i. 3.
15 Acts ii. 30.
16 Acts xiii. 23.
17 Heb. ii. 14.
18 Heb. ii. 16.
19 Eph. v. 30.
20 Heb. ii. 11. See Acts iii. 22; Deut. xviii. 15. Heb. i. 1.
21 John xvii. 19; Heb. v. 7—10, 12; Rom. v. 19; Eph. v. 2; Col. i 20; Eph. ii. 14—16; Rom. viii. 34; Heb. viii. 1, and ix. 24; 1 Peter ii. 5; John iv. 23, 24.

human nature; whence in Scripture it is attributed to his body, to his blood; yet the effectualness of this sacrifice did depend upon his Divine nature; therefore it is called the blood of God. He was the altar according to his Divine nature, it belonging to the altar to sanctify that which is offered upon it, and so it ought to be of greater dignity than the sacrifice itself.[1]

XIX. Concerning his kingly office, Christ being risen from the dead, and ascended into heaven, and having all power in heaven and earth, he doth spiritually govern his Church, and doth exercise his power over all, angels and men, good and bad, to the preservation and salvation of the elect, and to the overruling and destruction of his enemies. By this kingly power he applieth the benefits, virtue, and fruits of his prophecy and priesthood to his elect, subduing their sins, preserving and strengthening them in all their conflicts against Satan, the world, and the flesh, keeping their hearts in faith and filial fear by his Spirit; by this his mighty power he ruleth the vessels of wrath, using, limiting, and restraining them, as it seems good to his infinite wisdom.[2]

XX. This his kingly power shall be more fully manifested when he shall come in glory to reign among his saints, when he shall put down all rule and authority under his feet, that the glory of the Father may be perfectly manifested in his Son, and the glory of the Father and the Son in all his members.[3]

XXI. Jesus Christ by his death did purchase salvation for the elect that God gave unto him; these only have interest in him, and fellowship with him, for whom he makes intercession to his Father in the behalf of, and to them alone doth God by his Spirit apply this redemption unto; as also the free gift of eternal life is given to them, and none else.[4]

1 Heb. v. 6, vii. 16, etc., ix. 13, 14, x. 10, and xiii. 10, 12, 15; 1 Pet. i. 18, 19; Col. i. 20, 22; Acts xx. 28; Matt. xxiii. 17; John xvii. 19.

2 1 Cor. xv. 4; 1 Pet. iii. 21, 22; Matt. xxviii 18, 19, 20; Luke xxiv. 51; Acts i. 1, and v. 30, 31; John v. 26, 27, xix. 36 and xvi. 15; Rom. i. 21, v. 6—8, xiv. 9, 17; and xvii. 18; Gal. v. 22, 23; Mark i. 27; Heb. i. 14; Job. i. 8; Eph. iv. 17, 18; 2 Pet. ii.; John xvi. 15.

3 1 Cor. xv. 24, 28; Heb. ix. 28; 1 Thess. iv 15—17; 2 Thess. i. 9, 10; John xii. 21, 26.

4 Eph. i. 14; Heb. v. 9, and vii. 25; Matt. i. 21; John xvii. 6; 1 Cor. ii. 12; Rom. viii. 29, 30; 1 John v. 12; John xv. 13, and iii. 16.

XXII. Faith is the gift of God, wrought in the hearts of the elect by the Spirit of God; by which faith they come to know and believe the truth of the Scriptures, and the excellency of them above all other writings, and all things in the world, as they hold forth the glory of God in his attributes, the excellency of Christ in his nature and offices, and of the power and fulness of the Spirit in its workings and operations; and so are enabled to cast their souls upon this truth thus believed.[1]

XXIII. All those that have this precious faith wrought in them by the Spirit can never finally nor totally fall away, seeing the gifts of God are without repentance; so that he still begets and nourisheth in them faith, repentance, love, joy, hope, and all the graces of the Spirit, unto immortality; and though many storms and floods arise, and beat against them, yet they shall never be able to take them off that foundation and rock, which by faith they are fastened upon; notwithstanding, through unbelief, and the temptations of Satan, the sensible sight of this light and love be clouded and overwhelmed for a time; yet God is still the same, and they shall be sure to be kept by the power of God unto salvation, where they shall enjoy their purchased possession, they being engraven upon the palms of his hands, and their names having been written in the Book of Life from all eternity.[2]

XXIV. Faith is ordinarily begotten by the preaching of the Gospel, or Word of Christ, without respect to any power or agency in the creature; but it being wholly passive, and dead in trespasses and sins, doth believe and is converted by no less power than that which raised Christ from the dead.[3]

XXV. The preaching of the Gospel to the conversion of sinners is absolutely free; no way requiring, as absolutely necessary, any qualifications, preparations, or terrors of the law, or preceding ministry of the law, but only and alone the naked soul, a sinner and ungodly, to receive Christ crucified, dead, and buried, and risen

1 Eph. ii. 8; John iv. 10, vi. 29, 63, and xvii. 17; Phil. i. 29; Gal. v. 22; Heb. iv. 11, 12.

2 Matt. vii. 24, 25; John xiii. 10, and x. 28, 29; 1 Pet. i. 4—6; Isa. xlix. 13—16.

3 Rom. x. 17; 1 Cor. i. 28; Rom. i. 16, iii. 12, and ix. 16; Ezek. xvi. 16; Eph. i. 19; Col. ii. 12.

again; who is madè a prince and a saviour for such sinners as through the Gospel shall be brought to believe on him.[1]

XXVI. The same power that converts to faith in Christ carrieth on the soul through all duties, temptations, conflicts, sufferings; and whatsoever a believer is, he is by grace, and is carried on in all obedience and temptations by the same.[2]

XXVII. All believers are by Christ united to God; by which union God is one with them, and they are one with him; and that all believers are the sons of God, and joint heirs with Christ, to whom belong all the promises of this life, and that which is to come.[3]

XXVIII. Those that have union with Christ are justified from all their sins by the blood of Christ, which justification is a gracious and full acquittance of a guilty sinner from all sin, by God, through the satisfaction that Christ hath made by his death for all their sins, and this applied (in the manifestation of it) through faith.[4]

XXIX. All believers are a holy and sanctified people, and that sanctification is a spiritual grace of the new covenant, and an effect of the love of God manifested in the soul, whereby the believer presseth after a heavenly and evangelical obedience to all the commands which Christ, as head and king in his new covenant, hath prescribed to them.[5]

XXX. All believers, through the knowledge of that justification of life given by the Father, and brought forth by the blood of Christ, have, as their great privilege of that new covenant, peace with God, and reconciliation, whereby they that were afar off are made nigh by that blood, and have peace passing all understanding; yea, joy in God through our Lord Jesus Christ, by whom we have received the atonement.[6]

XXXI. All believers, in the time of this life, are in a continual warfare and combat against sin, self, the world, and the devil; and

1 John i. 12, and iii. 14, 15; Isa. iv. 1; John vii. 37; 1 Tim. i. 15; Rom. iv. 5, and v. 8; Acts v. 30, 31, and ii. 36; 1 Cor. i. 22, 24.

2 1 Pet. i. 5; 1 Cor. xv. 10; 2 Cor. xii. 9; Phil. ii. 12, 13; John xv. 5; Gal. ii. 19, 20.

3 1 Thess. i. 1; John xvii. 21; xx. 17; Heb. ii. 11; 1 John iv. 16; Gal. ii. 19, 20.

4 1 John i. 7; Heb. x. 14, and ix. 26; 2 Cor. v. 19; Rom. iii. 23, 25, 30, and v. 1; Acts xiii. 38, 39.

5 1 Cor. xi; 1 Pet. ii. 9; Eph. i. 4; 1 John iv. 16; Matt. xxviii. 20.

6 2 Cor. v. 19; Rom. v. 9, 10; Isaiah xxvi. 12, and liv. 10; Eph. ii. 13, 14, and iv. 7; Rom. v. 10, 11.

are liable to all manner of afflictions, tribulations, and persecutions, being predestinated and appointed thereunto; and whatsoever the saints possess or enjoy of God spiritually, is by faith; and outward and temporal things are lawfully enjoyed by a civil right by them who have no faith.[1]

XXXII. The only strength by which the saints are enabled to encounter with all oppositions and trials is only by Jesus Christ, who is the captain of their salvation, being made perfect through sufferings; who hath engaged his faithfulness and strength to assist them in all their afflictions, and to uphold them in all their temptations, and to preserve them by his power to his everlasting kingdom.[2]

XXXIII. Jesus Christ hath here on earth a spiritual kingdom, which is his Church, whom he hath purchased and redeemed to himself as a peculiar inheritance; which Church is a company of visible saints, called and separated from the world by the Word and Spirit of God, to the visible profession of the faith of the Gospel, being baptized into that faith, and joined to the Lord, and each to other, by mutual agreement, in the practical enjoyment of the ordinances commanded by Christ, their head and king.[3]

XXXIV. To this Church he hath made his promises, and given the signs of his covenant, presence, acceptation, love, blessing, and protection. Here are the fountains and springs of his heavenly graces flowing forth to refresh and strengthen them.[4]

XXXV. And all his servants of all estates are to acknowledge him to be their prophet, priest, and king; and called thither to be enrolled among his household servants, to present their bodies and souls, and to bring their gifts [that] God hath given them, to be under his heavenly conduct and government, to lead their lives in this walled

1 Rom. vii. 23, 24; and viii. 29; Eph. vi. 10, 11, etc.; Heb. ii. 9, 10; 2 Tim. iii. 12; 1 Thess. iii. 3; Gal. ii. 19, 20; 2 Cor. v. 7; Deut. ii. 5.

2 John xv. 5, and xvi. 33; Phil. iv. 11; Heb. ii. 9, 10; 2 Tim. iv. 18.

3 Matt. xi. 11; xviii. 19, 20; 2 Thess. i. 15; 1 Cor. i. 2; Eph. i. 1; Rom. i. 7. Acts xix. 8, 9, and xxvi. 18; 2 Cor. vi. 17; Rev. xviii. 4; Acts ii. 37, 42, ix. 26, and x. 37; Rom. x. 10; 1 Peter ii. 5.

4 Matt. xxviii. 18, etc.; 1 Cor. iii. 21, and xi. 24; 2 Cor. vi. 18; Rom. ix. 4, 5; Psalm cxxxiii. 3; Rom. iii. 7, 10; Ezek. xlvii. 2.

sheepfold and watered garden, to have communion here with his saints, that they may be assured that they are made meet to be partakers of their inheritance in the kingdom of God; and to supply each other's wants, inward and outward (and although each person hath a propriety in his own estate, yet they are to supply each other's wants, according as their necessities shall require, that the name of Jesus Christ may not be blasphemed through the necessity of any in the Church); and also being come, they are here by himself to be bestowed in their several order, due place, peculiar use, being fitly compact and knit together, according to the effectual working of every part, to the edifying of itself in love.[1]

XXXVI. Being thus joined, every Church hath power given them from Christ, for their well-being, to choose among themselves meet persons for elders and deacons, being qualified according to the Word, as those which Christ hath appointed in his Testament for the feeding, governing, serving, and building up of his Church; and that none have any power to impose on them either these or any other.[2]

XXXVII. That the ministers lawfully called, as aforesaid, ought to continue in their calling and place, according to God's ordinance, and carefully to feed the flock of God committed to them, not for filthy lucre, but of a ready mind.[3]

XXXVIII. The ministers of Christ ought to have whatsoever they shall need, supplied freely by the Church, that, according to Christ's ordinances, they that preach the Gospel should live of the Gospel by the law of Christ.[4]

XXXIX. Baptism is an ordinance of the New Testament, given by Christ, to be dispensed upon persons professing faith, or that are made disciples; who, upon profession of faith, ought to be baptized, and after to partake of the Lord's Supper.[5]

1 Acts ii. 41, 44, 45, 47; Isaiah iv. 3; 1 Cor. xii. 6, 7, etc.; Ezek. xx. 37, 40; Cant. iv. 12; Eph. ii. 19; Romans xii. 4—6; Col. i. 12, and ii. 5, 6, 19; Acts ii. 44, 45, iv. 34, 35, v. 4, and xix. 32; Luke xiv. 26; 1 Timothy vi. 1; Eph. iv. 16.

2 Acts i. 23, 26, vi. 3, and xv. 22, 25. Rom. xii. 7, 8; 1 Tim. iii. 2, 6, 7, 8; 1 Cor. xii. 8, 28; Heb. xiii. 7, 17; 1 Pet. v. 1—3; and iv. 15.

3 Heb. v. 4; John x. 3, 4; Acts xx. 28, 29; Rom. xii. 7, 8; Heb. xiii. 7, 17; 1 Pet. v. 1—3.

4 1 Cor. ix. 7, 14; Gal. vi. 8; Phil. iv. 15, 16; 2 Cor. x. 4; 1 Tim. i. 9; Ps. cx. 3.

5 Matt. xxviii. 18, 19; John iv. 1; Mark xvi. 15, 16; Acts ii. 37, 38, and viii. 36—33.

XL. That the way and manner of the dispensing this ordinance is dipping or plunging the body under water; it being a sign, must answer the things signified, which is, that interest the saints have in the death, burial, and resurrection of Christ; and that, as certainly as the body is buried under water, and risen again, so certainly shall the bodies of the saints be raised by the power of Christ, in the day of the resurrection, to reign with Christ.[1]

The word *baptizo* signifies to dip or plunge (yet so as convenient garments be both upon the administrator and subject with all modesty).

XLI. The person designed by Christ to dispense baptism, the Scripture holds forth to be a disciple; it being nowhere tied to a particular Church officer, or person extraordinarily sent, the commission enjoining the administration being given to them as considered disciples, being men able to preach the Gospel.[2]

XLII. Christ hath likewise given power to his Church to receive in and cast out any member that deserves it; and this power is given to every congregation, and not to one particular person, either member or officer, but in relation to the whole body, in reference to their faith and fellowship.[3]

XLIII. And every particular member of each Church, how excellent, great, or learned soever, is subject to this censure and judgment; and that the Church ought not, without great care and tenderness, and due advice, but by the rule of faith, to proceed against her members.[4]

XLIV. Christ, for the keeping of this Church in holy and orderly communion, placeth some special men over the Church, who, by their office, are to govern, oversee, visit, watch; so, likewise, for the better keeping thereof, in all places by the members, he hath given authority, and laid duty upon all to watch over one another.[5]

1 Matt. iii. 6, 16; Mark i. 5, verse 9 reads [into Jordan] in Greek; John iii. 23; Acts viii. 38; Rev. ii. 5, and vii. 14; Heb. x. 22; Rom. vi. 3—6; 1 Cor. xv. 28, 29.

2 Isa. viii. 16; Eph. iii. 7; Matt. xxviii. 19; John iv. 2; Acts x. 7, and xi. 20. 1 Cor. xi. 24, and x. 16, 17.

3 Rom. xvi. 2; Matt. xviii. 17; 1 Cor. v. 4, 11, 13, xii. 6, and ii. 3; 2 Cor. ii. 6, 7.

4 Matt. xviii. 16, and xvii. 18; Acts xi. ii. 3; 1 Tim. v. 19, etc.; Col. iv. 17; Acts xv. 1—3.

5 Acts xx. 27, 28; Heb. xiii. 17, 24; Matt. xxiv. 45; 1 Thess. v. 2, 14; Jude iii. 20; Heb. x. 34, 35, and xii. 15.

XLV. Also, such to whom God hath given gifts in the Church may and ought to prophecy, according to the proportion of faith, and so to teach publicly the Word of God, for the edification, exhortation, and comfort of the Church.[1]

XLVI. Thus, being rightly gathered, and continuing in the obedience of the Gospel of Christ, none are to separate for faults and corruptions (for as long as the Church consists of men subject to failings, there will be difference in the true constituted Church), until they have in due order and tenderness sought redress thereof.[2]

XLVII. And although the particular congregations be distinct, and several bodies, every one as a compact and knit city within itself, yet are they all to walk by one rule of truth: so also they (by all means convenient) are to have the counsel and help one of another, if necessity require it, as members of one body, in the common faith, under Christ, their head.[3]

XLVIII. A civil magistracy is an ordinance of God, set up by him for the punishment of evildoers, and for the praise of them that do well: and that in all lawful things commanded by them, subjection ought to be given by us in the Lord, not only for wrath but for conscience' sake; and that we are to make supplications and prayers for kings, and all that are in authority, that under them we may live a quiet and peaceable life, in all godliness and honesty.[4]

The supreme magistracy of this kingdom we acknowledge to be the king and parliament (now established) freely chosen by the kingdom, and that we are to maintain and defend all civil laws and civil officers made by them, which are for the good of the commonwealth. And we acknowledge with thankfulness, that God hath made this present king and parliament honorable in throwing down the prelatical hierarchy, because of their tyranny and oppression over us, under which this kingdom long groaned, for which we are ever engaged to bless God, and honor them for the same. And concerning the worship of God: there is but one lawgiver, which is able to save and destroy,[5] which is Jesus Christ, who hath given laws and rules

1 1 Cor. xiv. 3, etc.; Rom. xii. 6; 1 Pet. iv. 10, 11; 1 Cor. xii. 7; 1 Thess. v. 19, etc.

2 Rev. ii. and iii.; Acts xv. 12; 1 Cor. i. 10; Heb. x. 25; Jude 19; Rev. ii. 20, 21, 27; Acts xv. 1, 2; Rom. xiv. 1, and xv. 1—3.

3 1 Cor. iv. 17, xiv. 33, 36, and xvi. 1. Ps. cxxii. 3; Eph. ii. 12, 19; Rev. xxi.; 1 Tim. iii. 15, vi. 13, 14; 1 Cor. iv. 17; Acts xv. 2, 3; Cant. viii. 8, 9; 2 Cor. viii. 1, 4, 13, 14.

4 Rom. xiii. 1, 2, etc.; 1 Pet. ii. 13, 14; 1 Tim. ii. 1—3.

5 James iv. 12.

sufficient in his word for his worship; and for any to make more, were to charge Christ with want of wisdom, or faithfulness, or both, in not making laws enough, or not good enough, for his house: surely it is our wisdom, duty, and privilege, to observe Christ's laws only.[1] So it is the magistrates' duty to tender the liberty of men's consciences[2] (which is the tenderest thing unto all conscientious men, and most dear unto them, and without which all other liberties will not be worth the naming, much less enjoying), and to protect all under them from all wrong, injury, oppression, and molestation; so it is our duty not to be wanting in nothing which is for their honor and comfort, and whatsoever is for the well-being of the commonwealth wherein we live, it is our duty to do; and we believe it to be our express duty, especially in matters of religion, to be fully persuaded in our minds of the lawfulness of what we do, as knowing whatsoever is not of faith is sin. And as we cannot do anything contrary to our understandings and consciences, so neither can we forbear the doing of that which our understandings and consciences bind us to do. And if the magistrates should require us to do otherwise, we are to yield our persons in a passive way to their power, as the saints of old have done.[3] And thrice happy shall he be that shall lose his life for witnessing (though but for the least tittle) of the truth of the Lord Jesus Christ.[4]

XLIX. But in case we find not the magistrate to favor us herein, yet we dare not suspend our practice, because we believe we ought to go on in obedience to Christ, in professing the faith which was once delivered to the saints, which faith is declared in the holy Scriptures, and this our confession of faith a part of them, and that we are to witness to the truth of the Old and New Testaments unto the death, if necessity require, in the midst of all trials and afflictions, as his saints of old have done; not accounting our goods, lands, wives, children, fathers, mothers, brethren, sisters, yea, and our own lives, dear unto us, so we may finish our course with joy; remembering, always, that we ought to obey God rather than men, who will, when we have finished our course, and kept the faith, give us the crown of righteousness; to whom we must give an account of all our actions, and no man being able to discharge us of the same.[5]

L. It is lawful for a Christian to be a magistrate or civil officer;

1 Psalm ii. 6, 9, 10, 12.

2 Eccl. viii. 8.

3 James v. 4.

4 1 Peter v.; Gal. v.

5 Acts ii. 40, 41, iv. 19, v. 28, 29, and xx. 23; 1 Thess. iii. 3; Phil. i. 28, 29; Dan. iii. 16, 17, and vi. 7, 10, 22, 23; 1 Tim. vi. 13—15; Rom. xii. 1, 8; 1 Cor. xiv. 37; Rev. ii. 20; 2 Tim. iv. 6—8; Rom. xiv. 10, 12; 2 Cor. v. 10; Psalm xlix. 7, and l. 22.

and also it is lawful to take an oath, so it be in truth, and in judgment, and in righteousness, for confirmation of truth, and ending of all strife; and that by rash and vain oaths the Lord is provoked, and this land mourns.[1]

LI. We are to give unto all men whatsoever is their due, as their place, age, and estate, require; and that we defraud no man of anything, but to do unto all men as we would they should do unto us.[2]

LII. There shall be a resurrection of the dead, both of the just and unjust, and every one shall give an account of himself to God, that every one may receive the things done in his body, according to that he hath done, whether it be good or bad.[3]

THE CONCLUSION.

Thus we desire to give unto Christ that which is his; and unto all lawful authority that which is their due; and to owe nothing to any man but love; to live quietly and peaceably, as it becometh saints, endeavoring in all things to keep a good conscience, and to do unto every man (of what judgment soever) as we would they should do unto us, that as our practice is, so it may prove us to be a conscionable, quiet, and harmless people (no ways dangerous or troublesome to human society), and to labor and work with our hands, that we may not be chargeable to any, but to give to him that needeth, both friends and enemies, accounting it more excellent to give than to receive. Also, we confess that we know but in part, and that we are ignorant of many things which we desire and seek to know; and if any shall do us that friendly part, to show us from the Word of God that we see not, we shall have cause to be thankful to God and them; but if any man shall impose upon us anything that we see not to be commanded by our Lord Jesus Christ, we should in his strength rather embrace all reproaches and tortures of men, to be stripped of all outward comforts, and, if it were possible, to die a

[1] Acts. viii. 38, and x. 1, 2, 35, 44; Romans xvi. 23; Deut. vi. 13; Romans i. 9; 2 Cor. x. 11; Jer. iv. 2; Hebrews vi. 16.

[2] 1 Thess. iv. 6; Rom. xiii. 5—7; Matt. xxii. 21; Titus iii.; 1 Peter ii. 15, 17, and v. 5; Eph. v. 21, 23, and vi. 1, 9; Titus iii. 1—3.

[3] Acts xxiv. 15; 2 Cor. v. 10; Rom. xiv. 12.

thousand deaths, rather than to do anything against the least tittle of the truth of God, or against the light of our own consciences. And if any shall call what we have said heresy, then do we with the apostle acknowledge that, after the way they call heresy, worship we the God of our fathers, disclaiming all heresies, rightly so called, because they are against Christ, and to be steadfast and immovable, always abounding in obedience to Christ, as knowing our labor shall not be in vain in the Lord.[1]

Arise, O God, plead thine own cause; remember how the foolish man blasphemeth thee daily. Oh, let not the oppressed returned ashamed, but let the poor and needy praise thy name.

Come, Lord Jesus, come quickly.

1 Psalm lxxiv. 21, 22.

II.

A CONFESSION OF FAITH,

Put forth by the Elders and Brethren of many congregations of Christians (baptized upon profession of their faith), in London and the country. With an Appendix concerning Baptism.

We, the Ministers and Messengers of, and concerned for, upwards of one hundred baptized congregations in England and Wales (denying Arminianism), being met together in London, from the third of the seventh month to the eleventh of the same, 1689, to consider of some things that might be for the glory of God, and the good of these congregations; have thought meet (for the satisfaction of all other Christians that differ from us in the point of baptism) to recommend to their perusal the Confession of our Faith, printed for and sold by John Harris, at the *Harrow* in the *Poultry*, which Confession we own, as containing the doctrine of our faith and practice; and do desire that the members of our churches respectively do furnish themselves therewith.

Hanserd Knollys,
William Kiffin,
John Harris,
William Collins,
Hercules Collins,
Robert Steed,
Leonard Harrison,
George Barret,
Isaac Lamb,
Richard Adams,
Benjamin Keach,
Andrew Gifford,
Thomas Vaux,
Thomas Winnel,
James Hitt,
Richard Tidmarsh,
William Facey,
Samuel Buttal,
Christopher Price,
Daniel Finch,
John Ball,
Edmond White,
William Pritchard,
Paul Fruin,
Richard Ring,
John Tompkins,
Toby Willes,
John Carter,
James Webb,
Richard Sutton,
Robert Knight,
Edward Price,
William Phipps,
William Hawkins,
Samuel Ewer,
Edward Man,
Charles Archer.

In the name and behalf of the whole assembly.

TO THE JUDICIOUS AND IMPARTIAL READER.

COURTEOUS READER:

It is now many years since divers of us (with other sober Christians then living, and walking in the way of the Lord, that we profess) did conceive ourselves to be under a necessity of publishing a Confession of our Faith, for the information and satisfaction of those that did not thoroughly understand what our principles were, or had entertained prejudices against our profession, by reason of the strange representation of them, by some men of note who had taken very wrong measures, and accordingly led others into misapprehensions of us, and them: And this was first put forth about the year 1643, in the name of seven congregations then gathered in London; since which time, divers impressions thereof have been dispersed abroad, and our end proposed, in good measure answered, inasmuch as many (and some of those men eminent both for piety and learning) were thereby satisfied, that we were no way guilty of those heterodoxies, and fundamental errors, which had too frequently been charged upon us without ground, or occasion given upon our part. And forasmuch, as that Confession is not now commonly to be had, and also that many others have since embraced the same truth which is owned therein, it was judged necessary by us to join together in giving a testimony to the world, of our firm adhering to those wholesome principles, by the publication of this which is now in your hand.

And forasmuch as our method and manner of expressing our sentiments, in this, doth vary from the former (although the substance of the matter is the same) we shall freely impart to you the reason and occasion thereof. One thing that greatly prevailed with us to undertake this work was (not only to give a full account of ourselves to those Christians that differ from us about the subject of baptism, but also) the profit that might from thence arise, unto those that have any account of our labors, in their instruction and establishment in the great truths of the gospel; in the clear understanding and steady belief of which, our comfortable walking with God, and fruitfulness before him, in all our ways, is most nearly concerned. And therefore we did conclude it necessary to express ourselves the more fully and distinctly; and also to fix on such a method as might be most comprehensive of those things which we designed to explain our sense and belief of; and finding no defect in this regard in that fixed on by the Assembly, and after them by those of the Congregational way, we did readily conclude it best to retain the same order in our present Confession; and also when we observed that those last mentioned, did in their Confession (for reasons which seemed of weight both to themselves and others) choose not only to express their mind in words concurrent with the former in sense, concerning all those articles wherein they were agreed, but also for the most part without any variation of the terms, we did in like manner conclude it best to follow their example, in making use of the very same words with them both, in those articles (which are very many) wherein our faith and doctrine is the same with theirs; and this we did the more abundantly to manifest our consent with both, in all the fundamental articles of the Christian religion, as also with many others, whose orthodox confessions have been published to the world, on the behalf of the Protestants in divers nations and cities; and also to convince all that we have no itch to clog religion with new words, but do readily acquiesce in that form of sound words which hath been in consent with the Holy Scriptures, used by others before us; hereby declaring before God, angels and men, our hearty agreement with them in that wholesome Protestant doctrine which with so clear evidence of Scriptures they have asserted. Some things, indeed, are in some places added, some terms omitted, and some few changed; but these alterations are of that nature, as that we need not doubt any charge or suspicion of unsoundness in the faith from any of our brethren upon the account of them.

In those things wherein we differ from others, we have expressed ourselves with all candor and plainness, that none might entertain jealousy of aught secretly lodged in our breasts, that we would not the world should be acquainted with; yet we hope we have also observed those rules of modesty and humility as will render our freedom in this respect inoffensive, even to those whose sentiments are different from ours.

We have also taken care to affix texts of Scripture in the margin, for the confirmation of each article in our Confession; in which work we have studiously endeavored to select such as are most clear and pertinent for the proof of what is asserted by us; and our earnest desire is, that all into whose hands this may come, would follow that (never enough commended) example of the noble Bereans, who searched the Scriptures daily that they might find out whether the things preached to them were so or not.

There is one thing more which we sincerely profess and earnestly desire credence in, viz., that contention is most remote from our design in all that we have done in this matter; and we hope the liberty of an ingenuous unfolding our principles and opening our hearts unto our brethren, with the Scripture grounds on which our faith and practice leans, will by none of them be either denied to us, or taken ill from us. Our whole design is accomplished if we may obtain that justice, as to be measured in our principles and practice, and the judgment of both by others, according to what we have now published; which the Lord (whose eyes are as a flame of fire) knoweth to be the doctrine, which with our hearts we most firmly believe, and sincerely endeavor to conform our lives to. And, oh, that other contentions being laid asleep, the only care and contention of all, upon whom the name of our blessed Redeemer is called, might for the future be, to walk humbly with their God, and in the exercise of all love and meekness towards each other, to perfect holiness in the fear of the Lord, each one endeavoring to have his conversation such as becometh the gospel; and also suitable to his place and capacity, vigorously to promote in others the practice of true religion, and undefiled in the sight of God our Father. And that in this backsliding day, we might not spend our breath in fruitless complaints of the evils of others, but may every one begin at home, to reform in the first place our own hearts and ways, and then to quicken all, that we may have influence upon, to the same work; that if the will of God were so, none might deceive themselves by resting in, and trusting to, a form of godliness without the power of it, and inward experience of the efficacy of those truths that are professed by them.

And verily there is one spring and cause of the decay of religion in our day, which we cannot but touch upon, and earnestly urge a redress of, and that is the neglect of the worship of God in families, by those to whom the charge and conduct of them is committed. May not the gross ignorance and instability of many, with the profaneness of others, be justly charged upon their parents and masters, who have not trained them up in the way wherein they ought to walk when they were young; but have neglected those frequent and solemn commands which the Lord hath laid upon them, so to catechise and instruct them, that their tender years might be seasoned with the knowledge of the truth of God, as revealed in the Scriptures; and also by their own omission of prayer, and other duties of religion in their families, together with the ill example of their loose conversation, have inured them first to a neglect, and then contempt of all piety and religion? We know this will not excuse the blindness or wickedness of any; but certainly it will fall heavy upon those that have been thus the occasion thereof; they indeed die in their sins, but will not their blood be required of those under whose care they were, who yet permitted them to go on without warning, yea, led them into the paths of destruction? And will not the diligence of Christians, with respect to the discharge of these duties, in ages past, rise up in judgment against, and condemn many of those who would be esteemed such now?

We shall conclude with our earnest prayer, that the God of all grace will pour out those measures of his Holy Spirit upon us, that the profession of truth may be accompanied with the sound belief and diligent practice of it by us, that his name may in all things be glorified through Jesus Christ our Lord. AMEN.

CONTENTS.

CONFESSION OF FAITH.

CHAPTER I.

OF THE HOLY SCRIPTURES.

1. The Holy Scripture is the only sufficient, certain, and infallible[1] rule of all saving knowledge, faith and obedience; although the[2] light of nature, and the works of creation and providence do so far manifest the goodness, wisdom, and power of God, as to leave men unexcusable; yet are they not sufficient to give that knowledge of God and his will, which is necessary unto salvation. [3] Therefore it pleased the Lord at sundry times, and in divers manners, to reveal himself, and to declare that his will unto his church; and afterward, for the better preserving and propagating of the truth, and for the more sure establishment and comfort of the church, against the corruption of the flesh, and the malice of Satan, and of the world, to commit the same wholly unto[4] writing; which maketh the holy Scriptures to be most necessary, those former ways of God's revealing his will unto his people being now ceased.

2. Under the name of holy Scripture, or the word of God written, are now contained all the books of the Old and New Testament, which are these:

OF THE OLD TESTAMENT.

Genesis, Exodus, Leviticus, Numbers, Deuteronomy, Joshua, Judges, Ruth, 1 Samuel, 2 Samuel, 1 Kings, 2 Kings, 1 Chronicles, 2 Chronicles, Ezra, Nehemiah, Esther, Job, Psalms, Proverbs,

1 2 Tim. iii. 15, 16, 17, Isa. viii. 20; Luke xvi. 29, 31; Ephesians ii. 20.

2 Rom. i. 19, 20, 21, ii. 14, 15; Psalm xix. 1, 2, 3.

3 Hebrews i. 1.

4 Proverbs xxii. 19—21; Rom. xv. 4; 2 Peter i. 19, 20.

Ecclesiastes, The Song of Songs, Isaiah, Jeremiah, Lamentations, Ezekiel, Daniel, Hosea, Joel, Amos, Obadiah, Jonah, Micah, Nahum, Habakkuk, Zephaniah, Haggai, Zechariah, Malachi.

OF THE NEW TESTAMENT.

Matthew, Mark, Luke, John, The Acts of the Apostles, Paul's Epistles to the Romans, 1 Corinthians, 2 Corinthians, Galatians, Ephesians, Philippians, Colossians, 1 Thessalonians, 2 Thessalonians, 1 Timothy, 2 Timothy, to Titus, to Philemon, the Epistle to the Hebrews, the Epistle of James, the first and second Epistles of Peter, the first, second and third Epistles of John, the Epistle of Jude, the Revelation. All which are given by the [1] inspiration of God, to be the rule of faith and life.

3. The books commonly called Apocrypha, not being of [2] divine inspiration, are no part of the canon (or rule) of the Scripture, and therefore are of no authority to the church of God, nor to be any otherwise approved, or made use of than other human writings.

4. The authority of the holy Scriptures, for which it ought to be believed, dependeth not upon the testimony of any man, or church, but wholly upon [3] God (who is Truth itself), the author thereof; therefore it is to be received, because it is the word of God.

5. We may be moved and induced by the testimony of the church of God, to an high and reverent esteem of the holy Scriptures; and the heavenliness of the matter, the efficacy of the doctrine, and the majesty of the style, the consent of all the parts, the scope of the whole (which is to give all glory to God), the full discovery it makes of the only way of man's salvation, and many other incomparable excellencies, and entire perfections thereof, are arguments whereby it doth abundantly evidence itself to be the word of God; yet, notwithstanding our [4] full persuasion, and assurance of the infallible truth, and divine authority thereof, is from the inward

1 2 Tim. iii. 16.
2 Luke xxiv. 27, 44; Rom. iii. 2.
3 2 Peter i. 19, 20, 21; 2 Timothy iii. 16; 2 Thessalonians ii. 13; 1 John v. 9.
4 John xvi. 13, 14; 1 Cor. 2, 10, 11, 12; 1 John ii. 2, 20, 27.

work of the Holy Spirit, bearing witness by and with the word in our hearts.

6. The whole council of God concerning all things [1] necessary for his own glory, man's salvation, faith and life, is either expressly set down, or necessarily contained in the holy Scripture; unto which nothing at any time is to be added, whether by new revelation of the Spirit, or traditions of men.

Nevertheless we acknowledge the [2] inward illumination of the Spirit of God to be necessary for the saving understanding of such things as are revealed in the word, and that there are some circumstances concerning the worship of God, and government of the church, common to human actions and societies, which are to be [3] ordered by the light of nature, and Christian prudence, according to the general rules of the word, which are always to be observed.

7. All things in Scripture are not alike [4] plain in themselves, nor alike clear unto all; yet those things which are necessary to be known, believed, and observed for salvation, are so [5] clearly propounded, and opened in some place of Scripture or other, that not only the learned, but the unlearned, in a due use of ordinary means, may attain to a sufficient understanding of them.

8. The Old Testament in [6] Hebrew (which was the native language of the people of God of old) and the New Testament in Greek (which at the time of writing it was most generally known to the nations), being immediately inspired by God, and by his singular care and providence kept pure in all ages, are therefore [7] authentical; so as in all controversies of religion, the church is finally to appeal unto them.[8] But because these original tongues are not known to all the people of God, who have a right unto, and interest in the Scriptures, and are commanded in the fear of God to read [9] and search them, therefore they are to be translated into the vulgar language of every nation, unto which they [10] come, that the word of

1 2 Tim. iii. 15, 16, 17; Gal. i. 8, 9.
2 John vi. 45; 1 Cor. ii. 9—12.
3 1 Cor. xi. 13, 14, xiv. 26, 40.
4 2 Peter iii. 16.
5 Psalm xix. 7, cxix. 130.
6 Rom. iii. 2.
7 Isaiah viii. 20.
8 Acts xv. 15.
9 John v. 39.
10 1 Cor. xiv. 6, 9, 11, 12, 24, 28.

God dwelling [1] plentifully in all, they may worship him in an acceptable manner, and through patience and comfort of the Scriptures may have hope.

9. The infallible rule of interpretation of Scripture is the [2] Scripture itself. And therefore, when there is a question about the true and full sense of any Scripture (which is not manifold but one), it must be searched by other places, that speak more clearly.

10. The supreme judge by which all controversies of religion are to be determined, and all decrees of councils, opinions of ancient writers, doctrines of men, and private spirits, are to be examined, and in whose sentence we are to rest, can be no other but the holy Scripture delivered by the Spirit, into which [3] Scripture so delivered, our faith is finally resolved.

CHAPTER II.

OF GOD AND OF THE HOLY TRINITY.

1. The Lord our God is but [4] one only living and true God; whose [5] subsistence is in and of himself, [6] infinite in being and perfection, whose essence cannot be comprehended by any but himself; [7] a most pure Spirit, [8] invisible, without body, parts, or passions, who only hath immortality, dwelling in the light which no man can approach unto, who is [9] immutable, [10] immense, [11] eternal, incomprehensible, [12] almighty, every way infinite, [13] most holy, most wise, most free, most absolute, [14] working all things according to the counsel of his own immutable and most righteous will, [15] for his own glory, most loving, gracious, merciful, long-suffering, abundant in goodness and truth, forgiving iniquity, transgression and sin, [16] the rewarder of them that diligently seek him, and withal most just, [17] and terrible in

1 Col. iii. 16.
2 2 Peter i. 20, 21; Acts xv. 15, 16.
3 Matt. xxii. 29, 31; Eph. ii. 20; Acts xxviii. 23.
4 1 Cor. viii. 46; Deut. vi. 4.
5 Jer. x. 10; Isa. xlviii. 12.
6 Exodus iii. 14.
7 John iv. 24.
8 1 Tim. i. 17; Deut. iv. 15, 16.
9 Mal. iii. 6.
10 1 Kings viii. 27; Jer. xxiii. 23.
11 Psalm xc. 2.
12 Gen. xvii. 1.
13 Isa. vi. 3.
14 Psalm cxv. 3; Isa. xlvi. 10.
15 Prov. xvi. 4; Rom. xi. 36.
16 Exodus xxxiv. 6, 7; Heb. xi. 6.
17 Neh. ix. 32, 33.

his judgments,[1] hating all sin, and who will by no means clear the[2] guilty.

2. God having all[3] life,[4] glory,[5] goodness, blessedness, in and of himself, is alone in, and unto himself all sufficient, not[6] standing in need of any creature which he hath made, nor deriving any glory from them, but only manifesting his own glory in, by, unto, and upon them, he is the alone fountain of all being,[7] of whom, through whom, and to whom are all things, and he hath most sovereign[8] dominion over all creatures, to do by them, for them, or upon them, whatsoever himself pleaseth; in his sight[9] all things are open and manifest, his knowledge is[10] infinite, infallible, and independent upon the creature, so as nothing is to him contingent or uncertain; he is most holy in all his counsels,[11] all his works, and in all his commands; to him is due[12] from angels and men, whatsoever worship, service, or obedience, as creatures they owe unto the Creator, and whatever he is further pleased to require of them.

3. In this divine and infinite Being there are three subsistences,[13] the Father, the Word (or Son), and Holy Spirit, of one substance, power, and eternity, each having the whole divine essence,[14] yet the essence undivided; the Father is of none, neither begotten nor proceeding, the Son is[15] eternally begotten of the Father, the Holy Spirit[16] proceeding from the Father and the Son, all infinite, without beginning, therefore but one God, who is not to be divided in nature and being, but distinguished by several peculiar, relative properties and personal relations, which doctrine of the Trinity is the foundation of all our communion with God, and our comfortable dependence on him.

1 Psalm v. 5, 6.
2 Exodus xxxiv. 7; Nahum i. 2, 3.
3 John v. 26.
4 Psalm cxlviii. 14.
5 Psalm cxix. 68.
6 Job xxii. 2, 3.
7 Rom. xi. 34—36.
8 Daniel iv. 25, and v. 34, 35.
9 Heb. iv. 13.
10 Ezek. xi. 5; Acts xv. 18.
11 Psalm cxlv. 17.
12 Rev. v. 12—14.
13 1 John v. 7; Matt. xxviii. 19; 2 Cor. xiii. 14.
14 Exodus iii. 14; John xiv. 11; 1 Cor. viii. 6.
15 John i. 14, 18.
16 John xv. 26; Gal. iv. 6.

CHAPTER III.

OF GOD'S DECREES.

1. God hath [1] decreed in himself from all eternity, by the most wise and holy counsel of his own will, freely and unchangeably, all things whatsoever come to pass; yet so as thereby is God neither the author of sin, [2] nor hath fellowship with any therein, nor is violence offered to the will of the creature, nor yet is the liberty or contingency of second causes taken away, but rather [3] established, in which appears his wisdom in disposing all things, and power and faithfulness [4] in accomplishing his decree.

2. Although God knoweth whatsoever may, or can come to pass upon all [5] supposed conditions: yet hath he not decreed any thing [6] because he foresaw it as future, or as that which would come to pass upon such conditions.

3. By the decree of God, for the manifestation of his glory, [7] some men and angels are predestinated or foreordained to eternal life, through Jesus Christ, to the [8] praise of his glorious grace; others being left to act in their sin to their [9] just condemnation, to the praise of his glorious justice.

4. These angels and men thus predestinated, and foreordained, are particularly, and unchangeably designed; and their [10] number so certain, and definite, that it cannot be either increased or diminished.

5. Those of mankind [11] that are predestinated to life, God, before the foundation of the world was laid, according to his eternal and immutable purpose, and the secret counsel and good pleasure of his will, hath chosen in Christ unto everlasting glory, out of his mere free grace and love; [12] without any other thing in the creature as a condition or cause moving him thereunto.

1 Isa. xlvi. 10; Eph. i. 11; Heb. vi. 17; Rom. ix. 15, 18.
2 James i. 15, 17; 1 John i. 5.
3 Acts iv 27, 28; John xix. 11.
4 Numbers xxiii. 19; Ephesians i. 3—5.
5 Acts xv. 18.
6 Rom. ix. 11, 13, 16, 18.
7 1 Tim. v. 21; Matt. xxv. 41.
8 Eph. i. 5, 6.
9 Rom. ix. 22, 23; Jude 4.
10 2 Tim. ii. 19; John xiii. 18.
11 Eph. i. 4, 9, 11; Rom. viii. 30; 2 Tim. i. 9; 1 Thess. v. 9.
12 Rom. xix. 13, 16; Eph. i. 6, 12.

6. As God hath appointed the elect unto glory, so he hath by the eternal and most free purpose of his will, foreordained [1] all the means thereunto, wherefore they who are elected, being fallen in Adam, [2] are redeemed by Christ, are effectually [3] called unto faith in Christ, by his Spirit, working in due season, are justified, adopted, sanctified, and kept by his power through faith [4] unto salvation; neither are any other redeemed by Christ, or effectually called, justified, adopted, sanctified, and saved, but the elect [5] only.

7. The doctrine of this high mystery of predestination is to be handled with special prudence and care; that men attending the will of God revealed in his word, and yielding obedience thereunto, may, from the certainty of their effectual vocation, be assured of their [6] eternal election; so shall this doctrine afford matter [7] of praise, reverence, and admiration of God, and [8] of humility, diligence, and abundant [9] consolation, to all that sincerely obey the gospel.

CHAPTER IV.

OF CREATION.

1. In the beginning it pleased God the Father, [10] Son and Holy Spirit, for the manifestation of the glory of [11] his eternal power, wisdom, and goodness, to create or make the world, and all things therein, [12] whether visible or invisible, in the space of six days, and all very good.

2. After God had made all other creatures, he created [13] man, male and female, with [14] reasonable and immortal souls, rendering them fit unto that life to God, for which they were created, being [15] made after the image of God, in knowledge, righteousness, and true holiness, having the law of God [16] written in their hearts, and power

1 1 Peter i. 2; 2 Thess. ii. 13.
2 1 Thess. v. 9, 10.
3 Romans viii. 30; 2 Thess. ii. 13.
4 1 Peter i. 5.
5 John x. 26; xvii. 9; vi. 64.
6 1 Thess. i. 4, 5; 2 Peter i. 10.
7 Eph. i. 6; Rom. xi. 33.
8 Rom. xi. 5, 6.
9 Luke x. 20.
10 John i. 2, 3; Heb. i. 2; Job xxvi. 13.
11 Rom. i. 20.
12 Col. i. 16; Gen. ii. 1, 2.
13 Gen. i. 27.
14 Gen. ii. 7.
15 Eccl. vii. 29; Gen. i. 26.
16 Rom. ii. 14, 15.

to fulfil it; and yet under a possibility of transgressing, being left to the liberty of their own will, which was [1] subject to change.

3. Besides the law written in their hearts, they received [2] a command not to eat of the tree of knowledge of good and evil; which, whilst they kept, they were happy in their communion with God, and had dominion [3] over the creatures.

CHAPTER V.

OF DIVINE PROVIDENCE.

1. God, the good Creator of all things, in his infinite power and wisdom, doth [4] uphold, direct, dispose, and govern all creatures and things, from the greatest even to the [5] least, by his most wise and holy providence, to the end for the which they were created, according unto his infallible foreknowledge, and the free and immutable counsel of his [6] own will; to the praise of the glory of his wisdom, power, justice, infinite goodness and mercy.

2. Although in relation to the foreknowledge and decree of God, the first cause, all things come to pass [7] immutably and infallibly; so that there is not any thing befalls any [8] by chance, or without his providence; yet by the same providence he ordereth them to fall out according to the nature of second causes, either [9] necessarily, freely, or contingently.

3. God, in his ordinary providence, [10] maketh use of means; yet is free [11] to work without, [12] above, and [13] against them at his pleasure.

4. The almighty power, unsearchable wisdom, and infinite goodness of God, so far manifest themselves in his providence, that his determinate counsel [14] extendeth itself even to the first fall, and all other sinful actions both of angels and men; and that not by a

1 Gen. iii. 6.
2 Gen. vi. 17, iii. 8—10.
3 Gen. i. 26, 28.
4 Heb. i. 3; Job xxxviii. 11; Isa. xlvi. 10, 11; Psalm cxxxv. 6.
5 Matt. x. 29—31.
6 Eph. i. 11.
7 Acts ii. 23.
8 Prov. xvi. 33.
9 Gen. viii. 22.
10 Acts xxvii. 31, 44; Isa. lv. 10, 11.
11 Hosea i. 7.
12 Rom iv. 19—21.
13 Daniel iii. 27.
14 Rom. xi. 32—34; 2 Sam. xxiv. 1; 1 Chron. xxi. 1.

bare permission, which also he most wisely and powerfully [1] boundeth, and otherwise ordereth, and governeth, in a manifold dispensation to his most holy [2] ends: yet so as the sinfulness of their acts proceedeth only from the creatures, and not from God; who being most holy and righteous, neither is, nor can be, the author or [3] approver of sin.

5. The most wise, righteous, and gracious God, doth oftentimes leave for a season his own children to manifold temptations and the corruptions of their own heart, to chastise them for their former sins, or to discover unto them the hidden strength of corruption and deceitfulness of their hearts, [4] that they may be humbled; and to raise them to a more close and constant dependence for their support upon himself, and to make them more watchful against all future occasions of sin, and for other just and holy ends.

So that whatsoever befalls any of his elect is by his appointment, for his glory, [5] and their good.

6. As for those wicked and ungodly men, whom God as a righteous judge, for former sin doth [6] blind and harden; from them he not only withholdeth his [7] grace, whereby they might have been enlightened in their understanding, and wrought upon in their hearts, but sometimes also withdraweth [8] the gifts which they had, and exposeth them to such [9] objects as their corruptions make occasion of sin; and withall, [10] gives them over to their own lusts, the temptations of the world, and the power of Satan, whereby it comes to pass that they [11] harden themselves, even under those means which God useth for the softening of others.

7. As the providence of God doth in general reach to all creatures, so after a more special manner it taketh care of his [12] church, and disposeth of all things to the good thereof.

1 2 Kings xix. 28; Psalm lxxvi. 10.
2 Gen. l. 20; Isa. x. 6, 7, 12.
3 Psalm l. 21; 1 John ii. 16.
4 2 Chron. xxxii, 25, 26, 31; Samuel xxiv. 1; 2 Cor. xii. 7—9.
5 Rom. viii. 28.
6 Rom. i. 24, 26, 28, xi. 7, 8.
7 Deut. xxix. 4.
8 Matt. xiii. 12.
9 Deut. ii. 30; 2 Kings viii. 12, 13.
10 Psalm lxxxi. 11, 12; 2 Thess. ii. 10—12.
11 Exodus viii. 15, 32; Isa. vi. 9, 10; 1 Peter ii. 7, 8.
12 Tim. iv. 10; Amos ix. 8, 9; Isaiah lxiii. 3—5.

CHAPTER VI.

OF THE FALL OF MAN, OF SIN, AND OF THE PUNISHMENT THEREOF.

1. Although God created man upright, and perfect, and gave him a righteous law, which had been unto life had he kept it,[1] and threatened death upon the breach thereof; yet he did not long abide in this honor;[2] Satan using the subtlety of the serpent to seduce Eve, then by her seducing Adam, who, without any compulsion, did wilfully transgress the law of their creation, and the command given unto them, in eating the forbidden fruit, which God was pleased, according to his wise and holy counsel, to permit, having purposed to order it to his own glory.

2. Our first parents by this sin, fell from their[3] original righteousness and communion with God, and we in them, whereby death came upon all;[4] all becoming dead in sin, and wholly defiled,[5] in all the faculties and parts of soul and body.

3. They being the root,[6] and, by God's appointment, standing in the room and stead of all mankind, the guilt of the sin was imputed, and corrupted nature conveyed to all their posterity, descending from them by ordinary generation, being now[7] conceived in sin, and by nature children[8] of wrath, the servants of sin, the subjects[9] of death, and all other miseries, spiritual, temporal, and eternal, unless the Lord Jesus[10] set them free.

4. From this original corruption, whereby we are[11] utterly indisposed, disabled, and made opposite to all good, and wholly inclined to all evil, do[12] proceed all actual transgressions.

5. This corruption of nature, during this life, doth[13] remain in those that are regenerated; and although it be through Christ par-

1 Gen. ii. 16, 17.
2 Gen. iii. 12, x. 13; 2 Cor. i. 1—3.
3 Rom. iii. 23.
4 Rom. v. 12, etc.
5 Titus i. 15; Gen. vi. 5; Jere. xvii. 9; Rom. iii. 10—19.
6 Rom. v. 12—19; 1 Corinthians xv. 21, 22, 45, 49.
7 Psalm li. 5; Job xiv. 4.
8 Eph. ii. 3.
9 Rom. vi. 20, v. 12.
10 Heb. ii. 14; 1 Thes. i. 10.
11 Rom. viii. 7; Col. i. 21.
12 James i. 14, 15; Matt. xv. 19.
13 Rom. vii. 18, 23; Eccl. vii. 20; 1 John i. 8.

doned, and mortified, yet both itself, and the first motions thereof, are truly and properly[1] sin.

CHAPTER VII.

OF GOD'S COVENANT.

1. The distance between God and the creature is so great, that although reasonable creatures do owe obedience unto him as their Creator, yet they could never have attained the reward of life, but by some[2] voluntary condescension on God's part, which he hath been pleased to express, by way of covenant.

2. Moreover, man having brought himself[3] under the curse of the law by his fall, it pleased the Lord to make a covenant of grace, wherein he freely offereth unto sinners[4] life and salvation by Jesus Christ, requiring of them faith in him, that they may be saved; and[5] promising to give unto all those that are ordained unto eternal life, his Holy Spirit, to make them willing, and able to believe.

3. This covenant is revealed in the gospel, first of all to Adam, in the promise of salvation by the[6] seed of the woman, and afterwards by farther steps, until the full[7] discovery thereof was completed in the New Testament; and it is founded in that[8] eternal covenant transaction, that was between the Father and the Son about the redemption of the elect; and it is alone by the grace of this covenant, that all of the posterity of fallen Adam that ever were[9] saved did obtain life and blessed immortality; man being now utterly uncapable of acceptance with God upon those terms on which Adam stood in his state of innocence.

1 Romans vii. 24, 25; Galatians v. 17.

2 Luke xvii. 10; Job xxxv. 7, 8.

3 Gen. ii. 17; Gal. iii. 10; Rom. iii. 20, 21.

4 Rom. viii. 3; Mark xvi. 15, 16; John iii. 16.

5 Ezek. xxxiv. 26, 27; John vi. 44, 45; Psalm cx. 3.

6 Gen. iii. 15.

7 Heb. i. 1.

8 2 Tim. i. 9; Titus i. 2.

9 Heb. ii. 6, 13; Romans iv. 1, 2, etc.; Acts iv. 12; John viii. 56.

CHAPTER VIII.

OF CHRIST THE MEDIATOR.

1. It pleased God, in his eternal purpose, to choose and ordain the Lord Jesus, his only begotten Son, according to the covenant made between them both,[1] to be the Mediator between God and man; the [2] prophet, [3] priest, and [4] king, head and Saviour of his church, the heir of all things, and judge of the world; unto whom he did from all eternity [5] give a people to be his seed, and to be by him in time redeemed, called, justified, sanctified, and glorified.

2. The Son of God, the second person in the Holy Trinity, being very and eternal God, the brightness of the Father's glory, of one substance and equal with him; who made the world, who upholdeth and governeth all things he hath made; did when the fulness of time was come, take upon him [6] man's nature, with all the essential properties and common infirmities thereof, [7] yet without sin; being conceived by the Holy Spirit in the womb of the Virgin Mary, the Holy Spirit coming down upon her, and the power of the Most High overshadowing her,[8] and so was made of a woman, of the tribe of Judah, of the seed of Abraham and David, according to the Scriptures; so that two whole, perfect, and distinct natures, were inseparably joined together in one person, without conversion, composition, or confusion; which person is very God and very man, yet one [9] Christ, the only Mediator between God and man.

3. The Lord Jesus, in his human nature thus united to the divine, in the person of the Son, was sanctified and anointed [10] with the Holy Spirit, above measure; having in him [11] all the treasures of wisdom and knowledge; in whom it pleased the Father [12] that all fulness should dwell; to the end that, being [13] holy, harmless, unde-

1 Isa. xlii. 1; 1 Peter xix. 20.
2 Acts iii. 22.
3 Heb. v. 5, 6.
4 Psalm ii. 6; Luke i. 33; Eph. i. 23; Heb. i. 2; Acts. xvii. 31.
5 Isaiah liii. 10; John xvii. 6; Romans viii. 30.
6 John i. 1, 14; Gal. iv. 4.
7 Rom. viii. 3; Heb. ii. 14, 16, 17, and iv. 15.
8 Luke i. 27, 31, 35.
9 Rom. ix. 5; 1 Tim. ii. 5.
10 Psalm xlv. 7; Acts x. 38; John iii. 34.
11 Col. ii. 3.
12 Col. i. 19.
13 Heb. vii. 26.

filed, and full[1] of grace and truth, he might be thoroughly furnished to execute the office of a mediator and[2] surety; which office he took not upon himself, but was thereunto[3] called by his Father, who also put[4] all power and judgment in his hand, and gave him commandment to execute the same.

4. This office the Lord Jesus did most[5] willingly undertake, which that he might discharge he was made under the law,[6] and did perfectly fulfil it, and underwent the[7] punishment due to us, which we should have borne and suffered, being made[8] sin and a curse for us; enduring most grievous sorrows[9] in his soul, and most painful sufferings in his body; was crucified, and died, and remained in the state of the dead, yet saw no[10] corruption; on the[11] third day he arose from the dead, with the same[12] body in which he suffered; with which he also[13] ascended into heaven, and there sitteth at the right hand of his Father,[14] making intercession; and shall[15] return to judge men and angels, at the end of the world.

5. The Lord Jesus, by his perfect obedience and sacrifice of himself, which he through the eternal Spirit once offered up unto God,[16] hath fully satisfied the justice of God, procured reconciliation, and purchased an everlasting inheritance in the kingdom of heaven,[17] for all those whom the Father hath given unto him.

6. Although the price of redemption was not actually paid by Christ till after his incarnation,[18] yet the virtue, efficacy and benefit thereof, was communicated to the elect in all ages successively, from the beginning of the world, in and by those promises, types, and sacrifices, wherein he was revealed, and signified to be the seed of the woman, which should bruise the serpent's head,[19] and the Lamb

1 John i. 14.
2 Heb. vii. 22.
3 Heb. v. 5.
4 John v. 22, 27; Matt. xxviii. 18; Acts ii. 36.
5 Psalm xl. 7, 8; Heb. x. 5—11; John x. 18.
6 Gal. iv. 4; Matt. iii. 15.
7 Gal. iii. 13; Isa. liii. 6; 1 Peter iii. 18.
8 2 Cor. v. 21.
9 Matt. xxvi. 37, 38; Luke xxii. 44; Matt. xxvii. 46.
10 Acts xiii. 37.
11 1 Cor. xv. 3, 4.
12 John xx. 25, 27.
13 Mark xvi. 19; Acts i. 9—11.
14 Rom. viii. 34; Heb. ix. 24.
15 Acts x. 42; Rom. xiv. 9, 10; Acts i. 10.
16 Heb. ix. 14, x. 14; Romans iii. 25, 26.
17 John xvii. 2; Heb. ix. 15.
18 1 Cor. iv. 10; Heb. iv. 2; 1 Peter i. 10, 11.
19 Rev. xiii. 8.

slain from the foundation of the world; [1] being *the same yesterday, and to-day, and for ever.*

7. Christ, in the work of mediation acteth according to both natures, by each nature doing that which is proper to itself; yet by reason of the unity of the person, that which is proper to one nature is sometimes in Scripture attributed to the person [2] denominated by the other nature.

8. To all those for whom Christ hath obtained eternal redemption, he doth certainly and effectually [3] apply, and communicate the same, making intercession for them, uniting them to himself by his Spirit,[4] revealing unto them, in and by the word, the mystery of salvation, persuading them to believe and obey,[5] governing their hearts by his word and spirit, and [6] overcoming all their enemies by his almighty power and wisdom, in such manner and ways as are most consonant to his wonderful and [7] unsearchable dispensation; and all of free and absolute grace, without any condition foreseen in them, to procure it.

9. This office of mediator between God and man is proper [8] only to Christ, who is the prophet, priest, and king of the Church of God, and may not be, either in whole, or any part thereof, transferred from him to any other.

10. This number and order of offices is necessary; for in respect of our [9] ignorance we stand in need of his prophetical office, and in respect of our alienation from God [10] and imperfection of the best of our services, we need his priestly office to reconcile us, and present us acceptable unto God, and in respect of our averseness and utter inability to return to God, and for our rescue, and security from our spiritual adversaries, we need his kingly office,[11] to convince, subdue, draw, uphold, deliver, and preserve us to his heavenly kingdom.

1 Heb. xiii. 8.
2 John iii. 13; Acts xx. 28.
3 John vi. 37, x. 15, 16, and xvii. 9; Rom. v. 10.
4 John xvii. 6; Ephesians i. 9; 1 John v. 20.
5 Rom. viii. 9, 14.
6 Psalm cx. 1; 1 Cor. xv. 25, 26.
7 John iii. 8; Eph. i. 8.
8 1 Tim. ii. 5.
9 John i. 18.
10 Col. i. 21; Gal. v. 17.
11 John xvi. 8; Psalm cx. 3; Luke i. 74, 75.

CHAPTER IX.

OF FREE WILL.

1. God hath indued the will of man with that natural liberty and power of acting upon choice, that it is[1] neither forced, nor by any necessity of nature determined to do good or evil.

2. Man, in his state of innocency, had freedom and power to will and to do, that[2] which was good, and well pleasing to God, but yet[3] was mutable, so that he might fall from it.

3. Man, by his fall into a state of sin, hath wholly lost[4] all ability of will to any spiritual good accompanying salvation; so as a natural man, being altogether averse from that good,[5] and dead in sin, is not able, by his own strength, to[6] convert himself, or to prepare himself thereunto.

4. When God converts a sinner, and translates him into the state of grace,[7] he freeth him from his natural bondage under sin, and by his grace alone enables him[8] freely to will, and do that which is spiritually good; yet so as that, by reason of his[9] remaining corruptions, he doth not perfectly, nor only will that which is good, but doth also will that which is evil.

5. The will of man is made[10] perfectly and immutably free to God alone in the state of glory only.

CHAPTER X.

OF EFFECTUAL CALLING.

1. Those whom God hath predestinated unto life, he is pleased in his appointed and accepted time,[11] effectually to call by his word

1 Matthew xvii. 12; James i. 14; Deut. xxx. 19.
2 Eccl. vii. 29.
3 Gen. iii. 6.
4 Rom. v. 6, and viii. 7.
5 Eph. ii. 1, 5.
6 Titus iii. 3, 4, 5; John vi. 44.
7 Col. i. 13; John viii. 36.
8 Phil. ii. 13.
9 Rom. vii. 15, 18, 19, 21, 23.
10 Eph. iv. 13.
11 Romans viii. 30, and xi. 7; Ephesians i. 10, 11; 2 Thessalonians iii. 13, 14.

and Spirit, out of that state of sin and death in which they are by nature, to grace of salvation [1] by Jesus Christ, enlightening their minds, spiritually and savingly, to [2] understand the things of God, taking away their [3] heart of stone and giving unto them a heart of flesh, renewing their wills, and by his almighty power determining them [4] to that which is good, and effectually drawing them to Jesus Christ; yet so, as they come [5] most freely, being made willing by his grace.

2. This effectual call is of God's free and special grace alone,[6] not from anything at all foreseen in man, nor from any power or agency in the creature, co-working with his special grace,[7] the creature being wholly passive therein, being dead in sins and trespasses, until, being quickened and renewed by the Holy Spirit, he is thereby enabled to answer this call, and to embrace the grace offered and conveyed in it, and that by no less [8] power than that which raised up Christ from the dead.

3. Elect infants, dying in infancy, are [9] regenerated and saved by Christ through the Spirit, who worketh when, and where, and [10] how he pleaseth; so also are all other elect persons, who are incapable of being outwardly called by the ministry of the word.

4. Others not elected, although they may be called by the ministry of the word,[11] and may have some common operations of the Spirit, yet, not being effectually drawn by the Father, they neither will, nor can truly [12] come to Christ, and therefore cannot be saved; much less can men that receive not the Christian religion [13] be saved, be they never so diligent to frame their lives according to the light of nature, and the law of that religion they do profess.

1 Eph. ii. 1—6.
2 Acts xxvi. 18; Eph. i. 17, 18.
3 Ezekiel xxxvi. 26.
4 Deut. xxx. 6; Ezek. xxxvi. 27; Eph. i. 19.
5 Psalm cx. 3; Cant. i. 4.
6 2 Tim. i. 9; Eph. ii. 8.
7 1 Cor. ii. 14; Eph. ii. 5; John v. 25.
8 Eph. i. 19, 20.
9 John iii. 3, 5, 6.
10 John iii. 8.
11 Matt. xxii. 14, and xiii. 20, 21; Heb. vi. 4, 5.
12 John vi. 44, 45, 65; 1 John ii. 24, 25.
13 Acts iv. 12; John iv. 22, and xvii . 3.

CHAPTER XI.

OF JUSTIFICATION.

1. Those whom God effectually calleth, he also freely [1] justifieth, not by infusing righteousness into them, but by [2] pardoning their sins, and by accounting and accepting their persons as [3] righteous; not for anything wrought in them, or done by them, but for Christ's sake alone; not by imputing faith itself, the act of believing, or any other [4] evangelical obedience to them, as their righteousness, but by imputing Christ's active obedience unto the whole law, and passive obedience in his death, for their whole and sole righteousness, they [5] receiving, and resting on him, and his righteousness by faith; which faith they have not of themselves: it is the gift of God.

2. Faith, thus receiving and resting on Christ and his righteousness, is the [6] alone instrument of justification; yet it is not alone in the person justified, but is ever accompanied with all other saving graces, and is no dead faith, [7] but worketh by love.

3. Christ, by his obedience and death, did fully discharge the debt of all those that are justified; and did by the sacrifice of himself, in the blood of his cross, undergoing in their stead the penalty due unto them, make a proper, real and full satisfaction [8] to God's justice in their behalf; yet, inasmuch as he was given by the Father for them, and his obedience and satisfaction accepted in their stead, and both [9] freely, not for any thing in them, their justification is only of free grace, that both the exact justice and rich grace of God might be [10] glorified in the justification of sinners.

4. God did from all eternity decree to [11] justify all the elect, and

1 Rom. iii. 24, viii. 30.
2 Rom. iv. 5—8; Eph. i. 7
3 1 Corinthians i. 30, 31; Romans v. 17—19.
4 Phil. iii. 8, 9; Eph. ii. 8—10.
5 John i. 12; Rom. v. 17.
6 Rom. iii. 28.
7 Gal. v. 6; James ii. 17, 22, 26.
8 Heb. x. 14; 1 Peter i. 18, 19; Isa. liii. 5, 6.
9 Rom. viii. 32; 2 Cor. v. 21.
10 Rom. iii. 26; Eph. i. 6, 7, ii. 7.
11 Galatians iii. 8; 1 Peter i. 2; 1 Tim. ii. 6.

Christ did in the fulness of time die for their sins, and [1] rise again for their justification; nevertheless they are not justified personally until the Holy Spirit doth in due time [2] actually apply Christ unto them.

5. God doth continue to [3] forgive the sins of those that are justified; and although they can never fall from the state of [4] justification, yet they may by their sins fall under God's [5] fatherly displeasure; and in that condition, they have not usually the light of his countenance restored unto them, until they [6] humble themselves, confess their sins, beg pardon, and renew their faith and repentance.

6. The justification of believers under the Old Testament, was in all these respects [7] one and the same with the justification of believers under the New Testament.

CHAPTER XII.

OF ADOPTION.

1. All those that are justified, God vouchsafed in and for the sake of his only Son, Jesus Christ, to make partakers of the grace [8] of adoption; by which they are taken into the number, and enjoy the liberties and [9] privileges of children of God; have his [10] name put upon them, [11] receive the spirit of adoption, [12] have access to the throne of grace with boldness; are enabled to cry Abba, Father; are [13] pitied, [14] protected, [15] provided for, and [16] chastened

1 Rom. iv. 25.
2 Col. i. 21, 22; Titus iii. 4—7.
3 Matt. vi. 12; 1 John i. 7, 9.
4 John x. 28.
5 Psalm lxxxix. 31—33.
6 Psalm xxxii. 5, 51; Matthew xxvi. 75.
7 Gal. iii. 9; Rom. iv. 22—24.
8 Eph. i. 5; Gal iv. 4, 5.
9 John i. 12; Rom. viii. 17.
10 2 Corinthians vi. 18; Revelation iii. 12.
11 Rom. viii. 15.
12 Gal. iv. 6; Eph. ii. 18.
13 Psalm ciii. 13.
14 Prov. xiv. 26.
15 1 Peter v. 7.
16 Heb. xii. 6.

by him, as a father; yet never [1] cast off, but sealed, [2] to the day of redemption, and inherit the promises, [3] as heirs of everlasting salvation.

CHAPTER XIII.

OF SANCTIFICATION.

1. They who are united to Christ, effectually called, and regenerated, having a new heart and a new spirit created in them, through the virtue of Christ's death and resurrection; are also [4] further sanctified, really and personally, through the same virtue, [5] by his word and Spirit dwelling in them; [6] the dominion of the whole body of sin is destroyed, [7] and the several lusts thereof are more and more weakened and mortified; and they more and more quickened, and [8] strengthened in all saving graces, to the [9] practice of all true holiness, without which no man shall see the Lord.

2. This sanctification is [10] throughout, in the whole man, yet imperfect [11] in this life; there abideth still some remnants of corruption in every part, whence ariseth a [12] continual and irreconcilable war; the flesh lusting against the spirit, and the spirit against the flesh.

3. In which war, although the remaining corruption for a time may much [13] prevail, yet through the continual supply of strength, from the sanctifying Spirit of Christ, [14] the regenerate part doth overcome; and so the saints grow in grace, perfecting holiness in the fear of God, [15] pressing after an heavenly life, in evangelical obedience to all the commands which Christ, as head and king, in his word hath prescribed to them.

1 Isaiah liv. 8, 9; Lamentations iii. 31.
2 Eph. iv. 30.
3 Heb. i. 14, vi. 12.
4 Acts xx. 32; Rom. vi. 5, 6.
5 John xvii. 17; Eph. iii. 16—19; 1 Thess. v. 21—23.
6 Rom. vi. 14.
7 Gal. v. 24.
8 Col. i. 11.
9 2 Cor. vii. 1; Heb. xii. 14.
10 1 Thess. v. 23.
11 Rom. vii. 18, 23.
12 Gal. v. 17; 1 Pet. ii. 11.
13 Rom. vii. 23.
14 Rom. vi. 14.
15 Eph. iv. 5, 16; 2 Cor. iii. 18, vii. 1.

CHAPTER XIV.

OF SAVING FAITH.

1. The grace of faith, whereby the elect are enabled to believe to the saving of their souls, is the work of the Spirit of Christ [1] in their hearts, and is ordinarily wrought by the ministry of the [2] word; by which also, and by the administration of Baptism, and the Lord's Supper, prayer, and other means appointed of God, it is increased [3] and strengthened.

2. By this faith, a Christian believeth to be true [4] whatsoever is revealed in the word, for the authority of God himself; and also apprehendeth an excellency therein [5] above all other writings, and all things in the world; as it bears forth the glory of God in his attributes, the excellency of Christ in his nature and offices, and the power and fulness of the Holy Spirit in his workings and operations; and so is enabled to [6] cast his soul upon the truth thus believed; and also acteth differently upon that which each particular passage thereof containeth; yielding obedience to the [7] commands, trembling at the [8] threatenings, and embracing the [9] promises of God, for this life and that which is to come. But the principal acts of saving faith, have immediate relation to Christ, accepting, receiving, and resting upon [10] him alone, for justification, sanctification, and eternal life, by virtue of the covenant of grace.

3. This faith, although it be different in degrees, and may be weak, [11] or strong, yet it is in the least degree of it, different in the kind or nature of it (as is all other saving grace) from the faith [12] and common grace of temporary believers; and therefore, though it may be many times assailed and weakened, yet it gets [13] the victory, growing up in many to the attainment of a full [14] assurance through Christ, who is both the author [15] and finisher of our faith.

1 2 Cor. iv. 13; Eph. ii. 8.
2 Rom. x. 14, 17.
3 Luke xvii. 5; 1 Peter ii. 2; Acts xx. 32.
4 Acts xxiv. 14.
5 Psalm xix. 7—10, cxix. 72.
6 2 Tim. i. 12.
7 John xv. 14.
8 Isa. lxvi. 2.
9 Heb. xi. 13.
10 John i. 12; Acts xvi. 31; Gal. ii. 20; Acts xv. 11.
11 Heb. v. 13, 14; Mat. vi. 30; Ro. iv. 19, 20.
12 2 Peter i. 1.
13 Eph. vi. 16; 1 John v. 4, 5.
14 Heb. vi. 11, 12; Col. ii. 2.
15 Heb. xii. 2.

CHAPTER XV.

OF REPENTANCE UNTO LIFE AND SALVATION.

1. Such of the elect as are converted at riper years, having[1] sometime lived in the state of nature, and therein served divers lusts and pleasures, God, in their effectual calling, giveth them repentance unto life.

2. Whereas there is none that doth good, and sinneth[2] not, and the best of men may, through the power and deceitfulness of their corruption dwelling in them, with the prevalency of temptation, fall into greater sins and provocations, God hath in the covenant of grace mercifully provided that believers so sinning and falling,[3] be renewed through repentance unto salvation.

3. This saving repentance is an[4] evangelical grace, whereby a person, being by the Holy Spirit made sensible of the manifold evils of his sin, doth, by faith in Christ, humble himself for it, with godly sorrow, detestation of it, and self-abhorrency;[5] praying for pardon and strength of grace, with a purpose and endeavor by supplies of the Spirit, to[6] walk before God unto all well pleasing in all things.

4. As repentance is to be continued through the whole course of our lives, upon the account of the body of death, and the motions thereof; so it is every man's duty to repent of his[7] particular known sins, particularly.

5. Such is the provision which God hath made through Christ in the covenant of grace, for the preservation of believers unto salvation, that although there is no sin so small but it deserves[8] damnation, yet there is no sin so great that it shall bring damnation on them that[9] repent; which makes the constant preaching of repentance necessary.

1 Titus iii. 2—5.
2 Eccl. vii. 20.
3 Luke xxii. 31, 32.
4 Zech. xii. 10; Acts xi. 18.
5 Ezek. xxxvi. 31; 2 Cor. vii. 11.
6 Psalm cxix. 6, 128.
7 Luke xix. 8; 1 Tim. i. 13, 15.
8 Rom. vi. 23.
9 Isa. i. 16—18, lv. 7.

CHAPTER XVI.

OF GOOD WORKS.

1. Good works are only such as God hath [1] commanded in his holy word, and not such as, without the warrant thereof, are devised by men, out of blind zeal, [2] or upon any pretence of good intentions.

2. These good works done in obedience to God's commandments, are the fruits and evidences [3] of a true and lively faith; and by them believers manifest their [4] assurance, edify their [5] brethren, adorn the profession of the gospel, stop the mouths of the adversaries, and glorify [6] God, whose workmanship they are, created in Christ Jesus [7] thereunto, that having their fruit unto holiness, they may have the end [8] eternal life.

3. Their ability to do good works, is not at all of themselves, but wholly from the Spirit [9] of Christ; and that they may be enabled thereunto, besides the graces they have already received, there is necessary an [10] actual influence of the same Holy Spirit to work in them to will and to do of his good pleasure; yet are they not hereupon to grow negligent, as if they were not bound to perform any duty, unless upon a special motion of the Spirit, but they ought to be diligent in [11] stirring up the grace of God that is in them.

4. They who in their obedience attain to the greatest height which is possible in this life, are so far from being able to supererogate, and to do more than God requires, as that [12] they fall short of much which in duty they are bound to do.

5. We cannot by our best works merit pardon of sin, or eternal life at the hand of God, by reason of the great disproportion that is between them and the glory to come, and the infinite distance that

1 Micah vi. 8; Heb. xiii. 21.
2 Matt. xv. 9; Isa. xix. 13.
3 James ii. 18, 22.
4 Psalm cxvi. 12, 13; 1 John ii. 3, 5; 2 Peter i. 5—11.
5 Matt. v. 16.
6 1 Tim. vi. 1; 1 Peter ii. 15; Phil. i. 11.
7 Eph. ii. 10.
8 Rom. vi. 22.
9 John xv. 4, 6.
10 2 Cor. iii. 5; Phil. ii 13.
11 Phil. ii. 12; Heb. vi. 11, 12; Isaiah lxiv. 7.
12 Job ix. 2, 3; Gal. v. 17; Luke xvii. 10.

is between us and God, whom by them we can neither profit nor satisfy, for the debt of our[1] former sins, but when we have done all we can, we have done but our duty, and are unprofitable servants: and because as they are good, they proceed from his[2] Spirit, and as they are wrought by us, they are defiled,[3] and mixed with so much weakness and imperfection, that they cannot endure the severity of God's judgment.

6. Yet, notwithstanding, the persons of believers being accepted through Christ, their good works also are accepted in[4] him; not as though they were in this life wholly unblamable and unreprovable in God's sight, but that he, looking upon them in his Son, is pleased to accept and reward that which is[5] sincere, although accompanied with many weaknesses and imperfections.

7. Works done by unregenerate men, although for the matter of them they may be things which God commands, and of good use both to themselves and[6] others; yet because they proceed not from a heart purified by[7] faith, nor are done in a right manner according to the[8] word, nor to a right end, the[9] glory of God, they are therefore sinful, and cannot please God, nor make a man meet to receive grace from[10] God; and yet their neglect of them is more sinful, and[11] displeasing to God.

CHAPTER XVII.

OF PERSEVERANCE OF THE SAINTS.

1. Those whom God hath accepted in the Beloved, effectually called and sanctified by his Spirit, and given the precious faith of his elect unto, can neither totally nor finally fall from the state of

1 Rom. iii. 20; Eph. ii. 8, 9; Rom. iv. 6.
2 Gal. v. 22, 23.
3 Isa. lxiv. 6; Psalm cxliii. 2.
4 Eph. i. 6; 1 Peter ii. 5.
5 Matt. xxv. 21, 23; Heb. vi. 10.
6 2 Kings x. 30; 1 Kings xxi. 27, 29.
7 Gen. iv. 5; Heb. xi. iv. 6.
8 1 Cor. xiii. 1.
9 Matt. vi. 2, 5.
10 Amos v. 21, 22; Rom. ix. 16; Titus iii. 5.
11 Job xxi. 14, 15; Matt. xxv. 41—43.

grace,[1] but shall certainly persevere therein to the end, and be eternally saved, seeing the gifts and callings of God are without repentance (whence he still begets and nourisheth in them faith, repentance, love, joy, hope, and all the graces of the Spirit unto immortality); and though many storms and floods arise and beat against them, yet they shall never be able to take them off that foundation and rock which by faith they are fastened upon: notwithstanding, through unbelief and the temptations of Satan, the sensible sight of the light and love of God may for a time be clouded and obscured from [2] them, yet it is still the same,[3] and they shall be sure to be kept by the power of God unto salvation, where they shall enjoy their purchased possession, they being engraven upon the palm of his hands, and their names having been written in the book of life from all eternity.

2. This perseverance of the saints depends not upon their own free will, but upon the immutability of the decree of [4] election, flowing from the free and unchangeable love of God the Father, upon the efficacy of the merit and intercession of Jesus Christ [5] and union with him, the [6] oath of God, the abiding of his Spirit, and the [7] seed of God within them, and the nature of the [8] covenant of grace; from all which ariseth also the certainty and infallibility thereof.

3. And though they may, through the temptation of Satan, and of the world, the prevalency of corruption remaining in them, and the neglect of the means of their preservation, fall into grievous [9] sins, and for a time continue therein; whereby they incur [10] God's displeasure, and grieve his Holy Spirit, come to have their graces and [11] comforts impaired, have their hearts hardened, and their consciences wounded,[12] hurt and scandalize others, and bring temporal judgments [13] upon themselves, yet they shall renew their [14] repentance, and be preserved, through faith in Jesus Christ, to the end.

1 John x. 28, 29; Phil. i. 6; 2 Tim. ii. 19; 1 John ii. 19.
2 Psalm lxxxix. 31, 32; 1 Corinthians xi. 32.
3 Mal. iii. 6.
4 Rom. viii. 30, ix. 11, 16.
5 Rom. v. 9, 10; John xiv. 19.
6 Heb. vi. 17, 18.
7 1 John iii. 9.
8 Jer. xxxii. 40.
9 Matt. xxvi. 70, 72, 74.
10 Isa. lxiv. 5, 9; Ephesians iv. 30.
11 Psalm li. 10, 12.
12 Psalm xxxii. 3, 4.
13 2 Sam. xii. 14.
14 Luke xxii. 32, v. 61, 62.

CHAPTER XVIII.

OF THE ASSURANCE OF GRACE AND SALVATION.

1. Although temporary believers and other unregenerate men, may vainly deceive themselves with false hopes and carnal presumptions of being in the favor of God, and [in a] state of salvation,[1] which hope of theirs shall perish; yet such as truly believe in the Lord Jesus, and love him in sincerity, endeavoring to walk in all good conscience before him, may in this life be certainly assured,[2] that they are in the state of grace, and may rejoice in the hope of the glory of God which hope shall never make them [3] ashamed.

2. This certainty is not a bare conjectural and probable persuasion, grounded upon [4] a fallible hope, but an infallible assurance of faith founded on the blood and righteousness of Christ,[5] revealed in the gospel; and also upon the inward [6] evidence of those graces of the Spirit unto which promises are made, and on the testimony of the [7] Spirit of adoption, witnessing with our spirits that we are the children of God; and, as a fruit thereof, keeping the heart both [8] humble and holy.

3. This infallible assurance doth not so belong to the essence of faith, but that a true believer may wait long, and conflict with many difficulties, before he be [9] partaker of it; yet being enabled by the Spirit, to know the things which are freely given him of God, he may, without extraordinary revelation, in the right use of means [10] attain thereunto; and therefore it is the duty of every one to give all diligence to make their calling and election sure, that thereby his heart may be enlarged in peace and joy in the Holy Spirit, in love and thankfulness to God, and in strength and cheerfulness in the duties of obedience, the proper [11] fruits of this assurance; so far is it [12] from inclining men to looseness.

1 Job viii. 13, 14; Matt. vii. 22, 23.
2 1 John ii. 3; iii. 14, 18, 19, 21, 24, v. 13.
3 Rom. v. 2, 5.
4 Heb. vi. 11, 19.
5 Heb. vi. 17, 18.
6 2 Peter i. 4, 5, 10, 11.
7 Rom. viii. 15, 16.
8 1 John iii. 1—3.
9 Isa. l. 10; Psalms lxxxviii., lxxvii. 1—12.
10 1 John iv. 13; Heb. vi. 11, 12.
11 Romans v. 1, 2, 5, xiv. 17; Psalm cxix. 32.
12 Rom. vi. 1, 2; Titus ii. 11, 12, 14.

4. True believers may have the assurance of their salvation divers ways shaken, diminished, and intermitted; as [1] by negligence in preserving of it, by [2] falling into some special sin, which woundeth the conscience, and grieveth the Spirit, by some sudden or [3] vehement temptation, by God's withdrawing the [4] light of his countenance, and suffering even such as fear him to walk in darkness, and to have no light; yet they are never destitute of the [5] seed of God, and life [6] of faith, that love of Christ and the brethren, that sincerity of heart, and conscience of duty, out of which, by the operation of the Spirit, this assurance may in due time be [7] revived, and by the which in the mean time they are [8] preserved from utter despair.

CHAPTER XIX.

OF THE LAW OF GOD.

1. God gave to Adam a law of universal obedience,[9] written in his heart, and a particular precept of not eating the fruit of the tree of knowledge of good and evil; by which he bound him, and all his posterity, to personal, entire, exact and perpetual [10] obedience; promised life upon the fulfilling, and [11] threatened death upon the breach of it, and indued him with power and ability to keep it.

2. The same law that was first written in the heart of man,[12] continued to be a perfect rule of righteousness after the fall, and was delivered by God upon Mount Sinai, in [13] ten commandments, and written in two tables, the four first containing our duty towards God, and the other six our duty to man.

3. Besides this law, commonly called moral, God was pleased to give to the people of Israel ceremonial laws, containing several typical ordinances, partly of worship,[14] prefiguring Christ, his graces,

1 Cant. v. 2, 3, 6.
2 Psalm li. 8, 12, 14.
3 Psalm cxvi. 11; lxxvii. 7, 8, xxxi. 22.
4 Psalm xxx. 7.
5 1 John iii. 9.
6 Luke xxii. 32.
7 Psalm xlii. 5, 11.
8 Lam. iii. 26—31.
9 Gen. i. 17; Eccl. vii. 29.
10 Rom. x. 5.
11 Gal. iii 10, 12.
12 Rom. ii. 14, 15.
13 Deut. x. 4.
14 Heb. x. 1; Col. ii. 17.

actions, sufferings, and benefits; and partly holding forth divers instructions[1] of moral duties, all which ceremonial laws being appointed only to the time of reformation, are by Jesus Christ, the true Messiah, and only lawgiver, who was furnished with power from the Father for that end,[2] abrogated and taken away.

4. To them, also, he gave sundry judicial laws, which expired together with the state of that people, not obliging any now by virtue of that institution; their general[3] equity only being of moral use.

5. The moral law doth forever bind all,[4] as well justified persons as others, to the obedience thereof, and that not only in regard of the matter contained in it, but also in respect of the[5] authority of God the Creator who gave it; neither doth Christ in the gospel any way dissolve,[6] but much strengthen this obligation.

6. Although true believers be not under the law, as a covenant of works,[7] to be thereby justified or condemned, yet it is of great use to them as well as to others, in that, as a rule of life, informing them of the will of God and their duty, it directs and binds them to walk accordingly;[8] discovering also the sinful pollutions of their natures, hearts and lives, so as examining themselves thereby, they may come to further conviction of, humiliation for, and hatred against, sin, together with a clearer sight of the need they have of Christ, and the perfection of his obedience; it is likewise of use to the regenerate, to restrain their corruptions, in that it forbids sin; and the threatenings of it serve to show what even their sins deserve, and what afflictions in this life they may expect for them, although freed from the curse and unallayed rigor thereof. The promises of it likewise show them God's approbation of obedience, and what blessings they may expect upon the performance thereof, though not as due to them by the law as a covenant of works; so as man's doing good, and refraining from evil, because the law encourageth to the one, and deterreth from the other, is no evidence of his being[9] under the law, and not under grace.

1 1 Cor. v. 7.
2 Col. ii. 14, 16, 17; Eph. ii. 14, 16.
3 1 Cor ix. 8—10.
4 Rom. xiii. 8—10; James ii. 8, 10—12.
5 James ii. 10, 11.
6 Matt. v. 17—19; Rom. iii. 31.
7 Rom. vi. 14; Gal. ii. 16; Rom. viii. 1, x. 4.
8 Rom. iii. 20, vii. 7, etc.
9 Rom. vi. 12—14; 1 Peter iii. 8—13.

7. Neither are the forementioned uses of the law [1] contrary to the grace of the gospel, but do sweetly comply with it, the Spirit of Christ subduing [2] and enabling the will of man to do that freely and cheerfully, which the will of God revealed in the law requireth to be done.

CHAPTER XX.

OF THE GOSPEL, AND OF THE EXTENT OF THE GRACE THEREOF.

1. The covenant of works being broken by sin, and made unprofitable unto life, God was pleased to give forth the promise of Christ,[3] the seed of the woman, as the means of calling the elect, and begetting in them faith and repentance; in this promise, the [4] gospel, as to the substance of it, was revealed, and [is] therein effectual, for the conversion and salvation of sinners.

2. This promise of Christ, and salvation by him, is revealed only by [5] the word of God; neither do the works of creation, or providence, with the light of nature,[6] make discovery of Christ, or of grace by him, so much as in a general or obscure way; much less that men destitute of the revelation of him by the promise or gospel,[7] should be enabled thereby to attain saving faith or repentance.

3. The revelation of the gospel unto sinners, made in divers times, and by sundry parts, with the addition of promises and precepts, for the obedience required therein, as to the nations and persons to whom it is granted, is merely of the [8] sovereign will and good pleasure of God, not being annexed by virtue of any promise, to the due improvement of men's natural abilities, by virtue of common light received without it, which none ever did [9] make, or can so do: and therefore in all ages the preaching of the gospel hath been granted unto persons and nations, as to the extent or straightening of it, in great variety, according to the counsel of the will of God.

1 Gal. iii. 21.
2 Ezek. xxxvi. 27.
3 Gen. iii 15.
4 Rev. xiii. 8.
5 Rom. i. 17.
6 Rom. x. 14, 15, 17.
7 Proverbs xxix. 18; Isaiah xxv. 7, lx. 2, 3.
8 Psalm cxlvii. 20; Acts xvi. 7.
9 Rom. i. 18, etc.

4. Although the gospel be the only outward means of revealing Christ and saving grace, and is as such abundantly sufficient thereunto, yet that men who are born in trespasses may be born again, quickened or regenerated, there is moreover necessary, an effectual insuperable[1] work of the Holy Spirit upon the whole soul, for the producing in them a new spiritual life, without which no other means will effect[2] their conversion unto God.

CHAPTER XXI.

OF CHRISTIAN LIBERTY, AND LIBERTY OF CONSCIENCE.

1. The liberty which Christ hath purchased for believers under the gospel, consists in their freedom from the guilt of sin, the condemning wrath of God, the rigor and[3] curse of the law, and in their being delivered from this present evil[4] world, bondage to[5] Satan, and dominion[6] of sin, from the[7] evil of afflictions, the fear and sting[8] of death, the victory of the grave, and[9] everlasting damnation; as also in their[10] free access to God, and their yielding obedience unto him, not out of a slavish fear,[11] but a childlike love and willing mind.

All which were common also to believers under the law[12] for the substance of them; but under the New Testament the liberty of Christians is further enlarged in their freedom from the yoke of the ceremonial law, to which the Jewish Church was subjected, and in greater boldness of access to the throne of grace, and in fuller communications of the[13] free Spirit of God, than believers under the law did ordinarily partake of.

2. God alone is[14] Lord of the conscience, and hath left it free

1 Psalm cx. 3; 1 Cor. ii. 14; Eph. i. 19, 20.
2 John vi 44; 2 Cor. iv. 4, 6.
3 Gal. iii. 13.
4 Gal. i. 4.
5 Acts xxvi. 18.
6 Rom. viii. 3.
7 Rom. viii. 28.
8 1 Cor. xv. 54—57.
9 2 Thess. i. 10.
10 Rom. viii. 15.
11 Luke i. 74, 75; 1 John iv. 18.
12 Gal. iii. 9, 14.
13 John vii. 38, 39; Hebrews x. 19—21.
14 James iv. 12; Rom. xiv. 4.

from the doctrines and commandments of men[1] which are in anything contrary to his word, or not contained in it. So that to believe such doctrines, or obey such commands out of conscience,[2] is to betray true liberty of conscience; and the requiring of an[3] implicit faith, and absolute and blind obedience, is to destroy liberty of conscience, and reason also.

3. They who, upon pretence of Christian liberty, do practise any sin, or cherish any sinful lust, as they do thereby pervert the main design of the grace of the gospel[4] to their own destruction, so they wholly destroy[5] the end of Christian liberty; which is that, being delivered out of the hands of all our enemies, we might serve the Lord without fear, in holiness and righteousness before him, all the days of our life.

CHAPTER XXII.

OF RELIGIOUS WORSHIP AND THE SABBATH-DAY.

1. The light of nature shows that there is a God, who hath lordship and sovereignty over all; is just, good, and doth good unto all; and is therefore to be feared, loved, praised, called upon, trusted in, and served, with all the heart, and all the soul,[6] and with all the might. But the acceptable way of worshipping the true God, is[7] instituted by himself, and so limited by his own revealed will, that he may not be worshipped according to the imaginations and devices of men, or the suggestions of Satan, under any visible representations, or[8] any other way, not prescribed in the holy Scriptures.

2. Religious worship is to be given to God the Father, Son, and Holy Spirit, and to him[9] alone; not to angels, saints, or any other[10] creatures; and since the fall, not without a[11] mediator, nor in the mediation of any other but[12] Christ alone.

1 Acts iv. 19, v. 29; 1 Cor. vii. 23; Matt. xv. 9.
2 Col. ii. 20, 22, 23.
3 1 Cor. iii 5; 2 Cor. i. 24.
4 Rom. vi 1. 2.
5 Gal. v. 13; 2 Peter ii. 18—21.
6 Jer. x. 7; Mark xii. 33.
7 Deut. xii. 32.
8 Ex. xx. iv. 5, 6.
9 Matt. iv. 9, 10; John vi. 23; Matt. xxviii. 19.
10 Rom. i. 25; Col. ii 18; Rev. xix. 10.
11 John xiv. 6.
12 1 Tim. ii. 5.

3. Prayer with thanksgiving, being one special part of natural worship, is by God required of [1] all men. But that it may be accepted, it is to be made in the [2] name of the Son, by the help [3] of the Spirit, according to [4] his will; with understanding, reverence, humility, fervency, faith, love, and perseverance; and when with others, in a [5] known tongue.

4. Prayer is to be made for things lawful, and for all sorts of men living,[6] or that shall live hereafter; but not [7] for the dead, nor for those of whom it may be known that they have sinned [8] the sin unto death.

5. The [9] reading of the Scriptures, preaching, and [10] hearing the word of God, teaching and admonishing one another in psalms, hymns, and spiritual songs; singing with grace in our hearts to [11] the Lord; as also the administration [12] of baptism, and [13] the Lord's Supper, are all parts of religious worship of God, to be performed in obedience to him, with understanding, faith, reverence, and godly fear; moreover, solemn humiliation,[14] with fastings, and thanksgivings, upon [15] special occasions, ought to be used in an holy and religious manner.

6. Neither prayer, nor any other part of religious worship, is now, under the gospel, tied unto, or made more acceptable by any place in which it is [16] performed, or towards which it is directed; but God is to be worshipped everywhere in spirit and in truth; as in [17] private families [18] daily, and [19] in secret, each one by himself, so more solemnly in the public assemblies, which are not carelessly, nor wilfully to be [20] neglected or forsaken, when God by his word or providence calleth thereunto.

7. As it is of the law of nature, that in general a proportion of time, by God's appointment, be set apart for the worship of God, so

1 Psalm xcv. 1—71, xv. 2.
2 John xiv. 13, 14.
3 Rom. viii. 26.
4 1 John v. 14.
5 1 Cor. xiv. 16, 17.
6 1 Tim. ii. 1, 2; Sam. vii. 29.
7 2 Sam. xii. 21—23.
8 1 John v. 16.
9 1 Tim iv. 13.
10 2 Tim. iv. 2; Luke viii. 18.
11 Col. iii. 16; Eph. v. 19.
12 Matt. xxviii. 19, 20.
13 1 Cor. xi. 26.
14 Esther iv. 16; Joel ii. 12.
15 Ex. xv. 1, etc.; Psalm cvii.
16 John iv. 21; Mal. i. 11; 1 Tim. ii. 8.
17 Acts x. 2.
18 Matt. vi. 11; Psalm lv. 17.
19 Matt. vi. 6.
20 Heb. x. 25; Acts ii. 42.

by his word, in a positive, moral, and perpetual commandment, binding all men, in all ages, he hath particularly appointed one day in seven for a [1] Sabbath to be kept holy unto him, which from the beginning of the world, to the resurrection of Christ, was the last day of the week, and from the resurrection of Christ was changed into the first day of the week,[2] which is called the Lord's day; and is to be continued to the end of the world, as the Christian Sabbath; the observation of the last day of the week being abolished.

8. The Sabbath is then kept holy unto the Lord, when men, after a due preparation of their hearts, and ordering their common affairs aforehand, do not only observe an holy [3] rest all the day, from their own works, words, and thoughts, about their worldly employment and recreations, but also are taken up the whole time in the public and private exercises of his worship, and in the duties [4] of necessity and mercy.

CHAPTER XXIII.

OF LAWFUL OATHS AND VOWS.

1. A lawful oath is a part of religious worship [5] wherein the person swearing in truth, righteousness, and judgment, solemnly calleth God to witness what he sweareth,[6] and to judge him according to the truth or falseness thereof.

2. The name of God only is that by which men ought to swear, and therein it is to be used with all holy fear and reverence; therefore to swear vainly or rashly by that glorious and dreadful name, or to swear at all by any other thing, is sinful and to be [7] abhorred; yet as in matter of weight and moment, for confirmation of truth,[8] and ending all strife, an oath is warranted by the word of God; so a lawful oath being imposed,[9] by lawful authority, in such matters ought to be taken.

1 Exodus xx. 8.
2 1 Corinthians xvi. 1, 2; Acts xx. 7; Rev. i. 10.
3 Isa. lviii. 13; Neh. xiii. 15—23.
4 Matt. xii. 1—13.
5 Exodus xx. 7; Deut. x. 20; Jer. iv. 2.
6 2 Chron. vi 22, 23.
7 Matt. v. 34—37; James v. 12.
8 Heb. vi. 16; Cor. i. 23.
9 Neh. xiii. 25.

3. Whosoever taketh an oath, warranted by the word of God, ought duly to consider the weightiness of so solemn an act, and therein to avouch nothing but what he knoweth to be truth; for that by rash, false, and vain oaths, the [1] Lord is provoked, and for them this land mourns.

4. An oath is to be taken in the plain and [2] common sense of the words, without equivocation or mental reservation.

5. A vow, which is not to be made to any creature, but to God alone,[3] is to be made and performed with all religious care and faithfulness; but popish monastical vows,[4] of perpetual single life, professed [5] poverty, and regular obedience, are so far from being degrees of higher perfection, that they are superstitious,[6] and sinful snares, in which no Christian may entangle himself.

CHAPTER XXIV.

OF THE CIVIL MAGISTRATE.

1. God, the supreme Lord, and king of all the world, hath ordained civil [7] magistrates to be under him over the people, for his own glory, and the public good; and to this end hath armed them with the power of the sword, for defence and encouragement of them that do good, and for the punishment of evil-doers.

2. It is lawful for Christians to accept and execute the office of a magistrate, when called thereunto; in the management whereof, as they ought especially to maintain [8] justice, and peace, according to the wholesome laws of each kingdom and commonwealth; so for that end they may lawfully now under the New Testament [9] wage war upon just and necessary occasions.

3. Civil magistrates being set up by God, for the ends aforesaid, subjection in all lawful things commanded by them, ought to be yielded by us in the Lord, not only for wrath [10] but for conscience'

1 Lev. xix. 12; Jer. xxiii. 10.
2 Psalm xxiv. 4.
3 Psalm lxxvi. 11; Gen. xxviii. 20—22.
4 1 Cor. vii. 2, 9.
5 Eph. iv. 28.
6 Matt. xix. 11.
7 Rom. xiii. 1—4.
8 2 Sam. xxiii. 3; Psalm lxxxii. 3, 4.
9 Luke iii. 14.
10 Rom. xiii. 5, 6, 7; 1 Peter ii. 17.

sake; and we ought to make supplications and prayers for kings, and all that are in authority,[1] that under them we may live a quiet and peaceable life, in all godliness and honesty.

CHAPTER XXV.

OF MARRIAGE.

1. Marriage is to be between one man and one woman;[2] neither is it lawful for any man to have more than one wife, nor for any woman to have more than one husband at the same time.

2. Marriage was ordained for the mutual help[3] of husband and wife,[4] for the increase of mankind with a legitimate issue, and for[5] preventing of uncleanness.

3. It is lawful for[6] all sorts of people to marry, who are able with judgment to give their consent; yet it is the duty of Christians[7] to marry [only] in the Lord; and therefore such as profess the true religion should not marry with infidels,[8] or idolaters; neither should such as are godly be unequally yoked, by marrying with such as are wicked in their life, or maintain damnable heresy.

4. Marriage ought not to be within the degrees of consanguinity[9] or affinity forbidden in the word; nor can such incestuous marriage ever be made lawful, by any law of man or consent of parties[10] so as those persons may live together as man and wife.

CHAPTER XXVI.

OF THE CHURCH.

1. The catholic or universal church, which (with respect to the internal work of the Spirit and truth of grace) may be called invisi-

1 1 Tim. ii. 1, 2.
2 Gen. ii. 24; Mal. ii. 15; Matt. xix. 5, 6.
3 Gen. ii. 18.
4 Gen. i. 28.
5 1 Cor. vii. 2, 9.
6 Heb. xiii. 4; 1 Tim. iv. 3.
7 1 Cor. vii. 39.
8 Neh. xiii. 25—27.
9 Lev. xviii.
10 Matt. vi. 18; 1 Cor. v. 1.

ble, consists of the whole[1] number of the elect, that have been, are, or shall be gathered into one, under Christ, the head thereof; and is the spouse, the body, the fulness of him that filleth all in all.

2. All persons throughout the world, professing the faith of the gospel, and obedience unto God by Christ according unto it, not destroying their own profession by any errors everting the foundation, or unholiness of conversation,[2] are and may be called visible saints;[3] and of such ought all particular congregations to be constituted.

3. The purest churches under heaven are subject[4] to mixture and error; and some have so degenerated as to become[5] no churches of Christ, but synagogues of Satan; nevertheless Christ always hath had, and ever shall have, a[6] kingdom in this world, to the end thereof, of such as believe in him, and make professions of his name.

4. The Lord Jesus Christ is the head of the church, in whom, by the appointment of the Father,[7] all power for the calling, institution, order, or government of the church, is invested in a supreme and sovereign manner; neither can the Pope of Rome in any sense be head thereof, but is[8] [no other] than Antichrist, that man of sin, and son of perdition, that exalteth himself in the church against Christ, and all that is called God; whom the Lord shall destroy with the brightness of his coming.

5. In the execution of this power wherewith he is so entrusted, the Lord Jesus calleth out of the world unto himself, through the ministry of his word, by his Spirit,[9] those that are given unto him by his Father, that they may walk before him in all the[10] ways of obedience, which he prescribeth to them in his word. Those thus called, he commandeth to walk together in particular societies, or[11] churches, for their mutual edification, and the due performance of that public worship which he requireth of them in the world.

1 Heb. xii. 23; Col. i. 18; Eph. i. 20, 22, 23, v. 23, 27, 32.
2 1 Cor. i. 2; Acts xi. 26.
3 Rom. i. 7; Eph. i. 20—22.
4 1 Cor. xv.; Rev. ii., iii.
5 Revelation xviii. 2; 2 Thessalonians ii. 11, 12.
6 Matt. xvi. 18; Psalm lxxii. 17, cii. 28; Rev. xii. 17.
7 Col. i. 18; Matt. xxviii. 18—20; Eph. iv. 21, 22.
8 2 Thess. ii. 2—9.
9 John x. 16, xii. 32.
10 Matt. xxviii. 20.
11 Matt. xviii. 15—20.

6. The members of these churches are[1] saints by calling, visibly manifesting and evidencing (in and by their profession and walking) their obedience unto that call of Christ; and do willingly consent to walk together according to the appointment of Christ, giving up themselves to the Lord and one to another, by the will of God,[2] in professed subjection to the ordinances of the gospel.

7. To each of these churches thus gathered according to his mind, declared in his word, he hath given all that[3] power and authority, which is any way needful for their carrying on that order in worship and discipline, which he hath instituted for them to observe, with commands and rules, for the due and right exerting and executing of that power.

8. A particular church gathered, and completely organized, according to the mind of Christ, consists of officers and members: and the officers appointed by Christ to be chosen and set apart by the church (so called and gathered) for the peculiar administration of ordinances, and execution of power, or duty, which he entrusts them with, or calls them to, to be continued to the end of the world, are[4] bishops or elders, and deacons.

9. The way appointed by Christ for the calling of any person, fitted and gifted by the Holy Spirit, unto the office of bishop, or elder, in the church, is that he be chosen thereunto by the common[5] suffrage of the church itself; and solemnly set apart by fasting and prayer, with imposition of hands of the[6] eldership of the church, if there be any before constituted therein: and of a deacon[7] that he be chosen by the like suffrage, and set apart by prayer, and the like imposition of hands.

10. The work of pastors being constantly to attend the service of Christ, in his churches, in the ministry of the word, and prayer[8] with watching for their souls, as they that must give an account to him; it is incumbent on the churches to whom they minister, not only to give them all due respect,[9] but also to communicate to them

1 Rom. i. 7; 1 Cor. i. 2.
2 Acts ii. 41, 42, v. 13, 14; 2 Cor. ix. 13.
3 Matt. xviii. 17, 18; 1 Cor. v. 4, 5, 13; 2 Cor. ii. 6—8.
4 Acts xx. 17, v. 28; Phil. i. 1.
5 Acts xiv. 23. See the original.
6 1 Tim. iv. 14.
7 Acts vi. 3, 5, 6.
8 Acts vi. 4; Heb. xiii. 17.
9 1 Tim. v. 17, 18; Gal. vi. 6, 7.

cerned, or any one church, in their peace, union, and edification; or any member or members of any church are injured, in or by any proceedings in censures not agreeable to truth and order; it is according to the mind of Christ, that many churches holding communion together, do by their messengers meet to consider [1] and give their advice in or about that matter in difference, to be reported to all the churches concerned; howbeit these messengers assembled, are not entrusted with any church power, properly so called; or with any jurisdiction over the churches themselves, to exercise any censures either over any churches, or persons; or [2] to impose their determination on the churches or officers.

CHAPTER XXVII.

OF THE COMMUNION OF SAINTS.

1. All saints that are united to Jesus Christ, their head, by his Spirit and faith, although they are not made thereby one person with him, have [3] fellowship in his graces, sufferings, death, resurrection, and glory; and being united to one another in love, they [4] have communion in each other's gifts and graces, and are obliged to the performance of such duties, public and private, in an orderly way,[5] as to conduce to their mutual good, both in the inward and outward man.

2. Saints by profession, are bound to maintain an holy fellowship and communion in the worship of God, and in performing such other spiritual services,[6] as tend to their mutual edification; as also in relieving each other in [7] outward things, according to their several abilities and necessities; which communion according to the rule of the gospel, though especially to be exercised by them, in the relations wherein they stand, whether in [8] families or [9] churches, yet as God offereth opportunity, is to be extended to all the household of faith,

1 Acts xv. 2, 4, 6, 22, 23, 25.
2 2 Cor. i. 24; i. John iv. 1.
3 1 John i. 3; John i. 16; Phil. iii. 10; Rom. vi. 5, 6.
4 Eph. iv. 15, 16; 1 Corinthians xii. 7, iii. 21—23.
5 1 Thess. v. 11, 14; Rom. i. 12; 1 John iii. 17, 18; Gal. vi. 10.
6 Heb. x. 24, 25, iii. 12, 13.
7 Acts xii. 29, 30.
8 Eph. vi. 4.
9 1 Cor. xii. 14—27.

even all those who in every place call upon the name of the Lord Jesus; nevertheless their communion one with another as saints, doth not take away, or[1] infringe the title or propriety which each man hath in his goods and possessions.

CHAPTER XXVIII.

OF BAPTISM AND THE LORD'S SUPPER.

1. Baptism and the Lord's Supper are ordinances of positive and sovereign institution, appointed by the Lord Jesus, the only lawgiver, to be continued in his church[2] to the end of the world.

2. These holy appointments are to be administered by those only who are qualified, and thereunto called according[3] to the commission of Christ.

CHAPTER XXIX.

OF BAPTISM.

1. Baptism is an ordinance of the New Testament, ordained by Jesus Christ, to be unto the party baptized a sign of his fellowship with him in his death[4] and resurrection; of his being engrafted into him; of[5] remission of sins; and of his[6] giving up unto God, through Jesus Christ, to live and walk in newness of life.

2. Those who do actually profess[7] repentance towards God, faith in, and obedience to our Lord Jesus, are the only proper subjects of this ordinance.

3. The outward element to be used in this ordinance[8] is water, wherein the party is to be baptized, in the name of the Father, and of the Son, and of the Holy Spirit.

4. Immersion, or dipping of the person[9] in water, is necessary to the due administration of this ordinance.

1 Acts v. 4; Eph. iv. 28.
2 Matt. xxviii. 19, 20; 1 Cor. xi. 26.
3 Matt. xxviii. 19; 1 Cor. iv. 1.
4 Rom. vi. 3–5; Col. ii. 12; Galatians iii. 27.
5 Mark i. 4; Acts xxvi. 16.
6 Rom. vi. 2, 4.
7 Mark xvi. 16; Acts viii. 36, 37.
8 Matt. xxviii. 19, 20; Acts viii. 38.
9 Matt. iii. 16; John iii. 23.

CHAPTER XXX.

OF THE LORD'S SUPPER.

1. The Supper of the Lord Jesus was instituted by him the same night wherein he was betrayed, to be observed in his churches unto the end of the world for the perpetual remembrance, and showing forth the sacrifice of himself in his death,[1] confirmation of the faith of believers in all the benefits thereof, their spiritual nourishment and growth in him, their further engagement in and to all duties which they owe unto him;[2] and to be a bond and pledge of their communion with him, and with each other.

2. In this ordinance Christ is not offered up to his Father, nor any real sacrifice made at all for remission of sin, of the quick or dead, but only a memorial of that[3] one offering up of himself, by himself, upon the cross, once for all; and a spiritual oblation of all[4] possible praise unto God for the same. So that the popish sacrifice of the mass as (they call it) is most abominable, injurious to Christ's own only sacrifice, the alone propitiation for all the sins of the elect.

3. The Lord Jesus hath, in this ordinance, appointed his ministers to pray and bless the elements of bread and wine, and thereby to set them apart from a common to an holy use, and to take and break the bread; to take the cup,[5] and (they communicating also themselves) to give both to the communicants.

4. The denial of the cup to the people, worshipping the elements, the lifting them up or carrying them about for adoration, and reserving them for any pretended religious use,[6] are all contrary to the nature of this ordinance, and to the institution of Christ.

5. The outward elements in this ordinance, duly set apart to the uses ordained by Christ, have such relation to him crucified, as that truly, although in terms used figuratively, they are sometimes called by the name of the things they represent, to wit, the[7] body and

1 1 Cor. xv. 23—26.
2 1 Cor. x. 16, 17. 21.
3 Heb. ix. 25, 26, 28.
4 1 Cor. xi. 24; Matt. xxvi. 26, 27.
5 1 Cor. 11, 23—26, etc.
6 Matt. xxvi. 26—28, xv. 9; Exodus xx. 4, 5.
7 1 Cor. xi. 27.

blood of Christ, albeit in substance and nature, they still remain truly and only [1] bread and wine, as they were before.

6. That doctrine which maintains a change of the substance of bread and wine into the substance of Christ's body and blood (commonly called transubstantiation), by consecration of a priest, or by any other way, is repugnant not to Scripture [2] alone, but even to common sense and reason, overthroweth the [3] nature of the ordinance, and hath been and is the cause of manifold superstitions, yea, of gross idolatries.

7. Worthy receivers outwardly partaking of the visible elements in this ordinance, do then also inwardly, by faith really and indeed, yet not carnally and corporally, but spiritually receive, and feed upon Christ crucified [4] and all the benefits of his death; the body and blood of Christ being then not corporally, or carnally, but spiritually present to the faith of believers in that ordinance, as the elements themselves are to their outward senses.

8. All ignorant and ungodly persons, as they are unfit to enjoy communion [5] with Christ, so are they unworthy of the Lord's table, and cannot, without great sin against him, while they remain such, partake of these holy mysteries, [6] or be admitted thereunto: yea, whosoever shall receive unworthily, are guilty of the body and blood of the Lord, eating and drinking judgment to themselves.

CHAPTER XXXI.

OF THE STATE OF MAN AFTER DEATH, AND OF THE RESURRECTION OF THE DEAD.

1. The bodies of men after death return to dust, [7] and see corruption; but their souls, which neither die nor sleep, having an immortal subsistence, immediately [8] return to God who gave them: the souls of the righteous, being then made perfect in holiness, are

1 1 Cor. xi. 26, v 28.
2 Acts iii. 21; Luke xxiv. 6, v. 39.
3 1 Cor. xi. 24, 25.
4 1 Cor. x. 16, xi. 23—26.
5 2 Cor. vi. 14, 15.
6 1 Cor. xi. 29; Matt. vii. 6.
7 Gen. iii. 19; Acts xiii. 36.
8 Eccl. xii. 7.

received into paradise, where they are with Christ, and behold the face of God, in light [1] and glory, waiting for the full redemption of their bodies; and the souls of the wicked are cast into hell, where they remain in torment and utter darkness, reserved to [2] the judgment of the great day; besides these two places, for souls separated from their bodies, the Scripture acknowledgeth none.

2. At the last day, such of the saints as are found alive shall not sleep, but be [3] changed; and all the dead shall be raised up with the self-same bodies, and [4] none other; although with different [5] qualities, which shall be united again to their souls for ever.

3. The bodies of the unjust shall, by the power of Christ, be raised to dishonor; the bodies of the just, by his Spirit, unto honor,[6] and be made conformable to his own glorious body.

CHAPTER XXXII.

OF THE LAST JUDGMENT.

1. God hath appointed a day wherein he will judge the world in righteousness, by [7] Jesus Christ; to whom all power and judgment is given of the Father; in which day not only the [8] apostate angels shall be judged, but likewise all persons that have lived upon the earth, shall appear before the tribunal of Christ, [9] to give an account of their thoughts, words and deeds, and to receive according to what they have done in the body, whether good or evil.

2. The end of God's appointing this day, is for the manifestation of the glory of his mercy, in the eternal salvation of the elect; [10] and of his justice, in the eternal damnation of the reprobate, who are wicked and disobedient; for then shall the righteous go into ever-

1 Luke xxiii. 43; 2 Cor. v. 1, 6, 8; Phil. i. 23; Heb. xii. 23.
2 Jude vi. 7; 1 Peter iii. 19; Luke xvi. 23, 24.
3 1 Corinthians xv. 51, 52; 1 Thessalonians iv. 17.
4 Job xix. 26, 27.
5 1 Cor. xv. 42, 43.
6 Acts xxiv. 15; John v. 28, 29; Phil. iii. 21.
7 Acts xvii. 31; John v. 22, 27.
8 1 Cor. vi. 3; Jude 6.
9 2 Cor. v. 10; Eccl. xii. 14; Matt. xii. 36; Rom. xiv. 10, 12; Matt. xxv. 32, etc.
10 Rom. ix. 22, 23.

lasting life, and receive that fulness of joy and glory, with everlasting reward, in the presence [1] of the Lord; but the wicked who know not God, and obey not the gospel of Jesus Christ, shall be cast into eternal torments, and [2] punished with everlasting destruction, from the presence of the Lord, and from the glory of his power.

3. As Christ would have us to be certainly persuaded that there shall be a day of judgment, both [3] to deter all men from sin, and for the greater [4] consolation of the godly in their adversity, so will he have that day unknown to men, that they may shake off all carnal security, and be always watchful, because they know not at what hour the [5] Lord will come, and may ever be prepared to say, [6] *Come Lord Jesus, come quickly.* AMEN.

CHAPTER XXXIII.

AN APPENDIX CONCERNING BAPTISM.

Whosoever reads and impartially considers what we have in our foregoing confession declared, may readily perceive that we do not only concentre with all other true Christians on the word of God (revealed in the Scriptures of truth), as the foundation and rule of our faith and worship; but that we have also industriously endeavored to manifest, that in the fundamental articles of Christianity we mind the same things, and have therefore expressed our belief in the same words that have on the like occasion been spoken by other societies of Christians before us.

This we have done, that those who are desirous to know the principles of religion which we hold and practise may take an estimate from ourselves (who jointly concur in this work), and may not be misguided, either by undue reports, or by the ignorance or errors of particular persons, who, going under the same name with ourselves, may give an occasion of scandalizing the truth we profess.

1 Matthew xxv. 21, 34; 2 Timothy iv. 8.
2 Matt. xxv. 46; Mark ix. 48; 2 Thess. i. 7—10.
3 2 Cor. v. 10, 11.
4 2 Thess. i. 3, 6, 7.
5 Mark xiii. 35—37; Luke xiii. 35, 36.
6 Rev. xxii. 20.

And although we do differ from our brethren who are pædobaptists, in the subject and administration of baptism, and such other circumstances as have a necessary dependence on our observance of that ordinance, and do frequent our own assemblies for our mutual edification, and discharge of those duties and services which we owe unto God, and in his fear, to each other; yet we would not be from hence misconstrued, as if the discharge of our own consciences herein did any ways disoblige, or alienate our affections or conversations from any others that fear the Lord; but that we may and do, as we have opportunity, participate of the labors of those whom God hath endued with abilities above ourselves, and qualified and called to the ministry of the word, earnestly desiring to approve ourselves to be such as follow after peace with holiness; and therefore we always keep that blessed *Irenicum*, or healing word of the apostle before our eyes: *If in any thing ye be otherwise minded, God shall reveal even this unto you; nevertheless, whereto we have already attained, let us walk by the same rule, let us mind the same thing.*[1]

Let it not therefore be judged of us (because much hath been written on this subject, and yet we continue this our practice different from others) that it is out of obstinacy, but rather, as the truth is, that we do herein, according to the best of our understandings, worship God out of a pure mind, yielding obedience to his precept, in that method which we take to be most agreeable to the Scriptures of truth and primitive practice.

It would not become us to give any such intimation as should carry a semblance that what we do in the service of God is with a doubting conscience, or with any such temper of mind, that we do thus for the present with a reservation that we will do otherwise hereafter upon more mature deliberation; nor have we any cause so to do, being fully persuaded that what we do is agreeable to the will of God. Yet we do heartily propose this, that if any of the servants of our Lord Jesus shall, in the spirit of meekness, attempt to convince us of any mistake, either in judgment or practice, we shall diligently ponder his arguments, and account him our chiefest friend that shall be an instrument to convert us from any error

1 Phil. iii. 15, 16.

that is in our ways, for we cannot wittingly do any thing against the truth, but all things for the truth.

And therefore we have endeavored seriously to consider what hath been already offered for our satisfaction in this point; and are loth to say more, lest we should be esteemed desirous of renewed contests thereabout; yet, forasmuch as it may justly be expected that we show some reason why we cannot acquiesce in what hath been urged against us, we shall, with as much brevity as may consist with plainness, endeavor to satisfy the expectation of those that shall peruse what we now publish in this matter also.

1. As to those Christians who consent with us, that repentance from dead works and faith towards God and our Lord Jesus Christ, is required in persons to be baptized; and do therefore supply the defect of the infant (being incapable of making confession of either) by others, who do undertake these things for it. Although we do find by church history that this hath been a very ancient practice, yet considering that the same Scripture [1] which does caution us against censuring our brother, with whom we shall all stand before the judgment-seat of Christ, does also instruct us, that every one of us shall give an account of himself to God, and whatsoever is not of faith is sin; therefore we cannot for our own parts be persuaded in our own minds to build such a practice as this upon an unwritten tradition; but do rather choose, in all points of faith and worship, to have recourse to the holy Scriptures for the information of our judgment and regulation of our practice; being well assured that a conscientious attending thereto is the best way to prevent and rectify our defects and errors.[2] And if any such case happen to be debated between Christians, which is not plainly determinable by the Scriptures, we think it safest to leave such things undecided, until the second coming of our Lord Jesus; as they did in the church of old, until there should arise a priest with Urim and Thummim, that might certainly inform them of the mind of God thereabout.[3]

2. As for those our Christian brethren, who do ground their arguments for infants' baptism upon a presumed fœderal holiness or

1 Rom. xiv. 4, 10, 12, 23. 2 2 Tim. iii. 16, 17. 3 Ezra ii. 62, 63.

church membership, we conceive they are deficient in this — that, albeit this covenant holiness and membership should be as is supposed, in reference unto the infants of believers, yet no command for infant baptism does immediately and directly result from such a quality or relation.

All instituted worship receives its sanction from the precept, and is to be thereby governed in all the necessary circumstances thereof.

So it was in the covenant that God made with Abraham and his seed, the sign whereof was appropriated only to the male, notwithstanding that the female seed, as well as the male, were comprehended in the covenant, and part of the church of God; neither was this sign to be affixed to any male infant till he was eight days old, albeit he was within the covenant from the first moment of his life; nor could the danger of death, or any other supposed necessity, warrant the circumcising of him before the set time, nor was there any cause for it; the commination of being cut off from his people being only upon the neglect or contempt of the precept.

Righteous Lot was nearly related to Abraham in the flesh, and contemporary with him, when this covenant was made; yet, inasmuch as he did not descend from his loins, nor was of his household family (although he was of the same household of faith with Abraham), yet neither Lot himself nor any of his posterity (because of their descent from him) were signed with the signature of this covenant that was made with Abraham and his seed.

This may suffice to show that where there was both an express covenant and a sign thereof, such a covenant as did separate the persons with whom it was made and all their offspring from all the rest of the world, as a people holy unto the Lord, and did constitute them the visible church of God (though not comprehensive of all the faithful in the world), yet the sign of this covenant was not affixed to all the persons that were within this covenant, nor to any of them, till the prefixed season; nor to other faithful servants of God that were not of descent from Abraham. And, consequent'y, that it depends purely upon the will of the lawgiver to determine what shall be the sign of his covenant, unto whom, at what season, and upon what terms it shall be affixed.

If our brethren do suppose baptism to be the seal of the covenant which God makes with every believer (of which the Scriptures are altogether silent), it is not our concern to contend with them herein; yet we conceive the seal of that covenant is the indwelling of the Spirit of Christ in the particular and individual persons in whom he resides, and nothing else. Neither do they or we suppose that baptism is in any such manner substituted in the place of circumcision, as to have the same (and no other) latitude, extent, or terms than circumcision had. For that was suited only for the male children: baptism is an ordinance suited for every believer, whether male or female. That extended to all the males that were born in Abraham's house, or bought with his money, equally with the males that proceeded from his own loins; but baptism is not so far extended in any true Christian church that we know of, as to be administered to all the poor infidel servants that the members thereof purchase for their service, and introduce into their families, nor to the children born of them in their house.

But we conceive the same parity of reasoning may hold for the ordinance of baptism as for that of circumcision,[1] viz., one law for the stranger as for the home-born. If any desire to be admitted to all the ordinances and privileges of God's house, the door is open; upon the same terms that any one person was ever admitted to all or any of those privileges that belong to the Christian church, may all persons of right challenge the like admission.

As for that text of Scripture,[2] *He received circumcision, a seal of righteousness of the faith, which he had yet being uncircumcised;* we conceive, if the apostle's scope in that place be duly attended to, it will appear that no argument can be taken from thence to enforce infant baptism. And forasmuch as we find a full and fair account of those words given by the learned Dr. Lightfoot (a man not to be suspected of partiality in this controversy), in his Hor. Hebrai. on the 1 Cor. vii. 19, p. 42, 43, we shall transcribe his words at large, without any comment of our own upon them.

Circumcisio nihil est ratione habitâ temporis, jam enim evanuerat, adimpleto præcipuè ejus fine ob quem	Circumcision is nothing, if we respect the time, for now it was without use, that end of it being especially fulfilled

1 Exodus xii. 49.

2 Rom. iv. 11.

fuerat instituta; istum finem exhibet apostolus in verbis istis, Rom. iv. 11. σφραγῖδα τῆς δικαιοσύνης τῆς πίστεως τῆς ἐν ἀκροβυστίᾳ At vereor ne à plerisque versionibus non satis aptentur, ad finem circumcisionis, et scopum apostoli, dum ab iis interseritur aliquid de suo.

for which it had been instituted: this end the apostle declares in these words, Rom. iv. 11, σφραγίδα, etc. But I fear that by most translations they are not sufficiently suited to the end of circumcision and the scope of the apostle, whilst something of their own is by them inserted.

And after the doctor hath represented divers versions of the words, agreeing, for the most part, in sense with that which we have in our bibles, he thus proceeds:

Aliæ in eundem sensum, ac si circumcisio daretur Abrahamo in sigillum justitiæ istius, quam ille habuit, dum adhuc foret præputiatus; quod non negabimus aliqualiter verum esse, at credimus circumcisionem longè aliò præcipuè respexisse.

Other versions are to the same purpose; as if circumcision was given to Abraham for a seal of that righteousness which he had, being yet uncircumcised, which we will not deny to be in some sense true; but we believe that circumcision had chiefly a far different respect.

Liceat mihi verba sic reddere: et signum accepit circumcisionis, sigillum justitiæ fidei, quæ futura in præputio; quæ futura dico, non quæ fuerat. Non quæ fuerat Abrahamo adhuc præputiato, sed quæ futura semini ejus præputiato, id est, gentilibus, fidem olim Abrahami imitaturis.

Give me leave thus to render the words: And he received the sign of circumcision, a seal of the righteousness of faith, which was to be in the uncircumcision. Which was to be (I say), not which had been; not that which Abraham had whilst he was yet uncircumcised, but which his uncircumcised seed should have; that is, the Gentiles, who in time to come should imitate the faith of Abraham.

Nunc adverte bene quâ occasione instituta Abrahamo circumcisio, ponens tibi ante oculos historiam ejus. Gen. xvii.

Fit primò ei hæc promissio, Multatarum gentium eris tu pater (quonam sensu explicat apostolus, isto capite) et subinde subjungitur duplex sigillum rei corroborandæ; immutatio scilicet nominis Abrami in Abrahamum; et institutio circumcisionis: ver. 4. Ecce mihi tecum est fœdus, eris tu pater multarum gentium. Quare vocatum est nomen ejus Abrahamus! In sigillationem hujus promissionis. Tu pater eris multarum gentium. Et quare instituta ei circumcisio? In sigillationem ejusdem

Now, consider well on what occasion circumcision was instituted unto Abraham, setting before thine eyes the history thereof. Gen. xvii.

This promise is first made upto him, *Thou shalt be the father of many nations* (in what sense the apostle explaineth in that chapter), and then there is subjoined a double seal for the confirmation of the thing, to wit, the change of the name Abram into Abraham, and the institution of circumcision, ver. 4, *Behold, as for me, my covenant is with thee, and thou shalt be the father of many nations.* Wherefore was his name called Abraham? For the sealing of his promise. *Thou shalt be the father of many*

promissionis. Tu pater eris multarum gentium. Ita ut hic sit sensus apostoli, institutioni circumcisionis congruentissimus; accepit signum circumcisionis, sigillum justitiæ fidei, quam olim erat incircumcisio (vel Gentiles) habitura et adeptura.

nations. And wherefore was circumcision instituted to him? For the sealing of the same promise. *Thou shalt be the father of many nations*. So that this is the sense of the apostle, most agreeable to the institution of circumcision; he received the sign of circumcision, a seal of the righteousness of faith, which in time to come the uncircumcision (or the Gentiles) should have and obtain.

Duplex semen erat Abrahamo, naturale, Judæorum; et fidele, gentilium credentium: signatur naturale signo circumcisionis, primò quidem in sui distinctionem, ab omnibus aliis gentibus, dum eæ non adhuc forent semen Abrahami; at præcipue in memoriam justificationis gentium per fidem, cum tandem forent ejus semen. Cessatura ergo merito, erat circumcisio, cum introducerentur Gentiles ad fidem, quippe quod tunc finem suum ultimum ac præcipuum obtinuerat, et perinde ἡ περιτομὴ οὐδὲν.

Abraham had a twofold seed, natural, of the Jews; and, faithful, of the believing Gentiles; his natural seed was signed with the sign of circumcision, first, indeed, for the distinguishing of them from all other nations, whilst they as yet were not the seed of Abraham, but especially for the memorial of the justification of the Gentiles by faith, when at length they should become his seed. Therefore, circumcision was of right to cease when the Gentiles were brought into the faith, forasmuch as then it had obtained its last and chief end, and thenceforth circumcision is nothing.

Thus far he, which we earnestly desire may be seriously weighed, for we plead not his authority, but the evidence of truth in his words.

3. Of whatsoever nature the holiness of the children mentioned[1] be, yet they who do conclude that all such children (whether infants, or of riper years) have from hence an immediate right to baptism, do, as we conceive, put more into the conclusion than will be found in the premises.

For although we do not determine positively concerning the apostles' scope in the holiness here mentioned, so as to say, it is this or that, and no other thing; yet it is evident, that the apostle does by it determine not only the lawfulness, but the expedience also of a believer's cohabition with an unbeliever in the state of marriage.

And we do think that, although the apostle's asserting of the unbelieving yoke-fellow to be sanctified by the believer should carry

[1] 1 Cor. vii. 12.

in it somewhat more than is in the bare marriage of two infidels, because although the marriage covenant have a divine sanction so as to make the wedlock of two unbelievers a lawful action, and their conjunction and cohabition in that respect undefiled, yet there might be no ground to suppose from thence, that both or either of their persons are thereby sanctified; and the apostle urges the cohabition of a believer with an infidel in the state of wedlock from this ground, that the unbelieving husband is sanctified by the believing wife; nevertheless, here you have the influence of a believer's faith ascending from an inferior to a superior relation; from the wife to the husband, who is her head, before it can descend to their offspring. And, therefore, we say, whatever be the nature or extent of the holiness here intended, we conceive it cannot convey to the children an immediate right to baptism; because it would then be of another nature, and of a larger extent, than the root and original from whence it is derived. For it is clear, from the apostle's argument, that holiness cannot be derived to the child from the sanctity of one parent only; if either father or mother be (in the sense intended by the apostle) unholy or unclean, so will the child be also; therefore, for the production of a holy seed, it is necessary that both the parents be sanctified. And this the apostle positively asserts in the first place to be done by the believing parent although the other be an unbeliever, and then, consequentially, from thence argues, the holiness of their children. Hence, it follows, that as the children have no other holiness than what they derive from their parents, so neither can they have any right by this holiness to any spiritual privilege, but such as both their parents did also partake of; and therefore, if the unbelieving parent (though sanctified by the believing parent) have not thereby a right to baptism, neither can we conceive that there is any such privilege derived to the children by their birth-holiness.

Besides, if it had been the usual practice in the apostles' days for the father or mother, that did believe, to bring all their children with them to be baptized, then the holiness of the believing Corinthians' children would not at all have been in question when this epistle was written; but might have been argued from their passing under that ordinance, which represented their new birth, although they had derived no holiness from their parents by their first birth; and would have lain as an exception against the apostle's inference, *else were your children unclean*, etc. But of the sanctification of all the children of every believer by this ordinance, or any other way than what is before mentioned, the Scripture is altogether silent.

This may be also added, that if this birth-holiness do qualify all the children of every believer for the ordinance of baptism, why not for all other ordinances? for the Lord's supper, as was practiced for a long time together? for if recourse be had to what the Scriptures speak generally of this subject, it will be found that the same qualities which do entitle any person to baptism, do also for the participation of all the ordinances and privileges of the house of God that are common to all believers.

Whosoever can and does interrogate his good conscience towards God, when he is baptized (as every one must do that makes it to himself a sign of salvation), is capable of doing the same thing in every other act of worship that he performs.

4. The arguments and inferences that are usually brought for or against infant baptism, from those few instances which the Scriptures afford us of whole families being baptized, are only conjectural, and therefore cannot of themselves be conclusive on either hand; yet in regard most that treat on this subject of infant baptism do (as they conceive) improve these instances to the advantage of their argument, we think it meet (in like manner, as in the cases before mentioned, so in this) to show the invalidity of such inferences.

Cornelius worshipped God with all his house. The jailor and Crispus, the chief ruler of the synagogue, believed God with each of their houses. The household of Stephanus addicted themselves to the ministry of the saints: so that thus far worshipping and believing runs parallel with baptism. And if Lydia had been a married person when she believed, it is probable her husband would also have been named by the apostle, as in like cases, inasmuch as he would have been not only a part, but the head of that baptized household.

Who can assign any probable reason why the apostle should make mention of four or five households being baptized and no more? or why he does so often vary in the method of his salutations,[1] sometimes mentioning only particular persons of great note, other times such and the church in their house? the saints that were with them, and them belonging to Narcissus, who were in the Lord; thus saluting either whole families, or part of families, or only particular persons in families, considered as they were in the Lord. For if it had been a usual practice to baptize all children with their parents, there were then many thousands of the Jews which believed, and a great number of the Gentiles, in most of the principal cities in the world, and among so many thousands, it is more than probable there would have been some thousands of households baptized; why then should the apostle in this respect signalize one family of the Jews and three or four of the Gentiles, as particular instances in a case that was common? Whoever supposes that we do wilfully debar our children from the benefit of any promise or privilege that of right belongs to the children of believing parents, they do entertain over-severe thoughts of us. To be without natural affections is one of the characters of the worst of persons in the worst of times. We do freely confess ourselves guilty before the Lord, in that we have not with more circumspection and diligence trained up those that relate to us in the fear of the Lord; and do humbly and earnestly pray, that omissions herein may be remitted, and that they may not redound to the prejudice of ourselves or any of ours; but with respect to that duty that is incumbent on us, we acknowledge ourselves obliged by the precepts of God to bring up our children in the nurture and admonition of the Lord, to teach them his fear, both by instruction and example; and should we set light by this precept, it would demonstrate that we are more vile than the unnatural heathen, that like not to retain God in their knowledge; our baptism might then be justly accounted as no baptism to us.

There are many special promises that do encourage us, as well as precepts that do oblige us to the close pursuit of our duty herein; that God whom we serve, being jealous of his worship, threatens the visiting of the father's transgression upon the children, to the third and fourth generation of them that hate him; yet does more abun-

[1] Rom. i. 6.

dantly extend his mercy, even to thousands (respecting the offspring and succeeding generations) of them that love him and keep his commands.

When our Lord rebuked his disciples for prohibiting the access of little children that were brought to him that he might pray over them, lay his hands upon them, and bless them, [he] does declare, that of *such is the kingdom of God.* And the apostle Peter, in answer to their inquiry that desired to know what they must do to be saved, does not only instruct them in the necessary duty of repentance and baptism, but does also thereto encourage them, by that promise which had reference both to them and their children. If our Lord Jesus in the fore-mentioned place, do not respect the qualities of children (as elsewhere) as to their meekness, humility, and sincerity, and the like, but intend also, that those very persons, and such like, appertain to the kingdom of God; and if the apostle Peter, in mentioning the aforesaid promise, do respect not only the present and succeeding generations of those Jews that heard him (in which sense the same phrase doth occur in Scripture), but also the immediate offspring of his auditors; whether the promise relate to the gift of the Holy Spirit, or of eternal life, or any grace, or privilege tending to the obtaining thereof; it is neither our concern, nor our interest, to confine the mercies and promises of God to a more narrow or less compass than he is pleased graciously to offer and intend them; nor to have a light esteem of them; but are obliged in duty to God, and affection to our children, to plead earnestly with God, and use our utmost endeavors, that both ourselves and our offspring may be partakers of his mercies and gracious promises. Yet we cannot, from either of these texts, collect a sufficient warrant for us to baptize our children before they are instructed in the principles of the Christian religion.

For, as to the instance in little children, it seems, by the disciples forbidding them, that they were brought upon some other account, not so frequent as baptism must be supposed to have been, if from the beginning believers' children had been admitted thereto; and no account is given whether their parents were baptized believers or not. And as to the instance of the apostle, if the following words and practice may be taken as an interpretation of the scope of that promise, we cannot conceive it does refer to infant baptism, because the text does presently subjoin, *then they that gladly received the word were baptized.*

That there were some believing children of believing parents in the apostles' days is evident from the Scriptures, even such as were then in their father's family, and under their parents' tuition and education; to whom the apostle, in several of his epistles to the churches, giveth commands to obey their parents in the Lord; and does allure their tender years to hearken to this precept, by reminding them that it is the first command with promise.

And it is recorded by him for the praise of Timothy, and encouragement of parents, betimes to instruct, and children early to attend to godly instruction, that, ἀπὸ βρέφους, from a child he had known the holy Scriptures.

The apostle John rejoiced greatly when he found the children of the elect lady walking in the truth; and the children of her elect sister join with the apostle in his salutation.

But that this was not generally so, that all the children of believers were accounted for believers (as they would have been if they had been all baptized), may be collected from the character which the apostle gives of persons fit to be chosen to eldership in the church, which was not common to all believers; among others, this is expressly one, viz., if there be any having believing or faithful children, not accused of riot, or unruly; and we may, from the apostle's writings on the same subject, collect the reason of this qualification, viz., that in case the person designed for this office, to teach and rule in the house of God, had children capable of it, there might be first a proof of his ability, industry, and success in this work in his own family, and private capacity, before he was ordained to the exercise of this authority in the church in a public capacity, as a bishop in the house of God.

These things we have mentioned, as having a direct reference unto the controversy between our brethren and us; other things that are more abstruse and prolix, which are frequently introduced into this controversy, but do not necessarily concern it, we have purposely avoided, that the distance between us and our brethren may not be by us made more wide; for it is our duty and concern, so far as is possible for us (retaining a good conscience towards God) to seek a more entire agreement and reconciliation with them.

We are not insensible, that as to the order of God's house, and entire communion therein, there are some things wherein we (as well as others) are not at a full accord among ourselves; as, for instance, the known principle and state of the consciences of divers of us, that have agreed in this confession is such, that we cannot hold church communion with any other than baptized believers, and churches constituted of such; yet some others of us have a greater liberty and freedom in our spirits that way; and therefore we have purposely omitted the mention of things of that nature, that we might concur in giving this evidence of our agreement, both among ourselves, and with other good Christians, in those important articles of the Christian religion, mainly insisted on by us; and this, notwithstanding we all esteem it our chief concern, both among ourselves and all others that in every place call upon the name of the Lord Jesus Christ our Lord, both theirs and ours, and love him in sincerity, to endeavor to keep the unity of the Spirit in the bond of peace; and in order thereunto, to exercise all lowliness and meekness, with long-suffering, forbearing one another in love.

And we are persuaded, if the same method were introduced into frequent practice between us and our Christian friends, who agree with us in all the fundamental articles of the Christian faith (though they do not so in the subject and administration of baptism), it would soon beget a better understanding and brotherly affection between us.

In the beginning of the Christian church, when the doctrine of the baptism of Christ was not universally understood, yet those that knew only the baptism of John were the disciples of the Lord Jesus, and Apollos, an eminent minister of the gospel of Jesus.

In the beginning of the reformation of the Christian church, and recovery from that Egyptian darkness wherein our forefathers for many generations were held in bondage, upon recourse had to the Scriptures of truth, different apprehensions were conceived, which are to this time continued, concerning the practice of this ordinance.

Let not our zeal herein be misinterpreted; that God whom we serve is jealous of his worship. By his gracious providence the law thereof is continued amongst us; and we are forewarned, by what happened in the church of the Jews, that it is necessary for every generation, and that frequently in every generation, to consult the divine oracle, compare our worship with the rule, and take heed to what doctrines we receive and practise.

If the ten commandments exhibited in the popish idolatrous service-books had been received as the entire law of God, because they agree in number with his ten commands, and also in the substance of nine of them, the second commandment, forbidding idolatry, had been utterly lost.

If Ezra and Nehemiah had not made a diligent search into the particular parts of God's law and his worship, the feast of tabernacles (which for many centuries of years had not been duly observed according to the institution, though it was retained in the general notion) would not have been kept in due order.

So may it be now as to many things relating to the service of God, which do retain the names proper to them in their first institution, but yet through inadvertency (where there is no sinister design) may vary in their circumstances, from their first institution. And if by means of any ancient defection, or of that general corruption of the service of God and interruption of his true worship and persecution of his servants by the anti-christian bishop of Rome, for many generations, those who do consult the word of God cannot yet arrive at a full and mutual satisfaction among themselves, what was the practice of the primitive Christian church, in some points relating to the worship of God; yet inasmuch as these things are not of the essence of Christianity, but that we agree in the fundamental doctrines thereof, we do apprehend there is sufficient ground to lay aside all bitterness and prejudice, and in the spirit of love and meekness to embrace and own each other therein, leaving each other at liberty to perform such other services, wherein we cannot concur, apart unto God, according to the best of our understanding.

ADDITIONS

TO THE

CONFESSION OF 1689, BY THE PHILADELPHIA ASSOCIATION.

The following are the articles added by the Philadelphia Association, Sept. 15, 1742.

CHAPTER XXXIV.

OF THE SINGING OF PSALMS, ETC.

We believe that [1] singing the praises of God is a holy ordinance of Christ, and not a part of natural religion, or a moral duty only; but that it is brought under divine institution, it being enjoined on the churches of Christ to sing psalms, hymns, and spiritual songs; and that the whole church in their public assemblies (as well as private Christians) ought to [2] sing God's praises according to the best light they have received. Moreover, it was practised in the great representative church, by [3] our Lord Jesus Christ with his disciples, after he had instituted and celebrated the sacred ordinance of his holy supper, as a commemorative token of redeeming love.

CHAPTER XXXV.

OF LAYING ON OF HANDS.

1. We believe that [4] laying on of hands, with prayer, upon baptized believers, as such, is an ordinance of Christ, and ought to be submitted unto by all such persons that are admitted to partake of the Lord's Supper, and that the end of this ordinance is not for the extraordinary gifts of the Spirit, but for [5] a farther reception of the

1 Acts xvi. 25; Eph. v. 19; Col. iii. 16.
2 Heb. ii. 12; James v. 13.
3 Matt. xxvi. 30; Mark xiv. 26.
4 Heb. v. 12, vi. 1, 2; Acts viii. 17, 18, xix. 6.
5 Eph. i. 13, 14.

Holy Spirit of promise, or for the addition of the graces of the Spirit, and the influences thereof; to confirm, strengthen, and comfort them in Christ Jesus; it being ratified and established by the [1] extraordinary gifts of the Spirit in the primitive times, to abide in the church, as meeting together on the first day of the week was, [2] that being the day of worship, or Christian Sabbath, under the gospel; and as preaching the word was, [3] and as baptism was, [4] and prayer was, [5] and singing psalms, etc., was, [6] so this laying on of hands was, [7] for as the whole gospel was confirmed by [8] signs and wonders, and divers miracles and gifts of the Holy Ghost in general, so was every ordinance in like manner confirmed in particular.

1 Acts viii. 7, xix. 6.
2 Acts ii. 1.
3 Acts x. 44.
4 Matt. iii. 16.
5 Acts iv. 31.
6 Acts xvi. 25 26.
7 Acts viii xix.
8 Heb. ii. 3, 4.

NOTE.—The Discipline adopted by the Philadelphia Association, to accompany this Confession of Faith, will be found on page 199.

III.

THE NEW HAMPSHIRE DECLARATION OF FAITH.

I. OF THE SCRIPTURES.

We believe that the holy Bible was written by men divinely inspired, and is a perfect treasure of heavenly instruction;[1] that it has God for its author, salvation for its end,[2] and truth without any mixture of error for its matter;[3] that it reveals the principles by which God will judge us,[4] and therefore is, and shall remain to the end of the world, the true centre of Christian union,[5] and the supreme standard by which all human conduct, creeds, and opinions should be tried.[6]

II. OF THE TRUE GOD.

We believe that there is one, and only one, living and true God, an infinite, intelligent Spirit, whose name is Jehovah, the Maker and Supreme Ruler of heaven and earth;[7] inexpressibly glorious in holiness,[8] and worthy of all possible honor, confidence, and love;[9] that in the unity of the Godhead there are three persons, the Fa-

1 2 Tim. iii. 16, 17; 2 Peter i. 21; 2 Sam. xxiii. 2; Acts i. 16, iii. 21; John x. 35; Luke xvi. 29—31; Psalm cxix. 111; Rom. iii. 1, 2.

2 2 Tim. iii. 15; 1 Peter i. 10—12; Acts xi. 14; Rom. i. 16; Mark xvi. 16; John v. 38, 39.

3 Prov. xxx. 5, 6; John xvii. 17; Rev. xxii. 18, 19; Rom. iii. 4.

4 Rom. ii. 12; John xii. 47, 48; 1 Cor. iv. 3, 4; Luke x. 10—16, xii. 47, 48.

5 Philippians iii. 16; Ephesians iv. 3—6; Phil. ii. 1, 2; 1 Cor. i. 10; 1 Peter iv. 11.

6 1 John iv. 1; Isa. viii. 20; 1 Thess. v. 21; 2 Cor. xiii. 5; Acts xvii. 11; 1 John iv. 6; Jude 3; Eph. vi. 17; Psalm cxix. 59, 60; Phil. i. 9—11.

7 John iv. 24; Psalm cxlvii. 5, lxxxiii. 18; Heb. iii. 4; Rom. i. 20; Jer. x. 10.

8 Ex. xv. 11; Isa. vi. 3; 1 Peter i. 15, 16; Rev. iv. 6—8.

9 Mark xii. 30; Rev. iv. 11; Matt. x. 37; Jer. ii. 12, 13.

ther, the Son, and the Holy Ghost;[1] equal in every divine perfection,[2] and executing distinct but harmonious offices in the great work of redemption.[3]

III. OF THE FALL OF MAN.

We believe that man was created in holiness, under the law of his Maker;[4] but by voluntary transgression fell from that holy and happy state;[5] in consequence of which all mankind are now sinners,[6] not by constraint but choice;[7] being by nature utterly void of that holiness required by the law of God; positively inclined to evil; and therefore under just condemnation to eternal ruin,[8] without defence or excuse.[9]

IV. OF THE WAY OF SALVATION.

We believe that the salvation of sinners is wholly of grace;[10] through the mediatorial offices of the Son of God;[11] who by the appointment of the Father, freely took upon him our nature, yet without sin;[12] honored the divine law by his personal obedience,[13] and by his death made a full atonement for our sins;[14] that having risen from the dead, he is now enthroned in heaven;[15] and uniting in his wonderful person the tenderest sympathies with divine perfections, he is every way qualified to be a suitable, a compassionate, and an all-sufficient Saviour.[16]

1 Mat. xxviii. 19; John xv. 26; 1 Cor. xii. 4—6; 1 John v. 7.

2 John x. 30; John v. 17; xiv. 23, xvii. 5, 10; Acts v. 3, 4; 1 Cor. ii. 10, 11; Phil. ii. 5, 6.

3 Eph. ii. 18; 2 Cor. xiii. 14; Rev. i. 4, 5. Compare ii. 7.

4 Gen. i. 27; Gen. i. 31; Eccl. vii. 29; Acts xv. 26; Gen. ii. 16.

5 Gen. iii. 6—24; Rom. v. 12.

6 Rom. v. 19; John iii. 6; Psalm li. 5; Rom. v. 15—19; viii. 7.

7 Isa. liii. 6; Gen. vi. 12; Rom. iii. 9—18.

8 Eph. ii. 1—3; Rom. i. 18; Rom. i. 32, ii. 1—16; Galatians iii. 10; Matthew xx. 15.

9 Ezek. xviii. 19, 20; Rom. i. 20; Rom. iii. 19; Gal. iii. 22.

10 Eph. ii. 5; Matt. xviii. 11; 1 John iv. 10; 1 Cor. iii. 5—7; Acts xv. 11.

11 John iii. 16; John i. 1—14; Heb. iv. 14, xii. 24.

12 Phil. ii. 6, 7; Heb. ii. 9, ii. 14; 2 Cor. v. 21.

13 Isa. xlii. 21; Phil. ii. 8; Gal. iv. 4, 5; Rom. iii. 21.

14 Isa. liii. 4, 5; Matt. xx. 28; Rom. iv. 25, iii. 21—26; 1 John iv. 10, ii. 2; 1 Cor. xv. 1—3; Heb. ix. 13—15.

15 Heb. i. 8; Heb. i 3, viii. 1; Col. iii. 1—4.

16 Heb. vii. 25; Col. ii. 9; Heb. ii. 18; Heb. vii. 26; Psalm lxxxix. 19; Ps. xlv.

V. OF JUSTIFICATION.

We believe that the great gospel blessing which Christ[1] secures to such as believe in him, is justification;[2] that justification includes the pardon of sin,[3] and the promise of eternal life on principles of righteousness;[4] that it is bestowed, not in consideration of any works of righteousness which we have done, but solely through faith in the Redeemer's blood;[5] by virtue of which faith his perfect righteousness is freely imputed to us of God;[6] that it brings us into a state of most blessed peace and favor with God, and secures every other blessing needful for time and eternity.[7]

VI. OF THE FREENESS OF SALVATION.

We believe that the blessings of salvation are made free to all by the gospel;[8] that it is the immediate duty of all to accept them by a cordial, penitent, and obedient faith;[9] and that nothing prevents the salvation of the greatest sinner on earth, but his own determined depravity and voluntary rejection of the gospel;[10] which rejection involves him in an aggravated condemnation.[11]

VII. OF GRACE IN REGENERATION.

We believe that in order to be saved, sinners must be regenerated, or born again;[12] that regeneration consists in giving a holy disposition to the mind;[13] that it is effected in a manner above our comprehension by the power of the Holy Spirit, in connection with divine

1 John i. 16; Eph. iii. 8.

2 Acts xiii. 39; Isa. iii. 11, 12; Rom. viii. 1.

3 Rom. v. 9; Zech. xiii. 1; Matt. ix. 6; Acts x. 43.

4 Rom. v. 17; Titus iii. 5, 6; 1 Peter iii. 7; 1 John ii. 25; Rom. v. 21.

5 Rom. iv. 4, 5, v. 21, vi. 23; Phil. iii. 7—9.

6 Rom. v. 19; Rom. iii. 24—26; iv. 23—25; 1 John ii. 12.

7 Rom. v. 1, 2, v. 3, v. 11; 1 Cor. i. 30, 31; Matt. vi. 33; 1 Tim. iv. 8.

8 Isaiah lv. 1; Rev. xxii. 17; Luke xiv. 17.

9 Rom. xvi. 26; Mark i. 15; Rom. i. 15—17.

10 John v. 40; Matt. xxiii. 37; Rom. ix. 32; Prov. i. 24; Acts xiii. 46.

11 John iii. 19; Matt. xi. 20; Luke xix. 27; 2 Thess. i. 8.

12 John iii. 3, iii. 6, 7; 1 Cor. i. 14; Rev. viii. 7—9, xxi. 27.

13 2 Cor. v. 17; Ezek. xxxvi. 26; Deut. xxx. 6; Rom. ii. 28, 29, v. 5; 1 John iv. 7.

truth,[1] so as to secure our voluntary obedience to the gospel;[2] and that its proper evidence appears in the holy fruits of repentance, and faith, and newness of life.[3]

VIII. OF REPENTANCE AND FAITH.

We believe that repentance and faith are sacred duties, and also inseparable graces, wrought in our souls by the regenerating Spirit of God;[4] whereby, being deeply convinced of our guilt, danger, and helplessness, and of the way of salvation by Christ,[5] we turn to God with unfeigned contrition, confession, and supplication for mercy;[6] at the same time heartily receiving the Lord Jesus Christ as our Prophet, Priest, and King, and relying on him alone as the only and all-sufficient Saviour.[7]

IX. OF GOD'S PURPOSE OF GRACE.

We believe that election is the eternal purpose of God, according to which he graciously regenerates, sanctifies, and saves sinners;[8] that being perfectly consistent with the free agency of man, it comprehends all the means in connection with the end;[9] that it is a most glorious display of God's sovereign goodness, being infinitely free, wise, holy, and unchangeable;[10] that it utterly excludes boasting, and promotes humility, love, prayer, praise, trust in God, and active imitation of his free mercy;[11] that it encourages the use of means in the highest degree;[12] that it may be ascertained by its effects in all

1 John iii. 8, i. 13; James i. 16—18; 1 Cor. i. 30; Phil. ii. 13.

2 1 Peter i. 22—25; 1 John v. 1; Eph. iv. 20—24; Col. iii. 9—11.

3 Eph. v. 9; Rom. viii. 9; Gal. v. 16—23; Eph. iii. 14—21; Matt. iii. 8—10, vii. 20; 1 John v. 4, 18.

4 Mark i. 15; Acts xi. 18; Eph. ii. 8; 1 John v. 1.

5 John xvi. 8; Acts ii. 37, 38, xvi. 30, 31.

6 Luke xviii. 13, xv. 18—21; Jas. iv. 7—10; 2 Cor. vii. 11; Rom. x. 12, 13; Ps. li.

7 Rom. x. 9—11; Acts iii. 22, 23; Heb. iv. 14; Psalm ii. 6; Heb. i. 8; viii. 25; 2 Tim. 1, 12.

8 2 Tim. i. 8, 9; Eph. i. 3—14; 1 Peter i. 1, 2; Rom. xi. 5, 6; John xv. 16; 1 John iv. 19; Hosea xii. 9.

9 2 Thess. ii. 13, 14; Acts xiii. 48; John x. 16; Matt. xx. 16; Acts xv. 14.

10 Exodus xxxiii. 18, 19; Matt. xx. 15; Eph. i. 11; Rom. ix. 23, 24; Jer. xxxi. 3; Rom. xi. 28, 29; James i. 17, 18; 2 Tim. i. 9; Rom. xi. 32—36.

11 1 Cor. iv. 7, i. 26—31; Rom. iii. 27, iv. 16; Col. iii. 12; 1 Cor. iii. 5—7, xv. 10; 1 Peter v. 10; Acts i. 24; 1 Thess. ii. 13; 1 Peter ii. 9; Luke xviii. 7; John xv. 16; Eph. i. 16; 1 Thess. ii. 12.

12 2 Tim. ii. 10; 1 Cor. ix. 22; Rom. viii. 28—30; John vi. 37—40; 2 Pet. i. 10.

who truly believe the gospel;[1] that it is the foundation of Christian assurance;[2] and that to ascertain it with regard to ourselves demands and deserves the utmost diligence.[3]

X. OF SANCTIFICATION

We believe that sanctification is the process by which, according to the will of God, we are made partakers of his holiness;[4] that it is a progressive work;[5] that it is begun in regeneration;[6] and that it is carried on in the hearts of believers by the presence and power of the Holy Spirit, the Sealer and Comforter, in the continual use of the appointed means — especially, the word of God, self-examination, self-denial, watchfulness, and prayer.[7]

XI. OF THE PERSEVERANCE OF SAINTS.

We believe that such only are real believers as endure unto the end;[8] that their persevering attachment to Christ is the grand mark which distinguishes them from superficial professors;[9] that a special providence watches over their welfare;[10] and they are kept by the power of God through faith unto salvation.[11]

XII. OF THE HARMONY OF THE LAW AND THE GOSPEL.

We believe that the law of God is the eternal and unchangeable rule of his moral government;[12] that it is holy, just, and good;[13] and

1 Thess. i. 4—10.

2 Rom. viii. 28—30; Isa. xlii. 16; Rom. xi. 29.

3 2 Peter i. 10, 11; Phil. iii. 12; Heb. vi. 11.

4 1 Thess. iv. 3; 1 Thess. v. 23; 2 Cor. vii. 1; xiii. 9; Epis. i. 4.

5 Prov. iv. 18; 2 Cor. iii. 18; Heb. vi. 1; 2 Peter i. 5—8; Phil. iii. 12—16.

6 John ii 29; Rom. viii. 5; John iii. 6; Phil. i. 9—11; Eph. i. 13, 14.

7 Phil. ii. 12, 13; Eph. iv. 11, 12; 1 Peter ii. 2; 2 Peter iii. 18; 2 Cor. xiii. 5; Luke xi. 35, ix. 23; Matt. xxvi. 41; Eph. vi. 18; iv. 30.

John viii. 31; 1 John ii. 27, 28; iii. 9, v. 18.

9 1 John ii. 19; John xiii. 18; Matthew xiii. 20, 21; John vi. 66—69; Job xvii. 9.

10 Romans viii. 28; Matthew vi. 30—33: Jer. xxxii. 40; Psalm cxxi. 3; xci. 11, 12.

11 Phil. i. 6, ii. 12, 13; Jude 24, 25; Heb. i. 14; 2 Kings vi. 16; Heb. xiii. 5; 1 John iv. 4.

12 Rom. iii. 31; Matt. v. 17; Luke xvi. 17; Rom. iii. 20, iv. 15.

13 Rom. vii. 12, vii. 7, 14, 22; Gal. iii. 21; Psalm cxix.

that the inability which the Scriptures ascribe to fallen men to fulfil its precepts, arises entirely from their love of sin:[1] to deliver them from which, and to restore them through a mediator to unfeigned obedience to the holy law, is one great end of the gospel, and of the means of grace connected with the establishment of the visible church.[2]

XIII. OF A GOSPEL CHURCH.

We believe that a visible church of Christ is a congregation of baptized believers,[3] associated by covenant in the faith and fellowship of the gospel;[4] observing the ordinances of Christ;[5] governed by his laws;[6] and exercising the gifts, rights, and privileges invested in them by his word;[7] that its only scriptural officers are bishops or pastors, and deacons,[8] whose qualifications, claims, and duties are defined in the epistles to Timothy and Titus.

XIV. OF BAPTISM AND THE LORD'S SUPPER.

We believe that Christian baptism is the immersion in water of a believer,[9] into the name of the Father, and Son, and Holy Ghost;[10] to show forth, in a solemn and beautiful emblem, our faith in the crucified, buried, and risen Saviour, with its effect, in our death to sin and resurrection to a new life;[11] that it is pre-requisite to the privileges of a church relation; and to the Lord's Supper,[12] in which

1 Rom. viii. 7, 8; Josh. xxiv. 19; Jer. xiii. 23; John vi. 44, v. 44.

2 Rom. viii. 2, 4, x. 4; 1 Tim. i. 5; Heb. viii. 10; Jude 20, 21; Heb. xii. 14; Matt. xvi. 17, 18; 1 Cor. xii. 28.

3 1 Cor. i. 1—13; Matt. xviii. 17; Acts v. 11, viii. 1, xi. 31; 1 Cor. iv. 17, xiv. 28; 3 John 9; 1 Tim. iii. 5.

4 Acts ii. 41, 42; 2 Cor. viii. 5; Acts ii. 47; 1 Cor. v. 12, 43.

5 1 Cor. xi. 2; 2 Thess. iii. 6; Rom. xvi. 17—20; 1 Cor. xi. 23; Matt. xviii. 15—20; 1 Cor. v., vi.; 2 Cor. ii. 7; 1 Cor. iv. 17.

6 Matthew xxviii. 20; John xiv. 15, xv. 12; 1 John iv. 21; John xiv. 21; 1 Thessalonians iv. 2; 2 John 6; Gal. vi. 2. All the Epistles.

7 Eph. iv. 7; 1 Cor. xiv. 12; Phil. i. 27; 1 Cor. xii., xiv.

8 Phil. i. 1; Acts xiv. 23, xv. 22; 1 Tim. iii.; Titus i.

9 Acts viii. 36—39; Matt. iii. 5, 6; John iii. 22, 23, iv. i. 2; Matt. xxviii. 19; Mark xvi. 16; Acts ii. 38, viii. 12, xvi 32—34, xviii. 8.

10 Matt. xxviii. 19; Acts x. 47, 48; Gal. iii. 27, 28.

11 Rom. vi. 4; Col. ii. 12; 1 Peter iii. 20, 21; Acts xxii. 16.

12 Acts ii. 41, 42; Matt. xxviii. 19, 20. Acts and Epistles.

the members of the church by the sacred use of bread and wine, are to commemorate together the dying love of Christ;[1] preceded always by solemn self-examination.[2]

XV. OF THE CHRISTIAN SABBATH.

We believe that the first day of the week is the Lord's day, or Christian Sabbath;[3] and is to be kept sacred to religious purposes,[4] by abstaining from all secular labor and sinful recreations;[5] by the devout observance of all the means of grace, both private[6] and public;[7] and by preparation for that rest that remaineth for the people of God.[8]

XVI. OF CIVIL GOVERNMENT.

We believe that civil government is of divine appointment, for the interests and good order of human society;[9] and that magistrates are to be prayed for, conscientiously honored, and obeyed;[10] except only in things opposed to the will of our Lord Jesus Christ,[11] who is the only Lord of the conscience, and the Prince of the kings of the earth.[12]

XVII. OF THE RIGHTEOUS AND THE WICKED.

We believe that there is a radical and essential difference between the righteous and the wicked;[13] that such only as through faith are

1 1 Cor. xi. 26; Matt. xxvi. 26—29; Mark xiv. 22—25; Luke xxii. 14—20.

2 1 Corinthians xi. 28; 1 Corinthians v. 1, 8; x. 3—32; xi. 17—32; John vi. 26—71.

3 Acts xx. 7; Gen. ii. 3; Col. ii. 16, 17; Mark ii. 27; John xx. 19; 1 Cor. xvi. 1, 2.

4 Ex. xx. 8; Rev. i. 10; Ps cxvii. 24.

5 Isa. lviii. 13, 14, lvi. 2—8.

6 Ps. cxviii. 15.

7 Heb. x. 24, 25; Acts xi. 26; Acts xiii. 44; Lev. xix. 30; Ex. xlvi. 3; Luke iv. 16; Acts xvii. 2, 3; Psalm xxvi. 8; lxxxvii. 3.

8 Heb. iv 3—11.

9 Rom. xiii. 1—7; Deut. xvi. 18; 2 Sam. xxiii. 3; Exodus xviii. 23; Jer. xxx. 21.

10 Matt. xxii. 21; Titus iii. 1; 1 Peter ii. 13; 1 Tim. ii. 1—8.

11 Acts v. 29; Matt. x. 28; Dan. iii. 15—18; vi. 7—10; Acts iv. 18—20.

12 Matt. xxiii. 10; Rom. xiv. 4; Rev. xix. 16; Ps. lxxii. 11; Ps. ii.; Rom. xiv. 9—13.

13 Mal. iii. 18; Prov. xii. 26; Isa. v. 20; Gen. xviii. 23; Jer. xv. 19; Acts x. 34, 35; Rom. vi. 16.

justified in the name of the Lord Jesus, and sanctified by the Spirit of our God, are truly righteous in his esteem;[1] while all such as continue in impenitence and unbelief are in his sight wicked, and under the curse;[2] and this distinction holds among men both in and after death.[3]

XVIII. OF THE WORLD TO COME.

We believe that the end of this world is approaching;[4] that at the last day, Christ will descend from heaven,[5] and raise the dead from the grave to final retribution;[6] that a solemn separation will then take place;[7] that the wicked will be adjudged to endless punishment, and the righteous to endless joy;[8] and that this judgment will fix forever the final state of men in heaven or hell, on principles of righteousness.[9]

1 Rom. i. 17; Rom. vii. 6; 1 John ii. 29, iii. 7; Rom. vi. 18, 22; 1 Cor. xi. 32; Prov. xi. 31; 1 Peter iv. 17, 18.

2 1 John v. 19; Gal. iii. 10; John iii. 36; Isa. lvii. 21; Ps. x. 4; Isa. lv. 6, 7.

3 Prov. xiv. 32; Luke xvi. 25; John viii. 21—24; Prov. x. 24; Luke xii. 4, 5; ix. 23—26; John xii. 25, 26; Eccl. iii. 17; Matt. vii. 13, 14.

4 1 Peter iv. 7; 1 Cor. vii. 29—31; Heb. i. 10—12; Matt. xxiv. 35; 1 John ii. 17; Matt. xxviii. 20; xiii. 39, 40; 2 Peter iii. 3—13.

5 Acts i. 11; Rev. i. 7; Heb. ix. 28; Acts iii. 21; 1 Thes. iv. 13—18, v. 1—11.

6 Acts xxiv. 15; 1 Cor. xv. 12—59; Luke xiv. 14; Dan. xii. 2; John v. 28, 29, vi. 40; xi. 25, 26; 2 Tim. i. 10; Acts x. 42.

7 Matt. xiii. 49, xiii. 37—43; xxiv. 30, 31; xxv. 31—33.

8 Matt. xxv. 35—41; Rev. xxii. 11; 1 Cor. vi. 9, 10; Mark ix. 43—48; 2 Pet. ii. 9; Jude 7; Phi. iii. 19; Rom. vi. 22; 2 Cor. v. 10, 11; John iv. 36; 2 Cor. iv. 18.

9 Rom. iii. 5, 6; 2 Thess. i. 6—12; Heb. vi. 1, 2; 1 Cor. iv. 5; Acts xvii. 31; Rom. ii. 2—16; Rev. xx. 11, 12; 1 John ii. 28; iv. 17; 2 Peter iii. 11, 12.

IV.

DISCIPLINE ADOPTED BY THE PHILADELPHIA ASSOCIATION.

TO ALL THOSE INTO WHOSE HANDS THE FOREGOING CONFESSION OF FAITH,[1] UNTO WHICH THE FOLLOWING ABSTRACT CONCERNING OUR DISCIPLINE IS NOW ANNEXED, SHALL COME.

OUR last Association, met at Philadelphia, September 25, 1742, taking into consideration the general interest of the gospel, and especially the interest of the churches they were related unto and did then represent, judging it expedient to reprint the *Confession of Faith* put forth by the Elders and Brethren of upwards of one hundred Congregations baptized upon profession of faith in England and Wales, met in London, September 3, 1689, with the additions concerning Imposition of Hands, and singing of Psalms in the worship of God.

The Association likewise thought it proper to annex an abstract, or brief treatise concerning our Discipline; but not having, for some reasons, fixed upon any particular piece extant, they left it to Mr. Jenkin Jones and myself to prepare a short Narrative, in the most compendious manner we could; but Mr. Jones, by reason of his other avocations, not being able to prepare anything in due time, requested me to take it upon myself, which, after we had consulted on some particulars (though many other things at this juncture requiring my time and employing my thoughts, I could wish some other person had undertaken), I accepted, that I might prevent any disappointment, and have endeavored to perform as my small

[1] See page 190.

leisure would permit. And we having a small tract published by Elias Keach, and having also found a manuscript left by my brother Abel Morgan, deceased, which he intended, had he longer lived, to have revised and put in print for the benefit of our churches; I have transcribed some things out of said manuscript, and some other things out of Mr. Keach, some things without variation; besides which I have in some cases consulted Dr. Owen and Dr. Goodwin, and in some things I have followed the agreement that our Association came to some years ago, especially concerning the admission and dismission of members. I have endeavored to include the most material things in discipline (though very briefly) in the few following pages; and I desire the reader may be pleased to take the pains to peruse the Scriptures referred to in every particular, that the grounds of our practice may be better understood.

That this impartial account of our principles and practice may be accompanied with the blessing of God, to be beneficial unto men, is the hearty prayer of your well-wisher, and servant, in all gospel service,

BENJAMIN GRIFFITH.

TREATISE.

CONCERNING A TRUE AND ORDERLY GOSPEL CHURCH.

Before there can by any orderly discipline among a Christian assembly, they must be orderly constituted into a church state, according to the institution of Christ in the gospel.

1. A visible Gospel Church is made by gathering divers select persons into Jesus Christ, in a spiritual body, and relation to him as their political head,[1] himself being the great Shepherd that first seeks them, and prepares them by the work of renewing grace, for such spiritual building.

2. Christ as the mediator of the new covenant, ordereth the everlasting gospel to be preached, and accompanying it with his holy Spirit, blesseth it to the turning of men from darkness to light, working faith and love in them.[2]

3. When sinners are thus wrought upon effectually, to such a suitable number, as may be an essential church, *i. e.*, so many as may act properly and orderly as a church,[3] that then it will be proper for them, by their mutual consent, to propose to be constituted a church, or that others seeing the expediency thereof may encourage the same.[4]

4. For the accomplishment of so glorious a work, it is necessary that a day of fasting and prayer be appointed by and among such believers, and that such procure such neighboring helps as they can, especially of the ministry.[5]

5. The persons being first orderly baptized, according to the command of Christ,[6] and being all satisfied of the graces and qualifications of each other, and being willing in the fear of God to take the laws of Christ upon them, and do by one mutual consent give up

1 Ezek. xxxiv. 11; 2 Thess. ii. 1.
2 Eph. ii. 17; Acts xxvi. 18.
3 Matt. xvii. 15—17.
4 Acts xi.
5 Acts viii. 14; 1 Thess. iii. 2.
6 Matt. xxviii. 19.

themselves to the Lord, and to one another in the Lord,[1] solemnly submitting to the government of Christ in his church, and being united, they are to be declared a Gospel Church of Jesus Christ.[2]

6. A number of believers thus united under Christ their mystical head, are become a church essential; and as such is the first and proper subject of the keys, and have power and privilege to govern themselves, and to choose out their own ministerial officers.[3]

CONCERNING MINISTERS, ETC.

1. A church thus constituted, is not yet completed while wanting such ministerial helps as Christ hath appointed for its growth and well-being, and wanting elders and deacons to officiate among them. Men, they must be, that are qualified for the work; their qualifications are plainly and fully set down in holy Scripture,[4] all which must be found in them, in some good degree, and it is the duty of the church to try the persons by the rule of the Word.

Objection. But what shall a church do, in case they can have none among them fit to bear office according to the rule of the Word?

Answer. (1.) That to expect to have officers perfect in the highest degrees of those qualifications, were to expect apostolical and extraordinary ceased gifts in ordinary time. (2.) If none among the members of a church be found fit in some measure for the ministry, a neighboring church may and ought, if possible, to supply them.[5] (3.) Let such as they have, if they have any that seem hopeful, to be awhile upon trial; and the person that the Lord shall choose, will flourish in some good measure with Aaron's rod among the rods of the tribes.

2. A church being destitute of ministerial helps, may, after mature and often deliberate consultation, and serious prayers to God, pitch upon some person or persons in particular, giving him or them a solemn invitation to the work of the ministry, upon trial; and if such

1 2 Cor. viii. 5.
2 Phil. ii. 2—4; Rom. xv. 7, xii. 1; Acts ii. 41, 42.
3 Acts xiv. 23, vi. 3.
4 1 Tim. iii. 1—7; Titus iv. 5—10.
5 Cant. viii. 8.

accept of the church's call, let such be upon trial, to see if such fear God, make godliness their business, and be addicted to the work of the ministry, seeking to further the interest of Christ and the edification of his people in sound and wholesome doctrine; and to see if any vices or immorality appear in their advances.[1] Read the qualifications.[2] And in case a church should call a person to be their minister who is a member of some sister church, and he accept their call to be their minister, he must in the first place give himself a member with the church so calling him, that so they may choose him among themselves.[3]

3. After having taken all due care to choose one for the work of the ministry, they are, by and with the unanimous consent or suffrage of the church, to proceed to his ordination; which is a solemn setting apart of such a person for the sacred function, in this wise, by setting apart a day of fasting and prayer,[4] the whole church being present, he is to have the hands of the presbytery of that church, or of neighboring elders called and authorized by that church, whereof such a person is a member, solemnly laid upon him;[5] and thus such a person is to be recommended into the work of the Lord, and to take particular care of the flock of whom he is thus chosen.[6]

4. The minister being thus put upon his work, proceeds (1.) to preach the word of God unto them, thereby to feed the flock, and therein ought to be faithful and laborious, studying to show himself a workman that needeth not to be ashamed, rightly dividing the word of truth,[7] as he is a steward of God in the mysteries of the gospel,[8] and therefore ought to be a man of good understanding and experience, being sound in the faith, not a novice, or a double-minded, unstable man, nor such as is light-spirited or of a shallow understanding, but one that is learned in the mysteries of the kingdom, because he is to feed the people with knowledge and understanding.[9] He must be faithful in declaring the whole council of God.[10]

1 1 Cor. xvi. Phil. ii. 20, 21.
2 1 Tim. 3.
3 Acts vi. 3.
4 Acts xiii. 2, 3.
5 1 Tim. v. 22; Titus i. 5; Acts xiv. 23; 1 Tim. iv. 14.
6 Acts xx. 28.
7 2 Tim. ii. 15.
8 1 Cor. iv. 1, 2.
9 Jer. iii. 15.
10 Acts xx. 20.

He is to instruct them in all practical godliness, laying before them their manifold duties, and to urge them upon their consciences.[1] (2.) He must watch over them, as one that must give an account to God.[2] Such must have an eye upon every member to see how they behave in the house of God, where the presence of the Lord is more eminently, and where also the angels do always attend; and also their behaviour in the families they belong to, and their conversation abroad; according to their capacities, they are not to sleep under their charge. (3.) He is to visit his flock to know their state, in order to minister suitable doctrinal relief unto them, and that he may know what disorders there may be among them, that the unruly may be reproved.[3] (4.) He is to administer all the ordinances of Christ, amongst them: as Baptism, and the Lord's Supper, and herein he must be careful to follow the primitive pattern, thereby to hold forth the great end, wherefore they were ordained. (5.) He must be instant with God, in his prayers for and with them, as opportunity may serve. (6.) He must show them a good example in all respects, in conversation, sobriety, charity, faith, and purity,[4] behaving himself impartial unto all, not preferring the rich before the poor, nor lording it over God's heritage, nor assume greater power than God hath given him.[5]

OF RULING ELDERS.

Ruling elders are such persons as are endued with gifts to assist the pastor or teacher in the government of the church; it was as a statute in Israel.[6] The works of teaching and ruling belong both to the pastor; but in case he be unable, or the work of ruling too great for him, God hath provided such for his assistance, and they are called ruling elders,[7] helps,[8] governments, or he that ruleth. They are qualified for, and called unto, one part of the work; and experience teacheth us the use and benefit of such rulers in the

1 Titus ii. 1—15; 1 Tim. iv. 6.
2 Heb. xiii. 17.
3 Proverbs xxvii. 23; 1 Thessalonians v. 14, 15.
4 1 Tim. iv. 12.
5 Jas. ii. 4; 1 Tim. v. 21; 1 Pet. v. 3, 5.
6 Exod. xviii.; Deut. i. 9—13.
7 1 Tim. v. 17.
8 1 Cor. xii. 28.
9 Rom. xii. 8.

church, in easing the pastor or teacher, and keeping up the honor of the ministry. Their qualifications are such as are requisite to rule, as knowledge, judgment, prudence, etc.; and as to the manner of their ordination it is like ordination unto other offices in the church, with fasting and prayer, with imposition of hands. Their office only relateth to rule and order, in the church of God, and doth not include teaching; yet if the church findeth they have gifts and abilities to be useful in teaching, they may be put upon trial, and if approved, they may be called and solemnly set apart by ordination, it being wholly a distinct office from the former, which was only to rule well, and not to labor in word and doctrine.

OF DEACONS.

Deacons are men called forth by the church, to serve in the outward concerns thereof; whose office is to serve tables.[1] They are to be intrusted with the stock of the church, out of which stock they are to assist the poor members of the church, and to provide bread and wine for the Lord's table, and also to have regard to the minister's table; and moreover they should see that all the members of the church do contribute towards the proper uses of the church, that therefrom all necessary occasions may be supplied, as God hath given them, they to the poor, so that none be neglected,[2] by the faithful discharge of which office they shall purchase to themselves a good degree and great boldness in the faith.[3] The qualifications of these officers are laid down.[4]

OF THE ADMISSION OF CHURCH MEMBERS.

The Lord Jesus Christ hath committed the use and power of the keys, in matters of government, to every visible congregational church, to be used, according to the rules and directions that he hath given in his word, in his name, and to his glory. The keys are the power of Christ, which he hath given to every particular congregation, to open and shut itself by; and to do all things in order to the

1 Acts vi. 2—7.
2 1 Cor. xxvi. 2.
3 1 Tim. iii. 13.
4 1 Tim. iii. 8—13; Acts vi. 2—8.

great things proposed, viz., his glory and his people's spiritual benefit, in peace and purity.[1]

By virtue of the charter and the power aforesaid, which Christ hath given to his church, his spiritual corporation, they are enabled to receive members in, and to exclude unworthy members as occasion may require, as may appear by divers examples.[2]

In this case, a church hath to do, either with non-members, or those that are members of other churches; as to non-members proposing for admission into the church, the pastor, teacher, and elders of the church are to be acquainted therewith, and the body of the church also, in order that they may know the intent of such person or persons. A convenient meeting is necessary. When the church is come together, and the person proposing being present, after prayer to God for direction, the minister or pastor of the church is to put several questions to the person proposing. (1.) Concerning the ground and reason of his hope,[3] wherein is to be inquired, what experience he hath of the manifold graces of the holy Spirit, working in him repentance from dead works,[4] and faith towards our Lord Jesus Christ, in whom alone is salvation hoped for;[5] for without there be some good grounds, in the judgment of charity, that such a one is a new creature, the door of admission is not to be opened, for that would be abusing the privileges of the house of God. Therefore all due and regular care is to be taken.[6]

Secondly. What competency of knowledge, in the principal doctrines of faith and order, such hath acquired;[7] or whether such person be well instructed in the knowledge of God, in his glorious attributes, in the doctrine of the Trinity, or one God in three persons; the person, natures, and offices of Christ; the nature of the law; of original sin; of the pollution of man, by reason of sin, and lost and undone estate thereby, and of his being a child of wrath by nature; of the nature of the redemption wrought by Christ, his sufficiency to satisfy divine justice; of the reconciliation of sinners to

1 Isa. ix. 7, xxii.; Rev. iii. 7; Heb. iii. 6; Eph. ii. 19—22; Matt. xvi. 19; John xx. 23.

2 Rom. xiv. 1; Acts ii. 41; 1 Cor. x. 4, 5; Matt. xviii. 18; 2 Thess. ii. 6, 14.

3 1 Peter iii. 15.

4 Acts ii. 38; Heb. vi. 2.

5 Acts xx. 21; Philemon 5.

6 Psalm lxv. 16; Acts ix. 27.

1 Tim. ii. 4—6.

God, by the death of his Son; of our sins being imputed to Christ, and his righteousness imputed to us for justification, being received by faith alone; of the resurrection of Christ's body, and his ascension into heaven, and of his coming thence the second time, to judge the quick and the dead; and of the resurrection of the dead bodies of men; and of the eternal judgment; and of such proposing person's resolution to persevere in the profession of these truths unto the end. Such things are needful to be inquired into, by reason that too many in our day do build their conversion upon their convictions, and some general notions of the Christian religion, when indeed they are utter strangers unto, and very ignorant of the great mysteries of the gospel. Yet great care is to be taken that the weak be not discouraged, for the smoking flax is not to be quenched, nor the bruised reed to be broken, but such ignorant persons are to be taught by gentle instructions, and means ought to be used for their furtherance in the knowledge of divine truths,[1] and where there are the beginnings of true and saving grace in the heart, such will, with a spiritual appetite, receive the sincere milk of the word, that they may grow thereby,[2] and a church ought to be careful not to reject those, whom they judge to have the least degree of the work of saving grace wrought in them.[3]

Thirdly. Inquiry must be made whether such a person's life and conversation is answerable to such a profession, that he be likely to adorn the gospel with a holy conversation.[4] This regular carefulness is an indispensable duty of all regular churches, to use in the admission of members; and though all due care be used, yet some unsound and rotten professors will creep in unawares, and have crept into the purest churches,[5] and the fallibility of churches in this matter, is not to be urged, as an argument or ground to neglect the duty incumbent on the churches, according to the rule of the word.

And after such examination, the question is to be put to the church, whether they are all satisfied with the party's confession and conversation; and if the answer be in the affirmative, then the pas-

1 Matt. xxviii. 19.
2 1 Peter ii. 2.
3 Rom. xiv. 1.
4 Titus ii. 11—15, iii. 8.
5 Jude 4; 1 John ii. 19: Acts v., xx. 29, 30; Gal. ii. 4.

tor or minister is to proceed to ask the party proposing if he be willingly resolved, as God shall give ability, to walk in a professed subjection to the commands and institutions of Christ revealed in the gospel, and to give himself a member of that church in particular,[1] and to continue in the communion, faith, and order thereof, according to the gospel rules and directions; and after the person is baptized according to the institution and command of Christ, and come under the imposition of the hands of the elders of the church, according to the practice of the apostles,[2] the pastor, minister, or elders, as presiding in the acts of the church's power, do receive such a one into the communion and fellowship of that church in particular. But if the church is not satisfied with the person's confession or conversation, it is proper, if the objections be of any weight, to defer the party's admission until a more ample satisfaction can be given, that all, if possible, may receive such with freedom in love, and so to discharge all gospel duties towards him, as may promote his edification in the faith, and his increase in grace.[3]

And concerning those that are members of sister churches, their admission is either transient or occasional admission; or when any person is dismissed wholly from one church, and transmitted or recommended to another church of the same faith, order, and practice. (1.) Such as are and continue members of other regular churches, may, where they are well known, be admitted into transient communion, without a letter of recommendation from the church they belong unto: but from those a church hath no knowledge of, a testimonial letter is necessary, that a church may not be imposed on by any loose or disorderly persons. (2.) Those whose residence is removed, or place of abode is more convenient to be with another congregation than that of which they are members, are, upon their request made to the church whereof such are members, to be dismissed, and to have a letter from that church they are members of, subscribed by the officers and members, and directed to the church that the person is dismissed unto; whereby the party is discharged from his or her original relation of particular membership

1 Romans xii. 1, xv. 7—9; 2 Corinthians viii. 5.

2 Acts viii. 14—17; Heb. vi. 2.

3 2 Cor. i. 24; x. 8.

to that church, and is transferred to the constant communion, watch, and care of the other church: such persons are to be received upon their proposal, according to the credentials they bring; except the church they apply unto have a special reason to defer or refuse.

As it appears to have been the practice of believers, in the primitive times, to give themselves members of particular churches,[1] it appears also that in the apostles' days, there were many distinct and distant particular churches,[2] which churches are several corporations of men professing repentance from dead works, and faith in our Lord Jesus Christ, and incorporated by mutual consent, as before mentioned, whose end is to glorify God by obedience to his revealed will, and to their own edification in the faith, and the good of others, so it is the duty of believers to give themselves in particular membership, in such a particular church as shall appear by the word of God to be orthodox in the fundamental articles of the Christian religion, and to practise according to the mind of Christ declared in the New Testament, in all gospel institutions and worship.

From which considerations, it appears the reasonable duty of every believer to give himself a member to such an orderly church as is most conveniently situated, that is, meeting nighest the place of his or her residence, for which there are these apparent reasons. (1.) For men to give themselves members of a distant church, when another of the same faith and gospel order is nigher, is for such a person to put himself under a necessity of neglecting the ordinary appointed meetings of that church, whereof he is a member, and whereof the particular charge is given,[3] that he might attend and wait in the use of God's appointed means, for his edification by the ministry of that church. (2.) Such puts himself under a wilful necessity to neglect his duty of care over, and constant communion with his fellow-members, and wilfully deprives himself of their care over him, advice, Christian conversing, and brotherly loving instructions and counsels, that by the blessing of God might increase his knowledge, grace, and comfort. (3.) Such cannot be assistant to the church in discipline, contribution, and the like duties, nor cannot

1 Acts ii. 41, v. 13, 14.

2 1 Cor. i. 2; Gal. i. 2; 1 Cor. xvi. 1; Phil. i. 1.

3 Heb. x. 25.

be taken care of, and be assisted, without much unnecessary trouble, by the church, in case of need. (4.) Such a practice tends directly to the confusion of churches, and all church order, and suits well with the humor of noisy, lifeless, loose, or covetous, niggardly persons. (5.) It is a way that the church cannot find what useful talents such persons have, to the benefit of the body of the church. (6.) It is casting great contempt upon the nearer church, in her ministry and order, and the like.

And here it is further to be considered, that as it is expedient for persons to give themselves members of such regular churches, with which they may keep the most intimate fellowship and communion in all the parts of religious worship; so it is highly reasonable that they, that are members of such regular churches, where the word is purely preached, the ordinances of the gospel duly administered, and gospel discipline is impartially practised, should continue their membership with such church; although there be weakness, imperfection, and frailty, in the particular practical acts thereof; which, while the affairs of the church are managed by men, even their holy things will have iniquity as of old.[1] It is therefore unreasonable to dismiss any member from a church that is near to any one's residence to a church more remote, upon disgust taken at the management of some particular case, wherewith such is not well pleased, and for such cause, demands dismission; and it is unreasonable also to grant a dismission to such a member, who should demand a dismission in a peremptory manner, without giving a reason for such a demand; in either of which cases such a dismission is not to be granted. (1.) Because by so doing, the greatest confusion would be introduced; for one member would thus be dismissed to one distant church, and another to another distant church, and the other churches doing the like, it can end in nothing less than the confusion of every church. (2.) The same liberty that members have, pastors, ministers, ruling elders, and deacons have also, whereby any church may dismiss her members until she is unable to maintain worship and communion; for those that reside near, are become members of a remote body, and so unconcerned; and those that are members live remote, and

1 Exodus xxviii. 38.

so under an impossibility to occupy their place. (3.) This, in the tendency of it, is to remove the balance of churches, which is to consist of such members as can, with the utmost conveniency, meet together in one place, for both worship and government.[1] (4.) This hath a tendency to alter the constitution of particular churches, from being congregational corporations, into the national or universal notion of the church; which universal church we believe to be the mystical body of Jesus Christ, which as such is not the seat of instituted worship and ordinances. Also, it is not reasonable to dismiss to the world at large, nor to dismiss a member to a church, with which the church dismissing cannot hold communion.

OF THE DUTIES OF CHURCH MEMBERS.

The members of churches owe all their duties in a way of obedience to the will of God revealed in his word; and their duties are to be performed in love to our Lord Jesus Christ,[2] who is the great Prophet, Priest, and King of his church, which he hath purchased with his own blood,[3] unto whom all power in heaven and earth is given,[4] and is therefore our Lord and Lawgiver,[5] who alone is head of his church,[6] his person is to be honored, and all his commands are to be observed,[7] all worship is to be ascribed unto him, as God blessed forever;[8] all church members, therefore, are under the strictest obligations to do and observe whatsoever Christ enjoineth on them, as mutual duties towards one another.

The officers of the church, whom Christ hath appointed, are to be respected. (1.) The deacons of the church, though they officiate but in the outward concerns of the church, as in the section about deacons is noted, if they are faithful, do purchase unto themselves a good degree,[9] are therefore to be respected. (2.) Ruling elders also are to be respected, seeing they are fitted of God, and called by the church to go before the church, or to preside in acts of gov-

1 1 Cor. xi. 20, xiv. 33.
2 John xiv. 15.
3 Acts xx. 28; Rev. i. 5; 2 Cor. v. 15.
4 Matt. xxviii. 18.
5 Isa. xxxiii. 22.
6 Eph. i. 22.
7 Heb. i. 2; John v. 23.
8 Rom. ix. 4.
9 1 Tim. iii. 13.

ernment and rule.[1] (3.) Ministers, who are the stewards of the mysteries of the gospel, are in an eminent manner to be regarded as being the ambassadors of peace,[2] though they are not to hunt for it, as the pharisees of old.[3] The duties of church members towards their elders, teachers, ministers, and pastors, may be included in their (1.) praying for them, that God would open a door of utterance unto them, to unfold the mysteries.[4] (2.) To obey them in the Lord, in whatsoever they admonish them, according to the word of God.[5] (3.) In following their example and footsteps, as far as warranted by the word.[6] (4.) In standing by them in all their trials and afflictions, and in defending them in all good causes, as far as in them lies; those of Asia are blamed[7] for turning away, or not standing by the apostle. (5.) In not exposing their persons for their infirmities, as far as may be, considering the prosperity of the gospel much depends on their good report.[8] (6.) In contributing towards their maintenance, that they may attend wholly on teaching and give themselves to the ministry of the word, and to prayer,[9] the reason thereof is evident by a threefold law. (1.) The law of nature, from whence the apostle argues.[10] (2.) The Levitical law.[11] (3.) The gospel enjoineth and requireth the same.[12] Let these above cited places of Scripture be considered with many others of like importance, and the nature and tendency of the work of the ministry be well weighed, and it will be clear that it is a duty required of God himself; and that not in a way of alms, as to the poor, which is another standing ordinance of Christ, but it is to be performed in love to Christ, and obedience to his laws, in order to support and carry the interest of the gospel. Yet this is not to be given to any one that may pretend to be a minister, or thrust himself upon a church, or to such as run without a mission for filthy lucre's sake; but churches ought to take a special care who to call forth to the work of the ministry, according to the rule of instruction given by

1 1 Tim. v. 17.
2 2 Cor. v. 20.
3 Matt. xxiii. 5—7.
4 Eph. vi. 18—20.
5 Heb. xiii. 17—22.
6 1 Cor. iv. 16, xi. 1; Phil. iii. 17; Heb. xiii. 7.
7 2 Tim. i. 15.
8 Acts xxiii 5.
9 Acts vi. 4.
10 1 Cor. ix. 7—11.
11 1 Cor. ix. 13.
12 Gal. vi. 6; 1 Cor. ix. 14.

inspiration of God, be they learned or unlearned as to human learning, be they rich or poor as to worldly wealth.

The liberality of the people, if they be able, should surmount the necessity of the minister, so as that he may exercise those acts of love and hospitality, as is required of such, that therein he may be exemplary in good works, etc. Moreover, it is a duty on all those that attend on their ministry, to assist herein,[1] and as people do sow, so shall they reap.[2] When people neglect their duty towards their ministers, such ministers must of necessity neglect their studies, and betake to other secular employments to support themselves and families, or be worse than infidels; then such people must be great spiritual losers in their edification. Yet when and where a church is not able to raise a comfortable maintenance for to support their minister, there it is not only lawful, but the duty of such ministers to labor with their hands; for to leave such a congregation destitute, to languish without the ministry, would be very uncharitable, and smell very much of filthy lucre; and to expect from a people more than they are able, would be oppression or extortion.

OF THE MANIFOLD DUTIES OF CHRISTIANS, ESPECIALLY TO THE HOUSEHOLD OF FAITH.

Some of them are these. (1.) Love unfeigned and without dissimulation, for all their things ought to be done in love.[3] (2.) To labor to keep the unity of the Spirit in the bond of peace.[4] (3.) Endeavor for the edification and spiritual benefit of the whole body, that they all may grow up to be a holy temple in and for the Lord.[5] (4.) That they all watch over one another for good.[6] (5.) That they do pray with and for one another.[7] (6.) That they neglect not the assembling of themselves together, for the celebrating of divine worship, and so promote one another's spiritual benefit.[8]

1 Gal. vi. 6.
2 Gal. vi. 7, 8, vide *Confession of Faith*, 27, § 10.
3 John xiii. 34, 35; Rom. xii. 9, 10; xiii. 8–10.
4 Eph. iv. 3.
5 1 Cor. xiv. 12, 26; Eph. iv. 12, 29, ii. 21, 22.
6 Phil. ii. 3, 4.
7 James v. 16.
8 Heb. x. 25; Acts ii. 42.

(7.) That they use all means to keep the house of God in due order and cleanliness, walking inoffensive towards one another, and all others, with conscientious diligence, and so unanimously to contend for the faith and truth once delivered to the saints, in the purity thereof, according to the holy Scripture.[1]

OF CHURCH CENSURES.

Having spoken of the gathering together of a particular gospel church, and its officers, and the rules whereby we are to be guided in choosing and ordaining of them, and of the admission of members, etc., it is meet to give a short view of a church's duties and authority in respect of censures upon offenders.

First, of Admonition.

(1.) Admonition is a holy, tender, and wise endeavor, to convince a brother that he hath offended in matter of fact, or else is fallen into a way, wherein to continue is like to be prejudicial to the party himself, or some others; where the matter, whatever it be, and the sinfulness thereof, with the aggravating circumstances attending it, is to be charged on his conscience, in the sight of God, with due application of the word of God, which concerns his condition; thereby leading him to his duty and true reformation. (2.) Admonition is private by one or more of the brethren, or more public by the whole church. (1.) When one brother trespasses against another, the offended brother is not to divulge the offence, but to go in a gospel way to the offender, and to use his endeavor to reclaim his brother; and if he repents, the offended brother ought to forgive him.[2] But if the offending brother will not hear, then the offended brother ought to take two or three other brethren, and they such as may be the most likely to gain upon the offender; but if this admonition also takes no effect, it is to be brought before the church.[3] (2.) The church, when matters come thus before them, shall admonish and endeavor to reclaim the offender, in the spirit of meekness;

[1] Psalm xciii. 5; Zech. xiv. 21; 1 Cor. xiv. 33, 40; xi. 2.

[2] Matt. xviii. 15; Luke xvii. 3.

[3] Matt. xviii. 16, 17.

and if the brother that offended continues obstinate and impenitent, the church is directed to exclude him.[1]

(1.) From whence it follows, every church member has somewhat to do in his place.[2] (2.) In case of private offences, it is preposterous to publish them, or acquaint the church or the elders thereof therewith, before the two lower degrees of admonition are duly accomplished, and the offender has neglected to hear. (3.) That when matters are thus regularly brought to the church, then the private proceedings may cease. (4.) That when private offences are brought to the church without such proper private procedure, that the church may and ought to refuse it, as not coming according to gospel rule aforesaid.[3] (5.) But when those things that begin in private are thus regularly brought into the church, they must be received and adjudged according to the said rule.[4] So that it may and doth oftentimes fall out, that those things that begin with private admonition, do end in public excommunication.

Secondly, of Suspension.

(1.) A suspension may be, when the church is informed that a member hath acted amiss, either in matters of faith or practice, and not having satisfactory proof whether the information is true or false, and the case requiring time to inquire therein, it is expedient to suspend such a person from communion at the Lord's table, until the elders of the church can make suitable inquiry; as might be signified by the law in the case of leprosy.[5]

(2.) Suspension is rather to be looked upon to be, when a church doth debar a member from communion for some irregularity that he may be guilty of, which yet doth not amount so high as to be ripe for the great sentence of excommunication; but that the person, for such irregularity, ought to be debarred of the privilege of special communion and exercise of office, in order to his humiliation.[6] Such is not to be accounted as an enemy, but to be exhorted as a brother in union, though not in communion: but if such a one remain im-

1 Matt. xviii. 17.
2 Heb. xii. 15.
3 Matt. xviii.
4 Matt. xviii.
5 Lev. xiii., xiv.
6 2 Thess. iii. 6, 7, 10, 11, 14, 15.

penitent and incorrigible, the church, after due waiting for his reformation, is to proceed to excommunication;[1] for that would be a not hearing the church in the highest degree.

Thirdly, of Excommunication.

Excommunication is a judicial act or censure of the church, upon an offender, by the authority of Jesus Christ, and by his direction, delivered to his church by himself or his apostles, in the New Testament, which a gospel church ought to put in practice, when matters of fact require, according to gospel rule; as first, when a member, after all due admonition, continues obstinate, and will hear no reproof.[2] *Secondly*, when a member hath committed a gross sin, which is directly against the moral law, and being notorious and scandalous, and proved beyond dispute,[3] then a church is immediately to proceed unto censure, notwithstanding any present signs of conviction or remorse, for the necessary vindication of the glory of God, the vindication of the church, also, and their holy profession; and to manifest their just indignation and abhorrence against such wickedness.[4] *Thirdly*, when a member is found to be erroneous, defective, or heretical in some fundamental point, or to swerve from the right faith, in the principles of the Christian religion.[5]

The manner of proceeding unto this great and awful instituted ordinance, is: the church being gathered together, the offender also having notice to come to make his answer and defence (if he comes not, he aggravates his offence by despising the authority of Christ in his church), the body of the church is to have knowledge of the offender's crime fully, and the full proof thereof as of plain matter of fact; and after mature deliberate consideration, and consulting the rules of direction given in the word of God, whether the offender be present or absent, the minister or elder puts the question to the whole church, whether they judge the person guilty of such crime now proved upon him, is worthy of the censure of the church for

1 Matt. xviii. 17.
2 Matt. xviii 17.
3 1 Cor. v. 4, 5; 1 Tim. v. 24; 2 Cor. x. 6.
4 1 Cor. v. 1—13.
5 1 Tim. i. 19, 20.

the same? to which the members in general give their judgment; which, if it be in the affirmative, then the judgment of the members in general being had, or the majority of them, the pastor, minister, or elder, sums up the sentence of the church, opens the nature of the crime, with the suitableness of the censure, according to gospel rule; and having thus proceeded, a proper time is fixed to put the sentence in execution, at which time the pastor, minister, or elder of the church, as his place and duty requires, is to lay open the heinousness of such a sin, with all the aggravating circumstances thereof, and showing what an abominable scandal such an offender is become to religion, what dishonor it is to God, etc., applying the particular places of Scripture that are proper to the case, in order to charge the offence home upon the conscience of the offender if present, that others also may fear; showing also the awful nature of this great censure, and the main end thereof, for the salvation and not the destruction of the soul, and with much solemnity in the whole society, calling upon God for his gracious presence, and his blessing upon this his sacred ordinance; that the great end thereof may be obtained; still expressing the deep sense the church hath of the fall of this brother, with the great humiliation of the church, and great sorsow for, and detestation of, the sin committed. The said pastor, minister, or elder, in the name of the Lord Jesus Christ, in the presence of the congregation, and by and with the consent and according to the judicial sentence of the church, cuts off, and secludes such an offender by name, from the union and communion of the church, because of his offences; so that such a person is not thenceforth to be looked on, deemed or accounted as a brother or member of such a church, until God shall restore him again by repentance.

Which exclusion carries in it the full sense of our Lord's words,[1] *Let him be unto thee as an heathen man and a publican;* or of the apostle,[2] *to deliver such a one to Satan;* which is an authoritative putting of such a person out of the communion of the church, the kingdom of heaven, into the world, the kingdom of Satan, the prince of the power of the air, the spirit that now worketh in the children of disobedience, in order to his being humbled and broken under a

[1] Matt. xviii. 17. [2] 1 Cor. v. 5.

sight and sense of his sins, which is meant by the destruction of the flesh, and to the end that the spirit may be saved in the day of the Lord.

Amongst the many disorders which church members may be guilty of, and for the obstinate continuance therein, a church may and ought to use the power that Christ hath given to exclude them from her communion, that is one, which is when a member doth seclude himself, and that not in any regular way, but contrary to all rule and order; for when a church member, by reason of some offence he hath taken at the church, or some of the members thereof, and hath not done his duty according to the rule of the word, or else is a dying away in religion, by one means or another, as by the love of the world, change of condition in marriage, or not having his expected preferment in the church, or the like, doth, as it were excommunicate himself, the church, according to their duty, ought to use their endeavors to reclaim such; which endeavors, if they prove fruitless, and the party obstinate, the church ought not to acquiesce in his irregular departure from them, as if all their bonds of relation and duty were over, and no more was to be done, seeing the party has usurped the power of the keys to himself; the church, therefore, must maintain the power that Christ hath committed unto it, though it cannot hinder the inordinate and unruly passions of such a one, if God leaves him to it. He will run away from the church, rending himself schismatically off, breaking through all order and covenant obligations, in opposition to brotherly endeavors to hinder him, and to stay him in his place; the church is to proceed judicially to turn the key upon such a sinful, disorderly departure; and publicly declare, that as such a one by name hath been guilty of such a thing, naming his disorders, he is no longer in their communion, nor under their watch and care, etc., and that such a person is not to return to their communion until he hath given satisfaction to the church.[1] Such a separation or departure, is very sinful, for these and the like reasons. (1.) Because the church is a corporation privileged with laws and rules for admittance and dimittance, which ought to be observed.[2] (2.) Such a departure is rude and

1 Rom. xvi. 17. 2 Matt. xviii.; Rom. xii. 4, 5.

indecent, therefore dishonorable.[1] (3.) Because, if members may take this liberty, all the officers of the church, ministers, ruling elders, and deacons may take the same liberty, which would soon unchurch any church, or at least be destructive to its beauty, comfort, and edification.[2] (4.) All members do covenant the contrary,[3] and therefore it is a breach of covenant, which is a black character.[4] (5.) It destroys totally the relation between elders and people, which God hath ordained.[5] (6.) It is a usurping of the keys, or rather stealing of them.[6] (7.) It is schism; if there is such a thing in the world, it is of particular churches.[7] (8.) It is high contempt of Christ in the government of his church.[8] (9.) It is to break the staff of beauty [*covenant*] and of bands and brotherhood too.[9] (10.) It argues either some great undiscovered guilt lying on the party, or some by-ends in his first seeking admission into such a church. All which put together, it declares the great unity of a congregational gospel church, and the sinfulness of such disorderly persons in breaking off without a just cause: but if any church becomes heretical in principles, or idolatrous in worship, or immoral in life, it is lawful for persons, after they have discharged their conscience and duty in reproving and bearing witness against such gross defections, to depart.[10]

Other disorders and causes of discords in churches are these, and many of the like:

1. When members of churches, by their ignorance of the rules of discipline and right government of the church of Christ do not act according to their duty; particularly when that rule [11] is not observed; and that is, either (1.) When offended members instead of going to the offender to tell him his fault, will be divulging it disorderly to others, whether members or non-members. (2.) When offended members instead of acting according to the said rule, do conceal the matter from the offender and every body else, lest they should be looked upon as contentious persons: and thereby they suf-

1 1 Cor. xiv. 40.
2 John vi. 67.
3 Isa. xliv. 5.
4 2 Tim. iii. 3.
5 Matt. ix. 36.
6 Amos vi. 13.
7 1 Cor. xi. 18, xii. 25.
8 Jude xviii. 19; 2 Peter ii. 10, 11.
9 Zech. xi. 10, 14.
10 2 Cor. vi. 17, 18.
11 Matt. xviii. 15, 16.

fer sin upon their brother, and are become guilty of other men's sins, and thereby they suffer the name of God, their holy profession, and the church, to lie under a reproach by their neglect; either of which ways is very sinful, as being contrary to the express rule given by our Lord Jesus Christ; and such ought, as being thereby become offenders themselves, to be in a gospel way dealt with.

2. When an elder of a church do know that some of the members are immoral and scandalous in life, or heretical in matters of faith and judgment, and yet bear with them, or connive at them.

3. When members of churches take liberty to go to hear at other places, when the church is assembled to worship God, which is directly contrary to Hebrews 10 : 25, and is no less than breaking covenant with the church they belong unto, and may soon dissolve and unchurch any particular church; for, by the same rule that one member takes such liberty, another may, yea, all the members may, until their assembling entirely cease. And, moreover, it is casting great contempt on the ministry of such a church, and may cause others to be disaffected to the doctrine taught in such, though sound and orthodox. Yet no restraint ought to be laid on members going to hear at other places, where sound doctrine is taught, at other times.

4. When members take liberty to go to hear men that are corrupt in doctrine, and so suck in some unsound notions of religion, and endeavor to corrupt others with what they have imbibed themselves. And, alas! how many in our unhappy days are corrupted with *Arminianism*, *Socinianism*, and what not? Such cause trouble and great disorders.

5. Another disorder that may cause discord, is, when members are received without the general and unanimous consent of the church; or when any are admitted, with whose confession, or life and conversation, the generality of the members are not satisfied: or when elders and ministers, or leaders of the church, are remiss and careless in reception of members.

6. When a church shall receive a charge against a member, it being an offence given by one brother to another brother, before an orderly procedure has been made by the offended brother, according to the rule.[1]

[1] Matt. xviii.

7. When judgment passes with partiality, or some are connived at out of favor or affection, and others censured out of envy without due conviction. Levi was not to know his father, mother, or children in judgment.[1]

8. When the charges of a church are not equally borne by the members according to their several abilities, but some are burthened when others do little or nothing.

9. When accusations are received against an elder contrary to the rule,[2] which requires two or three witnesses as to matter of fact.

10. When any member shall divulge to persons not of the congregation, nor concerned in those matters, what is done in the church meetings: the church in this respect, as well as in others, is to be a garden enclosed, a spring shut up, a fountain sealed.[3] This often occasions great grief and trouble, and therefore such disorderly persons should be detected. Is it not a shame to any to divulge the secrets of a family? But far greater shame do such persons expose themselves unto.

11. When days of prayer, fasting, or thanksgiving, or days of discipline appointed by the church, are not carefully observed and kept.

In all these, and many other things of like nature, the members of particular churches ought to give all diligence to walk worthy of their vocation, and according to the rule and direction of the word of God, that disorders may be prevented, and that church communion may be maintained in peace and purity, to the edifying of the body of the church of Christ in love.

OF THE COMMUNION OF CHURCHES.

Every particular congregational church incorporated by and according to the institution of Christ in the gospel, and duly organized according to the pattern of the primitive churches, hath sufficient power from Christ to call and ordain its own officers; so that no man, or set of men, have authority to choose officers for them, or impose any officer on them, without their previous knowledge and

1 Deut. xxxiii. 9. 2 1 Tim. v. 16. 3 Cant. iv. 12.

voluntary consent.[1] Deacons are to be chosen by the multitude.[2] Elders were ordained in every church by election or suffrage of the church; and every particular church, as such, assembled with her proper elders, hath sufficient power to receive members.[3] And in the exercise of any acts of discipline, such a church being convened with her own officers or elders in the name of Christ, may act according to gospel rule in any case, even to excommunicate such members as are found to be obstinate in disorders, or heretical in principles, after due admonition, or such as are guilty of gross and scandalous immoralities in conversation, etc., independent on any other church power superior to itself, or higher judicatory lodged in any man or any set of men, by any institution of Christ: and therefore, the elders of a church, meeting in the absence of the members, or convened with the elders of other churches, are not intrusted with a power to act for a church in admission of members, ordination, or censures, etc., and it is the duty of such a church to admonish any of her members or officers, their teacher or pastor,[4] and exclude any too, when their crimes require, according to the rule of the gospel.

And such particular congregational churches, constituted and organized according to the mind of Christ revealed in the New Testament, are all equal in power and dignity, and we read of no disparity between them, or subordination among them, that should make a difference between the acts of their mutual communion, so as the acts of one church should be acts of authority, and the acts of others should be acts of obedience or subjection, although they may vastly differ in gifts, abilities, and usefulness.

Such particular distinct churches, agreeing in gospel doctrine and practice, may and ought to maintain communion together in many duties, which may tend to the mutual benefit and edification of the whole: and thereby one church that hath plenty of gifts, may and ought, if possible, to supply another that lacketh.[5] They may have mutual giving and receiving,[6] and mutual translation, recommendation, or dismission of members from one church to another, as occa-

1 Acts vi. 5.
2 Acts xiv. 23.
3 Acts ii. 41; Rom xiv. 7.
4 Col. iv. 17.
5 Cant. viii. 8.
6 Phil. iv. 15.

sion may require. It is to be noted that persons called to office are not to be dismissed as officers, but as members; though another church may call such to the same office again.

By virtue also of such communion, the members of one such church may, where they are known, occasionally partake at the Lord's table with a sister church. Yet, notwithstanding such communion of churches, by voluntary consent and confederation, the officers of one particular church may not act as officers in another church, in any act of government, without a particular call thereunto from the other church where they occasionally come.

It is expedient that particular churches constituted in the way and manner, and for the ends declared in the former part of this narrative, when they are planted by the providence of God, so as they may have opportunity and advantage so to do, should by their mutual agreement, appoint proper times and places, to meet by their respective messengers or delegates, to consider of such things as may be for the common benefit of all such churches, for their peace, prosperity, and mutual edification, and what may be for the furtherance of the gospel, and the interest of Christ in the world.

And forasmuch as it falls out many times that particular churches have to do with doubtful and difficult matters, or differences in point of doctrine or administration, like the church of Antioch of old, wherein either of the churches in general are concerned, or any one church in their peace, union, or edification; or any member or members of a church are injured, in or by any proceeding in censures not agreeable to gospel rule and order; it is according to the mind of Christ, that many churches holding communion together, should meet by their messengers and delegates to consider of and to give advice in or about such matters in difference; and their sentiments to be reported to all the churches concerned; and such messengers and delegates convened in the name of Christ, by the voluntary consent of the several churches in such mutual communion, may declare and determine of the mind of the Holy Ghost revealed in Scripture, concerning things in difference; and may decree the observation of things that are true and necessary, because revealed and appointed in the Scripture. And the churches will do well to receive, own, and observe such determinations, on the evidence and authority of the mind of the Holy Ghost in them.[1] Yet such delegates thus assembled, are not intrusted or armed with any coercive power, or any superior jurisdiction over the churches concerned, so as to impose their determinations on them or their officers, under the penalty of excommunication, or the like.[2]

Acts xv. 29.

2 See the *Confession*, Chap. 26, § 14, 15. See also Dr. OWEN, *On the Nature of the Gospel Church*, Chap. 11; and Dr. GOODWIN, Vol. IV. Chap. 8, 9, 10, etc., *Of the Government of the Churches of Christ.*

THE END.

WORKS FOR CHURCH MEMBERS.

THE CHRISTIAN'S DAILY TREASURY; a Religious Exercise for every Day in the Year. By Rev. E. Temple. A new and improved edition. 12mo, cloth, $1.00.

☞ A work for every Christian. It is indeed a "Treasury" of good things.

THE SCHOOL OF CHRIST; or, Christianity Viewed in its Leading Aspects. By the Rev. A. R. L. Foote, author of "Incidents in the Life of our Saviour," etc. 16mo, cloth, 50 cts.

THE CHRISTIAN PASTOR; His Work and the Needful Preparation. By Alvah Hovey, D. D., Prof. of Theology in the Newton Theol. Inst. 16mo, pp. 60; flexible cloth, 25 cents; paper covers, 12 cents.

APOLLOS; or, Directions to Persons just commencing a Religious Life. 32mo, paper covers, cheap, for distribution, per hundred, $6.00.

THE HARVEST AND THE REAPERS. Home Work for All, and how to do it. By Rev. Harvey Newcomb. 16mo, cloth, 63 cts.

This work is dedicated to the converts of 1858. It shows what *may* be done, by showing what has been done. It shows how much there is NOW to be done at home. It shows HOW to do it. Every man interested in the work of saving men, every professing Christian, will find this work to be for him.

THE CHURCH-MEMBER'S MANUAL of Ecclesiastical Principles, Doctrines, and Discipline. By Rev. William Crowell, D. D. Introduction by H. J. Ripley, D. D. Second edition, revised and improved. 12mo, cloth, 75 cts.

THE CHURCH-MEMBER'S HAND-BOOK; a Plain Guide to the Doctrines and Practice of Baptist Churches. By the Rev. William Crowell, D. D. 18mo, cloth, 38 cts.

THE CHURCH-MEMBER'S GUIDE. By the Rev. John A. James. Edited by J. O. Choules, D. D. New edition. With Introductory Essay, by Rev. Hubbard Winslow. Cloth, 33 cts.

"The spontaneous effusion of our heart, on laying the book down, was: 'May every church-member in our land possess this book, and be blessed with all the happiness which conformity to its evangelical sentiments and directions is calculated to confer.'" — *Christian Secretary.*

THE CHURCH IN EARNEST. By Rev. John A. James. 18mo, cloth, 40 cts.

"Its arguments and appeals are well adapted to prompt to action, and the times demand such a book. We trust it will be universally read." — *N. Y. Observer.*

"Those who have the means should purchase a number of copies of this work, and lend them to church-members, and keep them in circulation *till they are worn out!*" — *Mothers' Assistant.*

CHRISTIAN PROGRESS. A Sequel to the Anxious Inquirer. By John Angell James. 18mo, cloth, 31 cts.

☞ One of the best and most useful works of this popular author.

"It ought to be sold by hundreds of thousands, until every church-member in the land has bought, read, marked, learned, and inwardly digested a copy." — *Congregationalist.*

"So eminently is it adapted to do good, that we feel no surprise that it should make one of the publishers' excellent publications. It exhibits the whole subject of growth in grace with great simplicity and clearness." — *Puritan Recorder.*

VALUABLE NEW WORKS.

GOD REVEALED IN NATURE AND IN CHRIST; including a Refutation of the Development Theory contained in the "Vestiges of the Natural History of Creation." By Rev. JAMES B. WALKER, author of "THE PHILOSOPHY OF THE PLAN OF SALVATION." 12mo, cloth, $1.00.

PHILOSOPHY OF THE PLAN OF SALVATION; a Book for the Times. By an AMERICAN CITIZEN. With an Introductory Essay by CALVIN E. STOWE, D. D. ☞ New improved and enlarged edition. 12mo, cloth, 75 cts.

YAHVEH CHRIST; or, The Memorial Name. By ALEXANDER MACWHORTER. With an Introductory Letter by NATHANIEL W. TAYLOR, D. D., Dwight Professor in Yale Theol. Sem. 16mo, cloth, 60 cts.

SALVATION BY CHRIST. A Series of Discourses on some of the most Important Doctrines of the Gospel. By FRANCIS WAYLAND, D. D. 12mo, cloth, $1.00; cloth, gilt, $1.50.

CONTENTS. — Theoretical Atheism. — Practical Atheism. — The Moral Character of Man. — The Fall of Man. — Justification by Works Impossible. — Preparation for the Advent. — Work of the Messiah. — Justification by Faith. — Conversion. — Imitators of God. — Grieving the Spirit. — A Day in the Life of Jesus. — The Benevolence of the Gospel. — The Fall of Peter. — Character of Balaam. — Veracity. — The Church of Christ. — The Unity of the Church. — Duty of Obedience to the Civil Magistrate (three Sermons).

THE GREAT DAY OF ATONEMENT; or, Meditations and Prayers on the Last Twenty-four Hours of the Sufferings and Death of Our Lord and Saviour Jesus Christ. Translated from the German of CHARLOTTE ELIZABETH NEBELIN. Edited by MRS. COLIN MACKENZIE. Elegantly printed and bound. 16mo, cloth, 75 cts.

THE EXTENT OF THE ATONEMENT IN ITS RELATION TO GOD AND THE UNIVERSE. By Rev. THOMAS W. JENKYN, D. D., late President of Coward College, London. 12mo, cloth, $1.00.

This work was thoroughly revised by the author not long before his death, exclusively for the present publishers. It has long been a standard work, and without doubt presents the most complete discussion of the subject in the language.

"We consider this volume as setting the long and fiercely agitated question as to the extent of the Atonement completely at rest. Posterity will thank the author till the latest ages for his illustrious argument." — *New York Evangelist.*

THE SUFFERING SAVIOUR; or, Meditations on the Last Days of Christ. By FRED. W. KRUMMACHER, D. D., author of "Elijah the Tishbite." 12mo, cloth, $1.25.

"The narrative is given with thrilling vividness, and pathos, and beauty. Marking, as we proceeded, several passages for quotation, we found them in the end so numerous, that we must refer the reader to the work itself." — *News of the Churches (Scottish).*

THE IMITATION OF CHRIST. By THOMAS A KEMPIS. With an Introductory Essay, by THOMAS CHALMERS, D. D. Edited by HOWARD MALCOM, D. D. A new edition, with a LIFE OF THOMAS A KEMPIS, by Dr. C. ULLMANN, author of "Reformers before the Reformation." 12mo, cloth, 85 cts.

This may safely be pronounced the best Protestant edition extant of this ancient and celebrated work. It is reprinted from Payne's edition, collated with an ancient Latin copy. The peculiar feature of this new edition is the improved page, the elegant, large, clear type, and the NEW LIFE OF A KEMPIS, by Dr. Ullmann.

VALUABLE WORKS.

FOOTSTEPS OF OUR FOREFATHERS; What they suffered and what they sought. Describing Localities, and Portraying Personages and Events, conspicuous in the Struggles for Religious Liberty. By JAMES G. MIALL. Containing thirty-six Illustrations. 12mo, cloth, $1.00.

MEMORIALS OF EARLY CHRISTIANITY; Presenting, in a graphic, compact, and popular form, Memorable Events of Early Ecclesiastical History, &c. By Rev. J. G. MIALL, author of "Footsteps of our Forefathers." With numerous Illustrations. 12mo, cloth, $1.00.

☞ The above, by Miall, are both exceedingly interesting and instructive works.

REPUBLICAN CHRISTIANITY; or, True Liberty, as exhibited in the Life, Precepts, and early Disciples of the Great Redeemer. By the Rev. E. L. MAGOON, D. D., author of "Proverbs for the People," &c. Second edition. 12mo, cloth, $1.25.

"The author has at his command a rich store of learning, from which he skilfully draws abundant evidence for the support of the positions he assumes." — *Puritan Recorder.*

THE PERSON AND WORK OF CHRIST. By ERNEST SARTORIUS, D.D., Konigsberg, Prussia. Translated by Rev. OAKMAN S. STEARNS, A. M. 18mo, cloth, 42 cts.

"A work of much ability, and presenting the argument in a style that will be new to most of American readers. It will deservedly attract attention." — *New York Observer.*

CHRISTIANITY DEMONSTRATED; in four distinct and independent series of proofs; with an Explanation of the Types and Prophecies concerning the Messiah. By Rev. HARVEY NEWCOMB. 12mo, cloth, 75 cts.

THE SAINT'S EVERLASTING REST. By RICHARD BAXTER 16mo, cloth, 50 cts.

THE RELIGIONS OF THE WORLD, and their Relations to Christianity. By FREDERICK DENISON MAURICE, A. M., Professor of Divinity in King's College, London. 16mo, cloth, 60 cts.

THE CHRISTIAN WORLD UNMASKED. By JOHN BERRIDGE, A M., Vicar of Everton, Bedfordshire. With a Life of the Author, by Rev. THOMAS GUTHRIE, D. D., Minister of Free St. John's, Edinburgh. 16mo, cloth, 50 cts.

"The book," says DR. GUTHRIE, in his Introduction, "which we introduce anew to the public, has survived the test of years, and still stands towering above things of inferior growth, like a cedar of Lebanon. Its subject is all-important; in doctrine it is sound to the core; it glows with fervent piety; it exhibits a most skilful and unsparing dissection of the dead professor; while its style is so remarkable that he who could *preach* as Berridge has *written* would hold any congregation by the ears."

THE IMITATION OF CHRIST. By THOMAS A KEMPIS. Introductory Essay, by T. CHALMERS, D. D. Edited by the REV. HOWARD MALCOM, D. D. *Cheap edition.* 18mo, cloth, 38 cts.

GUIDO AND JULIUS. THE DOCTRINE OF SIN AND THE PROPITIATOR; or, the True Consecration of the Doubter. Exhibited in the Correspondence of two Friends. By FREDERICK AUGUSTUS O. THOLUCK, D. D. Translated from the German, by JONATHAN EDWARDS RYLAND. With an introduction by JOHN PYE SMITH, D. D. 16mo, cloth, 60 cts.

DR. JOHN HARRIS' WORKS.

THE GREAT TEACHER; or, Characteristics of our Lord's Ministry. By JOHN HARRIS, D. D. With an Introductory Essay by H. HUMPHREY, D. D. Sixteenth thousand. 12mo, cloth, 85 cents.

"DR. HARRIS is one of the best writers of the age; and this volume will not in the least detract from his well-merited reputation." — *American Pulpit.*

THE GREAT COMMISSION; or, the Christian Church constituted and charged to convey the Gospel to the World. A Prize Essay. With an Introductory Essay by W. R. WILLIAMS, D. D. Eighth thousand. 12mo, cloth, $1.00.

"This volume will afford the reader an intellectual and spiritual banquet of the highest order." — *Philadelphia Ch. Observer.*

THE PRE-ADAMITE EARTH. Contributions to Theological Science. By JOHN HARRIS, D. D. New and revised edition. 12mo, cloth, $1.00.

MAN PRIMEVAL; or, the Constitution and Primitive Condition of the Human Being. With a finely engraved Portrait of the Author. 12mo, cloth, $1.25.

PATRIARCHY; or, the Family, its Constitution and Probation. 12mo, cloth, $1.25.

This is the last of Dr. Harris' series entitled "Contributions to Theological Science."

SERMONS, CHARGES, ADDRESSES, &c., delivered by Dr. HARRIS in various parts of the country, during the height of his reputation as a preacher. Two elegant volumes, octavo, cloth, each, $1.00.

The immense sale of all this author's Works attests their intrinsic worth and great popularity.

DR. WILLIAMS' WORKS.

LECTURES ON THE LORD'S PRAYER. By WILLIAM R. WILLIAMS, D. D. Third edition. 12mo, cloth, 85 cts.

"We are constantly reminded, in reading his eloquent pages, of the old English writers, whose vigorous thought, and gorgeous imagery, and varied learning, have made their writings an inexhaustible mine for the scholars of the present day." — *Ch. Observer.*

RELIGIOUS PROGRESS; Discourses on the Development of the Christian Character. By WILLIAM R. WILLIAMS, D. D. Third edition. 12mo, cloth, 85 cts.

"His power of apt and forcible illustration is without a parallel among modern writers. The mute pages spring into life beneath the magic of his radiant imagination. But this is never at the expense of solidity of thought, or strength of argument. It is seldom, indeed, that a mind of so much poetical invention yields such a willing homage to the logical element." — *Harper's Monthly Miscellany.*

MISCELLANIES. By WILLIAM R. WILLIAMS, D. D. New and improved edition. *Price Reduced.* 12mo, cloth, $1.25.

☞ "Dr. Williams is a profound scholar and a brilliant writer." — *N. Y. Evangelist.*

BUNGENER'S WORKS.

THE PREACHER AND THE KING; or, Bourdaloue in the Court of Louis XIV.; being an Account of the Pulpit Eloquence of that distinguished era. Translated from the French of L. F. BUNGENER, Paris. Introduction by the Rev. GEORGE POTTS, D. D. *A new, improved edition,* with a fine LIKENESS and a BIOGRAPHICAL SKETCH OF THE AUTHOR. 12mo, cloth, $1.25.

THE PRIEST AND THE HUGUENOT; or, Persecution in the Age of Louis XV Translated from the French of L. F. Bungener. Two vols. 12mo, cloth, $2.25.

☞ This is not only a work of thrilling interest, — no fiction could exceed it, — but, as a Protestant work, it is a masterly production.

BIOGRAPHIES AND WORKS ON MISSIONS.

THE MISSIONARY ENTERPRISE; a Collection of the most important Discourses in the language, on Christian Missions, by distinguished American Authors. Edited by BARON STOW, D. D. Second Thousand. 12mo, cloth, 85 cts.

"You here see the high talent of the American church. The discourses by Dr. Beecher, Dr. Wayland, and the Rev. Dr. Stone, are among the very highest exhibitions of logical correctness, and burning, popular fervor." — *New Englander.*

A HISTORY OF AMERICAN BAPTIST MISSIONS, in Asia, Africa, Europe, and North America, from their earliest commencement to the present time. Prepared under the direction of the American Baptist Missionary Union. By WILLIAM GAMMELL, Professor in Brown University. With seven Maps. 12mo, cloth, at the low price of 75 cts.

This work was prepared at the request of the Executive Committee of the Missionary Union; and the Committee appointed by the Union to examine the manuscript, consisting of Doctors Cone, Sharp, and Chase, say: "It exhibits gratifying evidence of research, fidelity, and skill. It sets before the reader, in a lucid manner, facts that should never be forgotten. Some of them, in power to awaken attention and touch the heart, could scarcely be surpassed by fiction."

Rev. E. Kincaid says: "As I have labored more or less at *all* the stations in Burmah, I could but admire the singular accuracy with which all the leading facts of these missions are detailed in Prof. Gammell's History of American Baptist Missions. I have not found a *single error* of any importance."

Rev. J. Wade says: "I can most cordially recommend it to the public as being a very truthful and well-written work."

DR. GRANT AND THE MOUNTAIN NESTORIANS. By Rev. THOMAS LAURIE, his surviving associate in that Mission. With a Likeness, Map of the Country, and numerous Illustrations. Third edition. Revised and improved. 12mo, cloth, $1.25.

☞ A most valuable Memoir of a *remarkable man.*

THE KAREN APOSTLE; or, Memoir of KO-THAH-BYU, the first Karen Convert. With notices concerning his Nation. By Rev. FRANCIS MASON, D. D., Missionary. Edited by Prof. H. J. RIPLEY. 18mo, cloth, 25 cts.

"This is a work of thrilling interest, containing the history of a remarkable man, and giving, also, much information respecting the Karens, a people until recently but little known."

MEMOIR OF ANN H. JUDSON, late Missionary to Burmah. By Rev. J. D. KNOWLES. A new edition. Fifty-seventh thousand. 18mo, cloth, 58 cts.

FINE EDITION, with plates, 16mo, cloth, gilt, 85 cts.

MEMOIR OF GEORGE DANA BOARDMAN, late Missionary to Burmah, containing much intelligence relative to the Burman Mission. By Rev. A. KING. With an Introductory Essay, by W. R. WILLIAMS, D. D. New edition, with beautiful frontispiece. 12mo, cloth, 75 cts.

"One of the brightest luminaries of Burmah is extinguished." — REV. DR. JUDSON.

☞ The introduction alone is worth the price of the book, says a distinguished reviewer.

MEMOIR OF HENRIETTA SHUCK, first female Missionary to China. By Rev. J. B. JETER, D. D. With a likeness. Fifth thousand. 12mo, cloth, 50 cts.

"We have seldom taken into our hands a more beautiful book than this. It will be extensively read, and eminently useful." — *Family Visitor.*

MEMOIR OF REV. WILLIAM G. CROCKER, late Missionary to West Africa, among the Bassas. Including a History of the Mission. By R. B. MEDBERY. With a likeness. 18mo, cloth, 63 cts.

"This work is commended to the attention of every lover of the liberties of man." — *Watchman and Reflector.*

VALUABLE BIOGRAPHIES.

EXTRACTS FROM THE DIARY AND CORRESPONDENCE OF THE LATE AMOS LAWRENCE. With a brief account of some Incidents in his Life. Edited by his son, WM. R. LAWRENCE, M. D. With elegant Portraits of Amos and Abbott Lawrence, an Engraving of their Birthplace, an Autograph page of Handwriting, and a copious Index. One large octavo volume, cloth, $1.50 ; royal 12mo, cloth, $1.00.

A MEMOIR OF THE LIFE AND TIMES OF ISAAC BACKUS. By ALVAH HOVEY, Professor of Ecclesiastical History in Newton Theological Institution. 12mo, cloth, $1.25.

This work gives an account of a remarkable man, and of a remarkable movement in the middle of the last century, resulting in the formation of what were called the "Separate" Churches. It supplies an important deficiency in the history of New England affairs. For every Baptist, especially, it is a necessary book.

LIFE OF JAMES MONTGOMERY. By Mrs. H. C. KNIGHT, author of "Lady Huntington and her Friends," &c. Likeness and elegant Illustrated Title-Page on steel. 12mo, cloth, $1.25.

This is an original biography, prepared from the abundant but ill-digested materials contained in the seven octavo volumes of the London edition. The Christian public in America will welcome such a memoir of a poet whose hymns and sacred melodies have been the delight of every household.

MEMOIR OF ROGER WILLIAMS, Founder of the State of Rhode Island. By Prof. WILLIAM GAMMELL, A. M. 16mo, cloth, 75 cts.

PHILIP DODDRIDGE. His Life and Labors. By JOHN STOUGHTON, D. D. With an Introductory Chapter, by Rev. JAMES G. MIALL, Author of "Footsteps of our Forefathers," &c. With beautiful Illustrated Title-page and Frontispiece. 16mo, cloth, 60 cents.

THE LIFE AND CORRESPONDENCE OF JOHN FOSTER. Edited by J. E. RYLAND, with notices of Mr. FOSTER, as a Preacher and a Companion. By JOHN SHEPPARD. A new edition, two volumes in one, 700 pages. 12mo, cloth, $1.25.

"In simplicity of language, in majesty of conception, his writings are unmatched." — *North British Review.*

THE LIFE OF GODFREY WILLIAM VON LEIBNITZ. By JOHN M. MACKIE, Esq. On the basis of the German work of Dr. G. E. GUHRAUER. 16mo, cloth, 75 cts

"It merits the special notice of all who are interested in the business of education, and deserves a place by the side of Brewster's Life of Newton, in all the libraries of our schools, academies, and literary institutions." — *Watchman and Reflector.*

MEMORIES OF A GRANDMOTHER. By a Lady of Massachusetts. 16mo, cloth, 50 cts.

☞ "My path lies in a valley, which I have sought to adorn with flowers. Shadows from the hills cover it ; but I make my own sunshine." — *Author's Preface.*

THE TEACHER'S LAST LESSON. A Memoir of MARTHA WHITING, late of the Charlestown Female Seminary, with Reminiscences and Suggestive Reflections. By CATHARINE N. BADGER, an Associate Teacher. With a Portrait, and an Engraving of the Seminary. 12mo, cloth, $1.00.

The subject of this Memoir was, for a quarter of a century, at the head of one of the most celebrated female seminaries in the country. During that period she educated more than *three thousand* young ladies. She was a kindred spirit to Mary Lyon.

WORKS FOR BIBLE STUDENTS.

KITTO'S POPULAR CYCLOPÆDIA OF BIBLICAL LITERATURE. Condensed from the larger work. By the Author, JOHN KITTO, D. D. Assisted by JAMES TAYLOR, D. D., of Glasgow. With over five hundred Illustrations. One volume, octavo, 812 pp. Cloth, $3.00 ; sheep, $3.50 ; cloth, gilt, $4.00 ; half calf, $4.00.

A DICTIONARY OF THE BIBLE. Serving, also, as a COMMENTARY, embodying the products of the best and most recent researches in biblical literature in which the scholars of Europe and America have been engaged. The work, the result of immense labor and research, and enriched by the contributions of writers of distinguished eminence in the various departments of sacred literature, has been, by universal consent, pronounced the best work of its class extant, and the one best suited to the advanced knowledge of the present day in all the studies connected with theological science. It is not only intended for ministers and theological students, but it is also particularly adapted to parents, Sabbath-school teachers, and the great body of the religious public.

THE HISTORY OF PALESTINE, from the Patriarchal Age to the Present Time ; with Chapters on the Geography and Natural History of the Country, the Customs and Institutions of the Hebrews. By JOHN KITTO, D. D. With upwards of two hundred Illustrations. 12mo, cloth, $1.25.

☞ A work admirably adapted to the Family, the Sabbath, and the week-day School Library.

ANALYTICAL CONCORDANCE TO THE HOLY SCRIPTURES ; or, the Bible presented under Distinct and Classified Heads or Topics. By JOHN EADIE, D. D., LL D., Author of "Biblical Cyclopædia," "Ecclesiastical Cyclopædia," "Dictionary of the Bible," etc. One volume, octavo, 840 pp. Cloth, $3.00 ; sheep, $3.50 ; cloth, gilt, $4.00 ; half Turkey morocco, $4.00.

The object of this Concordance is to present the SCRIPTURES ENTIRE, under certain classified and exhaustive heads. It differs from an ordinary Concordance, in that its arrangement depends not on WORDS, but on SUBJECTS, and the verses *are printed in full*. Its plan does not bring it at all into competition with such limited works as those of Gaston and Warden ; for they select *doctrinal* topics principally, and do not profess to comprehend as this THE ENTIRE BIBLE. The work also contains a Synoptical Table of Contents of the whole work, presenting in brief a system of biblical antiquities and theology, with a very copious and accurate index.

The value of this work to ministers and Sabbath-school teachers can hardly be over-estimated ; and it needs only to be examined, to secure the approval and patronage of every Bible student.

CRUDEN'S CONDENSED CONCORDANCE. A Complete Concordance to the Holy Scriptures. By ALEXANDER CRUDEN. Revised and Re-edited by the Rev. DAVID KING, LL. D. Octavo, cloth backs, $1.25 ; sheep, $1.50.

The condensation of the quotations of Scripture, arranged under the most obvious heads, while it *diminshes the bulk* of the work, *greatly facilitates* the finding of any required passage.

"We have in this edition of Cruden the *best* made *better*. That is, the present is better adapted to the purposes of a Concordance, by the erasure of superfluous references, the omission of unnecessary explanations, and the contraction of quotations, &c. It is better as a manual, and is better adapted by its price to the means of many who need and ought to possess such a work, than the former large and expensive edition." — *Puritan Recorder.*

A COMMENTARY ON THE ORIGINAL TEXT OF THE ACTS OF THE APOSTLES. By HORATIO B. HACKETT, D. D., Prof. of Biblical Literature and Interpretation, in the Newton Theol. Inst. ☞ A new, revised, and enlarged edition. Royal octavo, cloth, $2.25.

☞ This most important and very popular work has been thoroughly revised ; large portions entirely re-written, with the addition of *more than one hundred pages of new matter ;* the result of the author's continued, laborious investigations and travels, since the publication of the first edition.

WORKS FOR BIBLE STUDENTS.

NOTES ON THE GOSPELS. Designed for Teachers in Sabbath Schools and Bible Classes, and as an Aid to Family Instruction. By HENRY J. RIPLEY, Prof. in Newton Theol. Inst. With Map of Canaan. Cloth, embossed, $1.25.

NOTES ON THE ACTS OF THE APOSTLES. With a beautiful Map, illustrating the Travels of the APOSTLE PAUL, with a track of his Voyage from Cesarea to Rome. By Prof. HENRY J. RIPLEY, D. D. 12mo, cloth, embossed, 75 cts.

NOTES ON THE EPISTLE OF PAUL TO THE ROMANS. Designed for Teachers in Sabbath Schools and Bible Classes, and as an aid to Family Instruction. By HENRY J. RIPLEY. 12mo, cloth, embossed, 67 cts.

The above works by Prof. Ripley should be in the hands of every student of the Bible, especially every Sabbath-school and Bible-class teacher. They are prepared with especial reference to this class of persons, and contain a mass of just the kind of information wanted.

MALCOM'S NEW BIBLE DICTIONARY of the most important Names, Objects, and Terms, found in the Holy Scriptures; intended principally for Sabbath-School Teachers and Bible Classes. By HOWARD MALCOM, D. D., late President of Lewisburg College, Pa. 16mo, cloth, embossed, 60 cts.

☞ The former Dictionary, of which more than *one hundred thousand copies* were sold, is made the basis of the present work; yet so revised, enlarged, and improved, by the addition of new material, a greatly increased number of articles, new illustrations, etc., as to render it essentially a NEW DICTIONARY.

THE EVIDENCES OF CHRISTIANITY, as exhibited in the writings of its apologists, down to Augustine. By W. J. BOLTON, of Gonville and Caius College, Cambridge 12mo, cloth, 80 cts.

HARMONY QUESTIONS ON THE FOUR GOSPELS, for the use of Sabbath Schools. By Rev. S. B. SWAIM, D. D. Vol. I. 18mo, cloth backs, 12½ cts.

The plan differs from all others in this, that it is based upon a HARMONY of the gospels. Instead of taking one of the gospels, — that of Matthew, for instance, — and going through with it, the author takes from ALL of the gospels those parts relating to the same event, and brings them together in the same lesson.

SABBATH-SCHOOL CLASS BOOK; comprising copious Exercises on the Sacred Scriptures. By E. LINCOLN. Revised and Improved by REV. JOSEPH BANVARD, author of "Topical Question Book," etc. 18mo, 12½ cts.

United testimony of Dr. Malcom, author of "Bible Dictionary," Dr. Stow, "Doctrinal Question Book," Dr. Hague, "Guides to Conversations on New Testament":

"It gives us pleasure to express our satisfaction with its design and execution. We think the work is well adapted to the end designed, having avoided, in a great degree, the evils of extreme redundance or conciseness."

LINCOLN'S SCRIPTURE QUESTIONS; with answers, giving, in the language of Scripture, interesting portions of the History, Doctrines, and Duties, exhibited in the Bible. 8⅓ cts. per copy; $1.00 per dozen.

☞ Where Bibles cannot be furnished to each scholar, this work will be found an admirable substitute, as the text is furnished in connection with the questions.

THE SABBATH-SCHOOL HARMONY; containing appropriate Hymns and Music for Sabbath Schools, Juvenile Singing Schools, and Family Devotion. By NATHANIEL D. GOULD. 12½ cts.

VALUABLE WORKS.

MOTHERS OF THE WISE AND GOOD. By JABEZ BURNS, D. D. 16mo, cloth, 75 cts.; cloth, gilt, $1.25.

☞ A sketch of the mothers of many of the most eminent men of the world, and showing how much they were indebted to maternal influence for their greatness and excellence of character.

MY MOTHER; or, Recollections of Maternal Influence. By a New England Clergyman. With a beautiful Frontispiece. 12mo, cloth, 75 cts.; cloth, gilt, $1.25.

A writer of wide celebrity says of the book: "It is one of those rare pictures painted from life with the exquisite skill of one of the *Old Masters*, which so seldom present themselves to the amateur."

THE EXCELLENT WOMAN, as Described in the Book of Proverbs With an Introduction by Rev. W. B. SPRAGUE, D. D. Containing twenty-four splendid Illustrations. Third thousand. 12mo, cloth, $1.00; cloth, gilt, $1.75; extra Turkey, $2.50.

☞ This elegant volume is an appropriate and valuable "Gift Book" for the husband to present the wife, or the child the mother.

THE SIGNET RING, AND ITS HEAVENLY MOTTO. From the German. Illustrated. 16mo, cloth, gilt, 31 cts.

☞ Seldom within so small a compass has such weighty teaching been presented with such exquisite and charming skill.

THE MARRIAGE RING; or, How to Make Home Happy. From the writings of JOHN ANGELL JAMES. Beautifully Illustrated edition. 16mo, cloth, gilt, 75 cts.

WORKS BY DR. TWEEDIE.

GLAD TIDINGS; or, the Gospel of Peace. A Series of Daily Meditations for Christian Disciples. By Rev. W. K. TWEEDIE, D. D. With an elegant illustrated title-page. 16mo, cloth, 63 cts.; cloth, gilt, $1.00.

A LAMP TO THE PATH; or, the Bible in the Heart, the Home, and the Market-place. With an elegant illustrated title-page. 16mo, cloth, 63 cts.; clo. gilt, $1.00.

SEED-TIME AND HARVEST; or, Sow Well and Reap Well. A Book for the Young. With an elegant illustrated title-page. 16mo, cloth, 63 cts.; cloth, gilt, $1.00.

☞ The above interesting works, by Dr. Tweedie, are of uniform size and style, and well adapted for "gift books."

GATHERED LILIES; or, Little Children in Heaven. By Rev. A. C. THOMPSON, Author of "The Better Land." 18mo, flexible cloth, 25 cts.; flexible cloth, gilt, 31 cts.; and cloth, gilt, 42 cts.

"My beloved has gone down into his garden to gather lilies." — *Song of Solomon.*

"In almost every household such a little volume as this will meet a tender welcome." — *N. Y. Evangelist.*

OUR LITTLE ONES IN HEAVEN. Edited by the Author of "The Aimwell Stories," &c. 18mo, cloth, 50 cts.; cloth, gilt, 75 cts.

This little volume contains a choice collection of pieces, in verse and prose, on the death and future happiness of young children.

SAFE HOME; or, the Last Days and Happy Death of Fannie Kenyon. With an Introduction by Prof. J. L. Lincoln, of Brown University. 18mo, flexible cloth cover, 25 cts.; gilt, 31 cts.

This is a delightful narrative of a remarkable little girl, and is recommended to the attention, particularly, of Sabbath Schools.

WORKS OF HUGH MILLER.

THE OLD RED SANDSTONE; or, New Walks in an Old Field. Illustrated with Plates and Geological Sections. NEW EDITION, REVISED AND MUCH ENLARGED, by the addition of new matter and new Illustrations, etc. 12mo, cloth, $1.25.

This edition contains over *one hundred pages of entirely new matter*, from the pen of Hugh Miller. It contains, also, several additional new plates and cuts, the old plates re-engraved and improved, and an Appendix of new Notes.

"It is withal one of the most beautiful specimens of English composition to be found, conveying information on a most difficult and profound science, in a style at once novel, pleasing, and elegant." — DR. SPRAGUE — *Albany Spectator*.

THE FOOT-PRINTS OF THE CREATOR; or, the Asterolepis of Stromness, with numerous Illustrations. With a Memoir of the Author, by LOUIS AGASSIZ. 12mo, cloth, $1.00.

DR. BUCKLAND *said he would give his left hand to possess such power of description as this man.*

TESTIMONY OF THE ROCKS; or, Geology in its Bearings on the two Theologies, Natural and Revealed. "Thou shalt be in league with the stones of the field." — *Job*. With numerous elegant Illustrations. One volume, royal 12mo, cloth, $1.25.

This is the largest and most comprehensive Geological Work that the distinguished author has yet published. It exhibits the profound learning, the felicitous style, and the scientific perception, which characterize his former works, while it embraces the latest results of geological discovery. But the great charm of the book lies in those passages of glowing eloquence, in which, having spread out his facts, the author proceeds to make deductions from them of the most striking and exciting character. The work is profusely illustrated by engravings executed at Paris, in the highest style of French art.

THE CRUISE OF THE BETSEY; or, a Summer Ramble among the Fossiliferous Deposits of the Hebrides. With Rambles of a Geologist; or, Ten Thousand Miles over the Fossiliferous Deposits of Scotland. 12mo, cloth, $1.25.

Nothing need be said of it save that it possesses the same fascination for the reader that characterizes the author's other works.

MY SCHOOLS AND SCHOOLMASTERS; or, the Story of my Education. AN AUTOBIOGRAPHY. With a full-length Portrait of the Author. 12mo, cloth, $1.25.

This is a personal narrative, of a deeply interesting and instructive character, concerning one of the most remarkable men of the age.

MY FIRST IMPRESSIONS OF ENGLAND AND ITS PEOPLE. With a fine Engraving of the author. 12mo, cloth, $1.00.

☞ A very instructive book of travels, presenting the most perfectly life-like views of England and its people to be found in any language.

☞ *The above six volumes are furnished in sets, printed and bound in uniform style:* viz.,

HUGH MILLER'S WORKS, SIX VOLUMES. Elegant embossed cloth, $7.00; library sheep, $8.00; half calf, $12.00; antique, $12.00.

MACAULAY ON SCOTLAND. A Critique, from the "Witness." 16mo, flexible cloth, 25 cts.

CHAMBERS' WORKS.

CHAMBERS' CYCLOPÆDIA OF ENGLISH LITERATURE. A Selection of the choicest productions of English Authors, from the earliest to the present time. Connected by a Critical and Biographical History. Forming two large imperial octavo volumes of 700 pages each, double column letter press; with upwards of 300 elegant Illustrations. Edited by ROBERT CHAMBERS. Cloth, $5.00; sheep, $6.00; full gilt, $7.50; half calf, $7.50; full calf, $10.00.

This work embraces about one thousand Authors, chronologically arranged, and classed as poets, historians, dramatists, philosophers, metaphysicians, divines, etc., with choice selections from their writings, connected by a Biographical, Historical, and Critical Narrative; thus presenting a complete view of English Literature from the earliest to the present time. Let the reader open where he will, he cannot fail to find matter for profit and delight. The selections are gems — infinite riches in a little room; in the language of another, "A WHOLE ENGLISH LIBRARY FUSED DOWN INTO ONE CHEAP BOOK!"

☞ THE AMERICAN edition of this valuable work is enriched by the addition of fine steel and mezzotint engravings of the heads of SHAKSPEARE, ADDISON, BYRON; a full-length portrait of DR. JOHNSON; and a beautiful scenic representation of OLIVER GOLDSMITH and DR. JOHNSON. These important and elegant additions, together with superior paper and binding, and other improvements, render the AMERICAN far superior to the English edition.

W. H. PRESCOTT, THE HISTORIAN, says, "Readers cannot fail to profit largely by the labors of the critic who has the talent and taste to separate what is really beautiful and worthy of their study from what is superfluous."

"I concur in the foregoing opinion of Mr. Prescott." — EDWARD EVERETT.

"A popular work, indispensable to the library of a student of English literature." — DR. WAYLAND.

"We hail with peculiar pleasure the appearance of this work." — *North American Review.*

CHAMBERS' MISCELLANY OF USEFUL AND ENTERTAINING KNOWLEDGE. Edited by WILLIAM CHAMBERS. With elegant Illustrative Engravings. Ten volumes. Cloth, $7.50; cloth, gilt, $10.00; library sheep, $10.00.

"It would be difficult to find any miscellany superior or even equal to it. It richly deserves the epithets 'useful and entertaining,' and I would recommend it very strongly, as extremely well adapted to form parts of a library for the young, or of a social or circulating library in town or country." — GEO. B. EMERSON, Esq. — *Chairman Boston School Book Committee.*

CHAMBERS' HOME BOOK; or, Pocket Miscellany, containing a Choice Selection of Interesting and Instructive Reading, for the Old and Young. Six volumes. 16mo, cloth, $3.00; library sheep, $4.00; half calf, $6.00.

This is considered fully equal, and in some respects superior, to either of the other works of the Chambers in interest; containing a vast fund of valuable information. It is admirably adapted to the School or Family Library, furnishing ample variety for every class of readers.

"The Chambers are confessedly the best caterers for popular and useful reading in the world." — *Willis' Home Journal.*

"A very entertaining, instructive, and popular work." — *N. Y. Commercial.*

"We do not know how it is possible to publish so much good reading matter at such a low price. We speak a good word for the literary excellence of the stories in this work; we hope our people will introduce it into all their families, in order to drive away the miserable flashy-trashy stuff so often found in the hands of our young people of both sexes." — *Scientific American.*

"Both an entertaining and instructive work, as it is certainly a very cheap one." — *Puritan Recorder.*

"If any person wishes to read for amusement or profit, to kill time or improve it, get 'Chambers' Home Book.'" — *Chicago Times.*

CHAMBERS' REPOSITORY OF INSTRUCTIVE AND AMUSING PAPERS. With Illustrations. A New Series, containing Original Articles. Two volumes. 16mo, cloth, $1.75.

THE SAME WORK, two volumes in one, cloth, gilt back, $1.50.

VALUABLE TEXT-BOOKS.

THE LECTURES OF SIR WILLIAM HAMILTON, BART., late Professor of Logic and Metaphysics, University of Edinburgh; embracing the METAPHYSICAL and LOGICAL COURSES; with Notes, from Original Materials, and an Appendix, containing the Author's Latest Development of his New Logical Theory. Edited by Rev. HENRY LONGUEVILLE MANSEL, B. D., Prof. of Moral and Metaphysical Philosophy in Magdalen College, Oxford, and JOHN VEITCH, M. A., of Edinburgh. In two royal octavo volumes, viz.,

I. METAPHYSICAL LECTURES (*now ready*). Royal octavo, cloth.

II. LOGICAL LECTURES (*in preparation*).

☞ G. & L., by a special arrangement with the family of the late Sir William Hamilton, are the Authorized American Publishers of this distinguished author's *matchless* LECTURES ON METAPHYSICS AND LOGIC, and they are permitted to print the same from advance sheets furnished them by the English publishers.

MENTAL PHILOSOPHY; Including the Intellect, the Sensibilities, and the Will. By JOSEPH HAVEN, Prof. of Intellectual and Moral Philosophy, Amherst College. Royal 12mo, cloth, embossed, $1.50.

It is believed this work will be found pre-eminently distinguished.

1. The COMPLETENESS with which it presents the whole subject. Text-books generally treat of only *one class* of faculties; this work includes the *whole*. 2. It is strictly and thoroughly SCIENTIFIC. 3. It presents a careful analysis of the mind, as a whole. 4. The history and literature of each topic. 5. The latest results of the science. 6. The chaste, yet attractive style. 7. The remarkable condensation of thought.

Prof. PARK, of Andover, says: "It is DISTINGUISHED for its clearness of style, perspicuity of method, candor of spirit, acumen and comprehensiveness of thought."

The work, though so recently published, has met with most remarkable success; having been already introduced into a large number of the leading colleges and schools in various parts of the country, and bids fair to take the place of every other work on the subject now before the public.

THESAURUS OF ENGLISH WORDS AND PHRASES, so classified and arranged as to facilitate the expression of ideas, and assist in literary composition. New and Improved Edition. By PETER MARK ROGET, late Secretary of the Royal Society, London, &c. Revised and edited, with a List of Foreign Words defined in English, and other additions, by BARNAS SEARS, D. D., President of Brown University. A NEW AMERICAN Edition, with ADDITIONS AND IMPROVEMENTS. 12mo, cloth, $1.50.

This edition is based on the London edition, recently issued. The first American Edition having been prepared by Dr. Sears for *strictly educational purposes*, those words and phrases properly termed "vulgar," incorporated in the original work, were omitted. These expurgated portions have, in the present edition, been *restored*, but by such an arrangement of the matter as not to interfere with the educational purposes of the American editor. Besides this, it contains important additions of words and phrases not in the English edition, making it in *all respects more full and perfect than the author's edition*. The work has already become one of standard authority, both in this country and in Great Britain.

PALEY'S NATURAL THEOLOGY. Illustrated by forty Plates, with Selections from the Notes of Dr. Paxton, and Additional Notes, Original and Selected, with a Vocabulary of Scientific Terms. Edited by JOHN WARE, M. D. Improved edition, with elegant newly engraved plates. 12mo, cloth, embossed, $1.25.

This work is very generally introduced into our best Schools and Colleges throughout the country. An entirely new and beautiful set of Illustrations has recently been procured, which, with other improvements, render it the best and most complete work of the kind extant.

VALUABLE WORKS.

THE LIMITS OF RELIGIOUS THOUGHT EXAMINED. By HENRY LONGUEVILLE MANSEL, B. D., Prof. of Moral and Metaphysical Philosophy, Magdalen College, Oxford, Editor of Sir William Hamilton's Lectures, etc. etc. With the COPIOUS NOTES of the volume translated for the American Edition. 12mo, cloth, $1.25.

☞ This is a *masterly* production, and may be safely said to be one of the most important works of the day.

FIRST THINGS; or, The Development of Church Life. By BARON STOW, D. D. 16mo, cloth, 75 cts.

HEAVEN. By JAMES WILLIAM KIMBALL. With an elegant vignette title-page. 12mo, cloth, $1.00.

"The book is full of beautiful ideas, consoling hopes, and brilliant representations of human destiny, all presented in a chaste, pleasing and very readable style." — *N. Y. Chronicle.*

THE PROGRESS OF BAPTIST PRINCIPLES IN THE LAST HUNDRED YEARS. By T. F. CURTIS, Professor of Theology in the Lewisburg University, Pa., and author of "Communion," &c. 12mo, cloth, $1.25.

Eminently worthy of the attention, not only of Baptists, *but of all other denominations.* In his preface the author declares that his aim has been to draw a wide distinction between *parties* and *opinions.* Hence the object of this volume is not to exhibit or defend the Baptists, *but their principles.* It is confidently pronounced the best exhibition of Baptist views and principles extant.

THOUGHTS ON THE PRESENT COLLEGIATE SYSTEM in the United States. By FRANCIS WAYLAND, D. D. 16mo, cloth, 50 cents.

SACRED RHETORIC; or, Composition and Delivery of Sermons. By H. J. RIPLEY, D. D., Prof. in Newton Theol. Inst. To which is added, DR. WARE'S HINTS ON EXTEMPORANEOUS PREACHING. Second thousand. 12mo, cloth, 75 cts.

THE PULPIT OF THE REVOLUTION; or, The Political Sermons of the Era of 1776. With an Introduction, Biographical Sketches of the Preachers and Historical Notes, etc. By JOHN WINGATE THORNTON, author of "The Landing at Cape Anne," etc. 12mo, cloth. *In press.*

THE EIGHTEEN CHRISTIAN CENTURIES. By the Rev. JAMES WHITE, author of "Landmarks of the History of England." 12mo, cloth. *In press.*

THE PLURALITY OF WORLDS. A NEW EDITION. With a SUPPLEMENTARY DIALOGUE, in which the author's Reviewers are reviewed. 12mo, cloth, $1.00.

This masterly production, which has excited so much interest in this country and in Europe, will now have an increased attraction in the addition of the Supplement, in which the author's reviewers are triumphantly reviewed.

THE CAMEL; His Organization, Habits, and Uses, considered with reference to his introduction into the United States. By GEORGE P. MARSH, late U. S. Minister at Constantinople. 12mo, cloth, 63 cts.

This book treats of a subject of great interest, especially at the present time. It furnishes a more complete and reliable account of the Camel than any other in the language ; indeed, it is believed that there is no other. It is the result of long study, extensive research, and much personal observation, on the part of the author, and it has been prepared with special reference to the experiment of domesticating the Camel in this country, now going on under the auspices of the United States government. It is written in a style worthy of the distinguished author's reputation for great learning and fine scholarship.

www.ingramcontent.com/pod-product-compliance
Lightning Source LLC
LaVergne TN
LVHW050518100826
845148LV00002B/375

* 9 7 8 1 4 2 5 5 2 0 6 5 6 *